BOYMOM

BOYMOM

REIMAGINING BOYHOOD IN THE AGE OF IMPOSSIBLE MASCULINITY

RUTH WHIPPMAN

HARMONY
NEW YORK

Boymom is a work of nonfiction. Some names and identifying details have been changed.

Published in the United States by Harmony Books, an imprint of Random House, a division of Penguin Random House LLC, New York.
HarmonyBooks.com | RandomHouseBooks.com

Harmony Books is a registered trademark, and the Circle colophon is a trademark of Penguin Random House LLC.

LIBRARY OF CONGRESS CATALOGING-IN-PUBLICATION DATA
Names: Whippman, Ruth, author.
Title: Boymom / by Ruth Whippman.
Identifiers: LCCN 2023039427 | ISBN 9780593577639 (hardcover) | ISBN 9780593577646 (ebook)
Subjects: LCSH: Child rearing. | Mothers and sons. | Child development. | Moral education. | Personality development. | Boys—Psychology. | Boys—Social conditions—21st century.
Classification: LCC HQ775 .W45 2024 | DDC 305.230811—dc23/eng/20230922
LC record available at https://lccn.loc.gov/2023039427

Printed in the United States of America

Cover design by Anna Bauer Carr
Cover illustration by Ola Jasionowska

2 4 6 8 9 7 5 3 1

First Edition

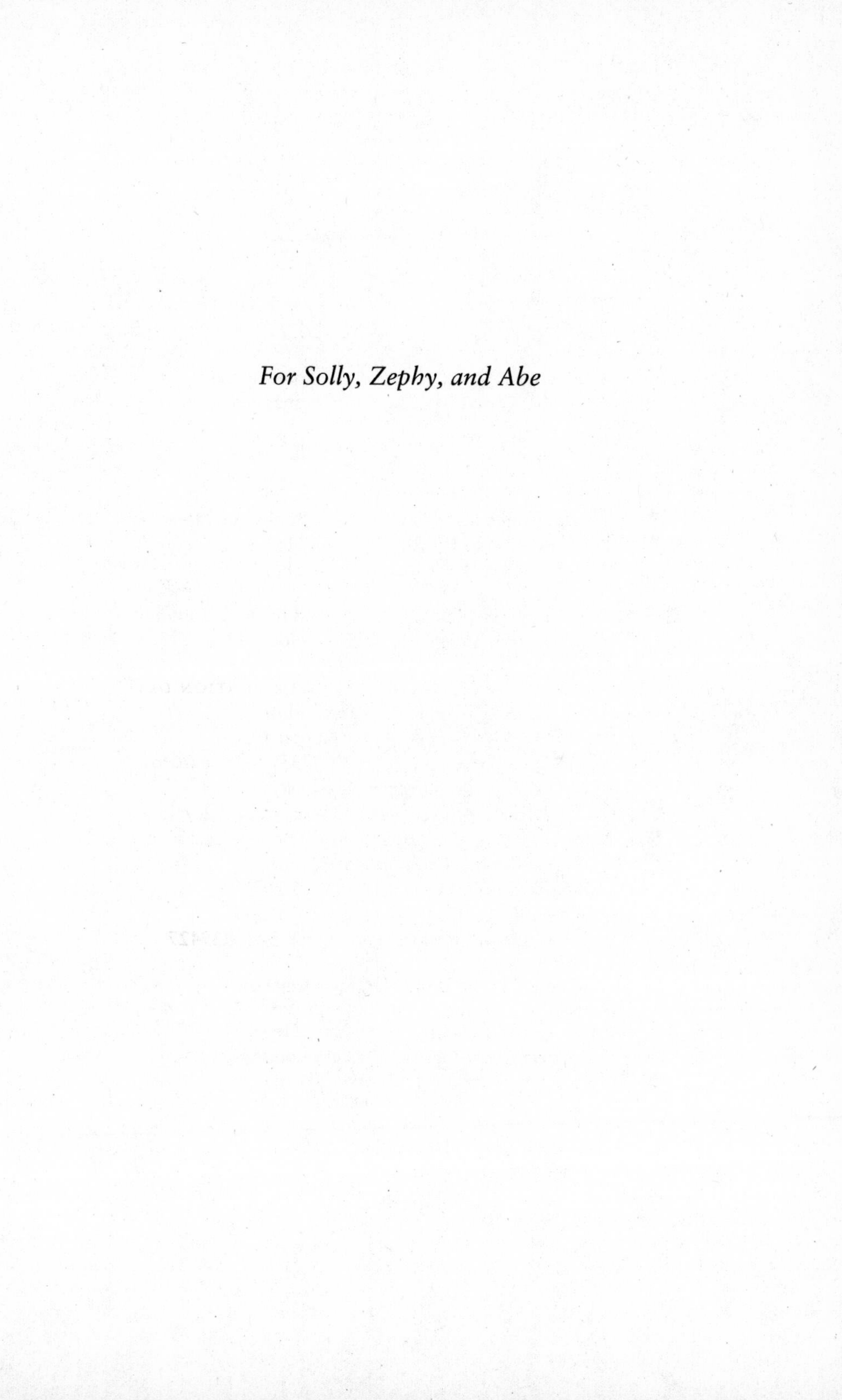

For Solly, Zephy, and Abe

"Boys need healthy self-esteem. They need love. And a wise and loving feminist politics can provide the only foundation to save the lives of male children. Patriarchy will not heal them. If that were so they would all be well."

—bell hooks, *Feminism Is for Everybody*

"And now," cried Max, "let the wild rumpus start!"

—Maurice Sendak, *Where the Wild Things Are*

CONTENTS

#METOO BABY

"I hope for your sake this one is a girl," said our mail carrier one morning as I sat out on the front step, nine months pregnant, my two sons buzzing hyperactively around me. Her eyes flicked between my giant bump and the boys, who were playing some generic mildly violent game, complete with gender essentialist soundtrack of "PEYEW PEYEW!! NEEEEOOOWWWWW!!! HIYUHHH!!" noises. When I told her that no, our third child was another boy, she let out an involuntary moan of compassion.

We had known this baby was male even before I got pregnant. "Known" not in some mystical feminine-intuition sense, but in the more concrete way that he had been a leftover frozen embryo from the IVF cycle that conceived his older brother, and we had done genetic tests.

Friends had told me I was crazy. "I could understand it for a girl," said one, when I told her we were going to defrost the embryo. "But why go through all that just for another boy?" The responses I got when I told people that I was pregnant with a third son tended to be less congratulatory than sympathetic, even veering into a kind of tetchy alarm—they backed away nervously, as though I had just told them that our family had all come down with the stomach flu.

This was late 2017, a year into the "Pussy Grabber" administration, and the news was a rolling horror show of male bad behavior. *The New York Times* had recently exposed film mogul Harvey Weinstein as a serial rapist and, within days, we seemed to have escalated from "Weinstein is a sex offender" to "every man in America is a sex offender." The abuses, and perhaps even worse, the decades of coddling and apathy that had enabled them, sat in a septic puddle of disgust at the back of my throat.

Even before this onslaught of bad news about men, in our liberal urban bubble, it was becoming increasingly clear that girls were now considered the prize. Boys, while cute and puppy-like, were generally viewed on some level as trouble—feral, hard to control, animalistic. *The New York Times* ran pieces with titles such as "Wanting Daughters, Getting Sons" and "It's a Boy, and It's Okay to be Disappointed."

"Boys are like dogs," said the mom in the park. So did the preschool teacher and the librarian patrolling quiet story time with a defeated, thousand-yard stare. "Just food and exercise and try your best to wear them out."

The comments stung. No one likes to be pitied, and it was hard to think that people saw my children as second best. I had also felt my fair share of sadness at the idea of never having a daughter, but as a feminist, I had always pushed back hard against gender stereotypes. Even apart from the sexism angle, the idea that a baby's biological sex could predict their personality or interests or life trajectory seemed so overly deterministic, even un-American, so fundamentally out of kilter with the "you can be anything you want to be" guiding story of American self-belief.

Anyway, surely no girl could be more different from them than my two boys were from each other. Seven-year-old Solly, intense and sensitive, lover of obscure marine animals and drawing; and four-year-old Zephy, big-hearted and rambunctious, whose two guiding passions were intricate bead art and karate chopping the sofa. Each of them had a mix of traits and interests—boyish, girlish, and neither. We were raising them (or so I believed) in a liberal, gender-neutral environment. Gender didn't matter.

But that was a while ago. Before Trump and Weinstein. Before incels and "masculinity influencers" and men's rights activists and white men waving tiki torches dominated the news. Now that postgender idealism was starting to feel like an artifact of an entirely different moral universe. Whatever unknowable mix of essential nature and socialization this all came down to, it was getting harder and harder to maintain the belief that men and women were fundamentally the same, and that raising a boy in this world was the same basic task as raising a girl.

Now the horrors in my news app mingled in my brain with the angsty neurochemicals of pregnancy, and for the first time, I was truly scared to be a mother of boys. Everywhere I turned there were bad men. I was frightened both for and of the tiny piece of patriarchy growing inside me, worried sick over what he and his brothers might become. The potential for darkness that I might be powerless to stop.

Patriarchy is the system in which men hold the bulk of power politically, economically, socially, and culturally; and male concerns are centered while others' are marginalized. It is the norm in almost every civilization on Earth, with only a small handful of exceptions. Simply by virtue of being born male, my sons would be part of this system and benefit from the unearned privilege it would bestow on them. No matter how much I wanted to, it wasn't possible to just opt out.

At night, as I battled insomnia, heaving my bump around the bed from one achy compromise to another, my pregnant brain churned out a ticker tape of bad outcomes for my unborn boy: rapist, school-shooter, incel, man-child, interrupter, mansplainer, boob-starer, birthday forgetter, frat boy, dude-bro, homophobe, self-important stoner, emotional-labor abstainer, nonwiper of kitchen counters. Trying to raise good sons suddenly felt like a hopeless task.

• • •

What I didn't know, as I lay there huge and bleak and defeated, was that within just a few days, I was about to witness one of the most momentous turning points in gender politics in recent history.

Just ten days after *The New York Times* published its exposé of Weinstein, the #MeToo movement would explode, and gender relations as we knew them would be upended. Although the basic structures of patriarchy would remain intact, the final weeks of my pregnancy would see a tectonic shift in the terms of the conversation, a fundamental rewriting of who got to speak and who had to shut up and listen. This in turn would spur a cycle of enraged backlash and digging in. For years to come we would be slugging it out, rethinking gender norms and power structures from the ground up. For good and for bad, my third son would be born into a very different world than the one his older brothers had entered just a few years earlier.

As a feminist, this moment in history would be one of the most clarifying, exhilarating times of my life. But as a mother of boys, it would twist my stomach into a knot of fear and hypocrisy, a tangle of competing envies and hopes and contradictions that would take a long time to fully unravel.

• • •

I watched #MeToo unfold live from the spare room of our house, a claustrophobic, jerry-rigged extension with knotted-pine walls the color of Donald Trump's face. Neil, my husband, had banished me from our shared bedroom, struggling to cope with my pregnancy insomnia and apocalyptic conversation.

I was lying on the bed, scrolling through Twitter on my phone and glugging Pepto-Bismol from the bottle when I noticed that the hashtag was trending. The tweets were in response to a plea from actress Alyssa Milano, herself a survivor of a violent sexual assault as a teenager: "If you have ever been sexually harassed or assaulted, write 'me too' as a reply to this tweet."

She was reviving a hashtag originally created by activist Tarana Burke a decade earlier to encourage solidarity and mutual support among survivors of sexual assault on the now defunct platform MySpace. Back then, the movement had stayed relatively niche. Sexual violence was still widely considered an aberration rather than a deep-rooted systemic problem, its survivors the victims of random bad luck rather than anything more sinister. But a yearlong national pileup of misogyny had propelled women into a new collective, more politicized headspace. Now we were ready to receive the #MeToo message in an entirely different way.

The sewage that had always been contained out of sight, in underground pipes, was now spewing into the streets. Suddenly we had the drive, the vocabulary, and the social permission to talk about men in a whole new way. All at once, across the world, women had wrested control of the conversation, and now we were thinking in terms of systems, not just individuals. Every unwanted touch or grope or boob stare or inappropriate comment was no longer just a creepy one-off, but part of a systemic, ingrained pattern of male behavior.

As much as it was a revolution of substance, #MeToo was a revolution of storytelling. Perhaps the ultimate power available to any human being is to have control of the narrative. To be the one who gets to decide which story to tell, and how to tell it. And with #MeToo, that power subtly shifted.

For all of recorded history, men had set the terms of the discussion, and women had worked around them. Even when we were ostensibly fighting sexism, women were still responding to a male agenda. Now, within a matter of days, it seemed as though that dynamic had reversed. For maybe the first time ever, women were dictating the boundaries of the national conversation, and men were on the defensive, scrambling to respond.

All at once, we had crowbarred the Overton window out of the men's locker room and reinstalled it in the gender studies department.

• • •

It felt as though society was fracturing along gender lines. Conservatives were rallying around men, leaping to their defense.

#NotAllMen, they tweeted, willfully denying the systemic nature of the problem; even going so far as to claim that men were the real victims of #MeToo. Liberals, my natural clan, allied themselves with girls and women. In a strange politicization of gender itself, men and boys somehow became the very symbol of conservative values, and women and girls of progressive ones. Although obviously there were still countless individual conservative women and progressive men, as a political class, females started to represent change and hope, while males symbolized the status quo, injustice and harm. It was, of course, a false dichotomy, but at a gut, tribal level it felt real. My tribe was rejecting my kids. I found myself stranded on one side of the symbolic divide, with my own children on the other.

While the left branded masculinity as toxic, the right sold it as the answer to all our problems, with both politicians and online influencers peddling a new brand of wounded, furious manhood, drawn from a combination of superhero fantasies and defensive rage.

Everywhere I turned inside my own brain I found contradiction and hypocrisy. In the fevered, absolutist climate of #MeToo, it was hard not to start to see men as the enemy. The sheer volume of evidence of male bad behavior was impossible to deny. I was angry with men and boys, horrified at the harm they had caused. But I was the mother of two of them. I was growing one inside my own body. Did my feminist principles require me to condemn the entire gender that included my own children? I feared what it would do to my sons and other boys psychologically, to grow up hearing that who they were was inherently toxic, their sexuality so potentially harmful.

Disorientated, I veered wildly between disgust and defensiveness. While the feminist part of me yelled *"Smash the patriarchy!"* the mother part of me wanted to wrap the patriarchy up in its blankie and read it a story.

At times I would dig in, spitting defensive maternal poison and finding shameful comfort in the ideological tropes of the right—whataboutery and #NotAllMen-ism. I would look at my sons' sweet faces in denial, finding it almost impossible to imagine that they could ever cause harm. Instinctively, it all felt like a pile on. I could see why so many young men felt attacked, and how easily, in immature brains, that could curdle into anger and self-victimization, even radicalism.

At other times, my defensiveness turned to disgust. One of the hardest parts of parenting for me had always been the sheer boisterous physicality of my boys, often teetering right on the precipice of violence or total loss of control. I had tended to dismiss this raucous energy (perhaps self-servingly) as boyish rowdiness, but now I had a whole new uncomfortable filter through which to view their behavior. When Solly hit Zephy for taking bricks from his Lego model, was this normal sibling conflict or toxic male aggression? When they begged me for Nerf guns, was this a sign of an emergent desire to shoot up a high school? When Zephy's preschool teacher emailed to say that he and a group of his classmates had become "interested in private parts," was this healthy exploration or the first signs of something abusive?

Not for the first time, I felt jealous of my feminist friends with daughters. They could ride the breathtaking wave of #MeToo unconflicted, their political beliefs and parenting interests aligned. All around me, mothers of girls were finding a new energy. Their daughters went to "Go Girls" camp, dressed up as Ruth Bader Ginsburg for Halloween, and carried Girl Power water bottles. I cheered them on, truly agreeing that it was time for men to step back and hand over the reins of power. But still, somehow, every time I saw a little girl in a THE FUTURE IS FEMALE T-shirt, I felt a secret, shameful stab. What did this mean for my boys?

The guiding tropes of modern American parenting—reach for the stars, let nothing stand in your way, seize every opportunity—now seemed wildly tonally off-key when talking about raising future white men. But both instinct and conditioning made it hard to let go. I wanted to raise sons who were confident and secure and motivated to dream big, if that's what they chose. But should I really be teaching them to aim low, to step aside and make way for their female peers?

• • •

Meanwhile, another huge cultural shift was underway. After decades of work by activists, the younger generation was radically rethinking the very meaning of gender itself, and these ideas were entering the mainstream. The changes came with their own backlash, with trans rights under threat in much of the country. But at least in our liberal bubble, kids and adolescents no longer felt obliged to stick to the gender category that was assigned to them at birth; their biology no longer the determinant of their identity. More and more of the kids we knew were identifying as nonbinary, or gender-fluid, or trans. My sons' teachers and coaches now routinely asked children to share their pronouns. Along with the wider push to break down barriers and stereotypes for girls, it felt as though gender roles were being turned on their heads for almost everyone.

But not quite everyone. The one gender category that seemed almost impervious to all this dazzling change was the one that included my own sons: cisgender boys. For those who had been raised as boys and still identified as them, gender expectations and norms were shifting at a much more glacial pace.

Society was at full throttle, encouraging girls to break free of constricting stereotypes, with communities funding after-school programs and camps to encourage them to be fearless and brave, to become engineers and computer programmers. But there was little on offer designed to help boys challenge masculine stereotypes, to be more empathetic or relational or nurturing. Even in the progressive Bay Area, I couldn't find any empowerment camps to teach boys how to become caregivers or nurses or fashion designers. Attempts to shift the norms for boys fell to individual parents, with little societal support or backing. All around people were encouraging young girls to be "anything a boy can be," but encouraging your son to behave more like a girl still felt vaguely emasculating, even irresponsible.

And as much as they harmed women and girls, traditional masculine norms seemed like a prison for boys, pressurizing them into a kind of rigid, aggressive stoicism while cutting them off from their own emotions and those of other people. Patriarchy would, without a doubt, bring significant unearned privilege to my sons and their peers throughout their lives, but increasingly I was also realizing that this would come at a high cost.

It all seemed like some kind of soul-compromising bargain from a Greek myth. Boys and men automatically receive substantial material life advantages by virtue of their maleness, but at the cost of their morality, their freedom to access the full range of human feeling and connection.

The research certainly seems to back this up. Boys in America are going through something of a crisis. Academically, they are now trailing behind girls at every level of schooling. They make up the majority of both the perpetrators and, I was surprised to see, the victims of violent crimes. They are significantly more likely than girls to engage in serious antisocial behavior. Mental health issues are reaching epidemic levels for both male and female adolescents, but teenage boys now commit suicide at close to four times the rate of their female peers.

The last thing I wanted was to align myself emotionally with the men's rights activists, the right-wing "boys are the real victims," #HimToo apologists. Was there a way to square this and offer real empathy to boys, give them a more expansive story about their own possibilities, without betraying any feminist principles?

Understanding where we are going wrong with raising boys, and trying to change those patterns, is one of our most urgent cultural projects as a society. A couple of generations of feminists have scrutinized and politicized girlhood, pouring their energies into raising a cohort of strong, powerful young women. Meanwhile, we have been mostly ignoring boyhood. Boy socialization is still barely seen as socialization at all, just the default normal, the standard to which everyone should aspire.

This is a half-finished revolution.

We need to do for boys what my mother's generation started for girls: to truly dig into the subtle and not so subtle forces of socialization at work, to attempt to expand our sense of who and what boys can be.

How did we get to a point where sexual violence was just a routine part of daily life? What are the million subtle signs that boys receive that let them internalize this behavior as normal, and how do we turn that around? What is behind the groundswell of rage and violence among young men that is making them turn to misogynistic YouTubers, threaten feminists online, and in the most extreme cases, even shoot up their high schools? What are the myriad ways in which we suppress the emotional lives of boys, limiting who they can be and become?

There are, of course, dozens of parenting books out there about raising boys. Almost invariably written by experts, they tend to come with clear, bullet-pointed advice that seems to crumble in the face of the messy reality, never quite acknowledging the complicated swill of best intentions and worst selves.

They are also usually written by men. Much of the advice tends to sideline mothers, pitching boyhood as something so momentous and delicate and unknowable that it can only truly competently be handled by fathers or other males.

Mothers are often invisible in this story. It's hard to find much that addresses the experience of raising boys from the mother's point of view, that gives voice to the peculiar, joyful, terrifying, conflicted reality of being a mother and a feminist with a son at this particular moment in history.

I am lucky in that I am not doing this alone. My husband, Neil, is a phenomenal father and partner and is equally committed to unpacking these norms and giving our boys a more freeing, more open-ended story about who they can be.

Because neither of us wants our guiding parenting goal to be "just make sure he doesn't become a rapist." We also want to give our sons a more inspirational narrative about their own lives and possibilities: To thrive and feel pride, not shame, in their boyhood. To find their tribe and their identity. We want to raise them to understand and acknowledge their many, many advantages and privileges as young males and to learn to navigate those with awareness and compassion. We want to hold our boys accountable but not make them feel so defensive that they get angry or depressed. And I especially want to do all this with both my feminist principles and my mental health intact.

• • •

As I got closer to my due date, it was still hard to tell whether the bile pooling in the back of my throat was pregnancy heartburn, or just a normal physiological response to the abuses of the patriarchy. Each night, the sour swill rose higher and higher, gagging me and burning my tongue. My limbs felt heavy, my brain foggy.

Eventually, I caved and took an Uber to my doctor's office, feeling so dreadful I was barely able to walk. The doctor took my vital signs and sent me straight to the hospital. It was preeclampsia, a dangerous late-pregnancy complication and the leading cause of maternal death. My blood pressure was sky-high and the placenta was starting to fail. I stayed in the hospital for a week, connected to monitors, buying time for my baby to grow as much lung tissue as possible as I flitted in and out of consciousness.

By Sunday, my blood pressure had risen uncontrollably high. My baby and I were in danger. They rushed me into the operating theater and snatched him out of my body. The first thing I saw of my newest boy was a giant pair of testicles, wildly disproportionate to the tiny premature newborn they were attached to.

My third son. My Abe. My beloved. We'd made it. But we were only just beginning.

• • •

I was euphoric after Abe's birth. He had a special sweetness. Born a month early, he was tiny, a third smaller than my previous two babies, and too new to be in this world. His hair was still a soft fuzz and would take another month to grow in.

In the early days, my mangled post C-section body could barely lift him out of the plastic hospital crib. A kind nurse put him in the crook of my arm, and he nuzzled there for days, sleeping and eating round the clock, warm and safe next to my beating heart.

His brothers loved him on sight. Solly made him a card out of red construction paper, with a crayon drawing of Abe wearing a superhero T-shirt and looking like a first grader himself. "Wellekom to the family," he wrote. "I love you allreddy."

At four, Zephy was warier, more jealous. But one morning in the supermarket, when a slightly unhinged man approached the stroller and started cooing at his three-week-old brother in an overly intense and scary manner, Zephy puffed himself up to his full forty-two inches and roared, "GET AWAY FROM OUR BABY!"

Now I had three boys. Three adorable, irrepressible, anarchic, creative, rambunctious, aggressive, big-hearted boys, the loves of my life. I still had time, but not much. Just a few years with them, to get this right, to help them learn to be good in a world that wanted to make them bad.

I was out of my depth. I wanted this book, needed this book, but it didn't exist. So I had to write it.

BOYMOM

CHAPTER 1

BOYS WILL BE BOYS

OFF TO A BAD START

About three months after we bring baby Abe home from the hospital, a biblical plague of rage and vengeance befalls our household.

We have had a few weeks' grace. Abe is the kind of easy newborn that I had envied from afar when the older two were babies. In his early days, he is more like a cute clutch purse than a demanding human infant, lying quietly next to me wherever I put him, an adorable accessory to family life who doesn't ask for much in return.

Our fridge, the hub for our family photo collection, is now living its best life as a millennial's Instagram page, proudly displaying a fanatically curated vision board of life as a family of five. There are the two big boys perched on the sofa, their brand-new brother draped across their laps, still scrunchy eyed and burrito-wrapped in the regulation hospital blanket. There is Solly, nose to nose with a three-week-old Abe, staring into his eyes with exquisite tenderness. There is me, caught at an unfeasibly flattering angle on the Santa Cruz boardwalk, a curly haired boy holding each hand, the baby carrier neatly obscuring my bulging postpartum stomach.

But then, at around the three-month mark, Abe's crumpled little womb eyes pop open, his tiny chalky mouth spreads into a winning gummy grin, and he presents us with his list of demands. Enraged by the sudden reduction in parental attention, his brothers are instantly gripped by a violent, uncontrolled jealousy.

Both Solly and Zephy adore their baby brother and are surprisingly gentle and nurturing with him. But when they realize that the overall pie of attention is now to be divided three ways instead of two, they turn on each other, in a bloody pact to fight to the death for the remaining sliver.

Solly, my sensitive, thoughtful eldest, who had been a model big brother when Zephy was born and who, as far as I could remember, even in deepest toddlerhood had never hit or bitten or pushed another child, now becomes angry and dysregulated.

Zephy, always a good-hearted, rufty-tufty little bundle of energy, now takes on an alter ego he calls Dino Slash, an outlet for his most out-of-control impulses. He can assume the Dino Slash persona without warning, flailing wildly, biting and karate chopping anyone who comes near.

They fight constantly and brutally. If I leave the room for three minutes, at speed, to change the baby's diaper or go to the bathroom, by the time I race back, still zipping up my jeans, at least one of the older boys is wailing and clutching an injured body part. When I get out of the car, in the time it takes me to walk round to open the back door and unbuckle the baby from his car seat, the other two have locked themselves together in a fevered wrestling match, bones and feelings cracking. When I pick them up from school, the moment they lay eyes on each other, one of them starts pushing or punching the other, while crowds of parents and teachers look on. We are constantly one snatched Lego brick away from a crushed skull.

Their "love language" is light physical violence. So is their hate language. And also their "I'm actually pretty indifferent to this situation, but I might as well just hit you anyway" language. They rarely communicate with each other in words. My sole job as a mother quickly becomes just getting to the end of each day with everyone alive. Any hopes for a higher order of parenting—chores, etiquette, craft projects, how to handle both a fork and a knife during the same meal, let alone teaching them the meaning of consent or the nuances of feminism—quickly fall away.

Now the fridge fantasy photo montage is obscured by a new gallery. The Apology Letter collection.

IM SORREE I HIT U WIV A SHUVL
IM SORREE I BASHD U INTO THE WOL
IM SORREE I KIKD U
IM SORREE I PUNCHT U
IM SORREE I YELD AT U
IM SORREE UR HED IS SMASHT

Not that the letters I make them write after every incident do any good. Nothing does. Not extra attention or clear limits or "special time." Not "logical consequences" or empathetic listening or sticker charts or time-outs or less screen time or more exercise or an "authoritative voice." None of the dozens of parenting strategies I try even touch this angry, boisterous mess.

At night, as I spiral deeper into a mental sinkhole of inadequacy, I read parenting books on my Kindle. Positive Parenting Solutions! Negative Parenting Solutions! Be more lenient! Be stricter! Fill their power buckets! Don't give them too much power! Time-outs are abusive! If you don't enforce time-outs, you are raising an entitled monster! The only thing they seem to agree on is that I am doing it all wrong.

It isn't just the hitting. It is the constant wild energy, the complete lack of moments of calm or reflection. During this time, my boys do sometimes seem more animal than human, but they aren't like dogs. Dogs can be trained to follow commands, walk to heel, rescue children from wells, and perch coquettishly in fancy purses. At times my boys seem more like rabid wolves. And ever present in the back of my mind is the cold dread that it will be a straight line from this grade-school house of horrors to pussy grabbing and school shooting.

I had always pushed back hard against the idea of gender essentialism, the idea that boys are predestined to be rambunctious or aggressive. The only differences between boys and girls are genitals and socialization, my pre-kids self had maintained ferociously. But now, I am not so sure.

All of my lofty ambitions about raising sons who are different—who use their words and not their fists, who are empathetic and sensitive and mindful of their own privilege—have been exposed as pathetic vanities. I had prided myself on avoiding this exact situation, formed an entire feminist identity around it, and now my worst fears are coming true. This is toxic masculinity, junior edition, live in my own home.

• • •

Meanwhile, on the other side of the Rocky Mountains, my friend Hanna is taping a sweet drawing of a rainbow to her fridge.

Hanna had been my neighbor for a couple of years when Solly was a toddler, and we had become close friends. She had a girl the same age, and we had slogged through the long days of early motherhood together, in one or the other of our living rooms. I hadn't noticed a huge difference between the behavior of her daughter Sky and Solly. They both had tantrums and gave cuddles and hated sitting still. They both played with trains and dolls. If anything, Sky had been the more aggressive of the pair, enthusiastically adopting the role of hair puller to Solly's hair "pullee."

Then Hanna moved with her family to Colorado, and now she has three girls, roughly lining up with our boys in age, including a new baby just a few weeks older than Abe. But despite having the same basic family ingredients, the same potential for chaos and conflict, life in the Simmons household as a new family of five is playing out very differently.

Like any good social media nemesis, Hanna's online self-presentation speaks directly to my own insecurities; her particular strain of perfection communicates at some deep cellular level with my own failings. As I help Zephy to sound out the word B-L-E-E-D-I-N-G for his third apology note of the morning, I log onto social media and see a post from Hanna: pictures of her girls together, peacefully doing crafts, playing house or school, and cooperating on art projects they had devised themselves. One of them is an elaborate painting of a rainbow-colored elephant that her two older daughters spent the morning on, working together before she had even woken up. "Sky outlined it and Siena colored it in!" she had written. She might as well have said that they bred live elephants themselves in their bedrooms for all I can relate.

I convince myself that this is probably all social media hype, that the actual reality is less idyllic. After all, I post my fair share of blissful kid pictures, too. People probably think my own life is pretty perfect. But then Hanna brings the girls to visit me in our hometown, and I realize that the difference between our experiences is even starker than I had feared.

We meet for breakfast at a local café. My boys are at school, but Hanna has brought her daughters with her. I am initially a bit disappointed when I see them walking through the door—I had wanted to catch up with Hanna properly and couldn't imagine sitting and chatting for ten seconds if my own boys were around. But we end up lingering for nearly two hours, while the girls join in the conversation, draw pictures, play quiet games with each other, and generally self-regulate.

Wow! I think to myself. *Girls are like humans.*

• • •

Of course, the differences between my experience of parenting and Hanna's hardly constitute a double-blind randomized controlled study. We are just two families, six children. The fact that our children conform to gender stereotypes doesn't make those stereotypes universal or even real. I know plenty of exceptions. Another friend with three daughters is at her wit's end with all their fighting, some of it physical. My friend Elissa's two boys are about as calm as any two children I have ever met. Meghan's three sons are best friends.

Our struggles could have nothing to do with gender at all, and everything to do with individual temperament or parenting. But I have heard enough from other mothers of boys to think my own experiences aren't completely random either. It is the sheer physicality of the experience, the rowdiness, the boisterous energy, the hair-triggered hitting. So many of us seem to share a similar level of exhaustion and nagging self-doubt.

I know that the world is judging me, too. One afternoon at school pickup, I chat with a mom who has two daughters a few years older than my boys. She tells me a story about how she had recently taken them to an orientation dinner at the local middle school. All the girls at the dinner had apparently been sitting nicely, eating and making conversation, while all the boys had been racing around, shouting and throwing food, and their parents had done nothing to stop them, she complains.

"Parents of boys just don't parent their children," she says. I look over at Zephy, who is pulling the flowers off a nearby plant and stomping on them. "Girls are held to higher standards. We expect them to be polite and compliant, whereas people just say, 'boys will be boys' and let them get away with anything."

Just a year or so earlier, I would have enthusiastically agreed with her. Now I am horribly conflicted. My feminist value system tells me she is right, but inside I am screaming: *You try a formal dinner with my boys! Do you know how many times I've told them not to behave this way? How many limits I've set, how many times I've changed my approach, threatened, bribed, cajoled? It's not that easy!* It seemed in that moment as though mothers of girls had the perfect sweet spot—both the easier parenting task and the moral high ground.

What are these mothers of girls doing that I am not doing? Are they just more competent parents? Am I shrugging and allowing my sons to behave like wild animals? It doesn't feel like it. It seems as though I have tried everything, that I am just dealing with an inherently more difficult situation, the basic ingredients just harder to control. But what are my blind spots? Have I in fact inflicted a million invisible acts of boy socialization to get to this point?

• • •

If I am fully honest with myself, my longstanding belief that there were no essential differences between boys and girls had sprung not just from abstract feminist principles but also from a kind of defensive envy. I don't have daughters, and I hate the idea that I have somehow gotten a raw deal, that my sons are biologically preprogrammed to be brutish, insensitive, and exhausting. I had railed against the idea that gender was destiny, in part because if I accepted it, I was accepting some kind of dismal inevitability about my own children.

Perhaps at heart, I just don't want them to be too "boyish." Even the nontoxic version of masculinity doesn't hold a huge amount of appeal for me. I'm sure the world is full of mothers who don't just tolerate the rambunctious physicality of boyhood, but thrive on it, and enjoy the wild ride. But for me, one of two bookish sisters, whose childhood was spent on cello lessons and industrious overachievement, it is a struggle. Even my boys' more lovable rough and tumble moments feel stressful to me. I identify much more strongly with quiet coloring, reading, "using my words," and slightly anxious compliance. When my sons are at their least boyish is when I find them easiest to be around. Like many mothers in the strange liberal bubble of Berkeley, California, where we live, I am more comfortable buying my boys a princess dress than a Nerf gun.

Even the "good" parts of the boy stereotype rankle. In the gender narrative I hear most often, boys are rowdy, animalistic, hard to control, but the flip side is that they are essentially uncomplicated and loving (with the misogynistic subtext "unlike those scheming, devious witches, girls"). On the internet, mothers of boys self-identify under the hashtag #boymom and share "hilarious" stories about mud and farts and pee-stained toilets. But these posts often hit a false note of defensive overcompensation. The narrative has a bit too much of a consolation prize flavor to it, a barely concealed attempt by mothers of boys to convince themselves that they got the better deal. The whole description still feels slightly subhuman—more cute naughty pet than fully realized human relationship.

So I had always pushed back hard against the stereotypes. None of this is innate, I had maintained. If boys and girls behave differently, it's only because we raise them differently. The logic had given me a sense of control, of possibility. It had also chimed well with my feminist principles. "Boys will be boys" is the story that created toxic masculinity in the first place, a get-out-of-jail-free card that we use to excuse and enable bad male behavior, from toddler hitting to frat boy rape. I refused to be part of that story.

But now, exhausted and overwhelmed, I feel as though I have walked into my own ideological trap. In the worldview I had so painstakingly crafted and defended, in which boys behaved badly only because we let them, my own sons' behavior must be, in large part at least, my fault.

• • •

The wider conversation around gender and sex differences has historically stalled in this same territory of nature versus nurture. Both the popular discussion and the science have consistently looped back to the same questions of how much is innate and how much is socialized. As if knowing the answer would somehow provide the key to either solving gender inequality or resigning ourselves to the prospect that it is essentially unsolvable.

The debate itself is deeply loaded and can easily become a highly politicized proxy for a more high-stakes fight. This is the ongoing battle between those who want to expand women's access to power in the world, and those who want to find justifications for limiting it. Because hovering in the background of every pop-psychology article about who can read maps and who can read emotions is the poisonous disparity between men's and women's actual status in the real world. The question of why a single toddler might prefer dolls or diggers, sitting still and coloring or wreaking havoc at circle time comes heavily freighted with the baggage of inequality—of the pay gap and double standards and the distribution of household chores and mansplaining and rape culture and the fights for bodily autonomy and trans rights. This makes it hard for anyone to have the nature-nurture debate in a neutral or fully honest way.

Taken as a whole, the research on gender differences is complicated and often contradictory. It is possible to mine the available studies for innate differences between the sexes and find them. It is also possible to read the same research looking for the idea that these differences are largely socialized or inconsequential and find that, too. People of good faith can look at this body of evidence and draw wildly differing conclusions. It is relatively easy to co-opt individual studies in service of either nature or nurture and to do so with a reasonable claim to objectivity and scientific inquiry.

As both a journalist and a parent, I have done both at different points in my life, first scouring for evidence that there were few essential differences between the sexes, that nurture was everything, and I could star in my own "choose your own parenting adventure" story, carefully socializing any unwanted gender stereotypes out of my children with a high degree of control.

Later when, unsurprisingly, my children refused to cooperate with my hubris, I went back to the same research looking for absolution, for proof that my boys' raucous or aggressive behavior was determined entirely before birth by some premixed neurohormonal cocktail and that I was blameless.

Ultimately, how our sex and our gender affect our personality, identity, and behaviors is an intricate mix of genetics, epigenetics, hormones, socialization, and cultural forces that interact with each other in complex ways that scientists still don't fully understand. What we do know for certain is that there are differences, on average, between the ways boys and girls behave, play, communicate, mature, and respond to the world. These are, of course, population-level trends and don't necessarily apply to any given person—there is a huge amount of individual variation within genders as well as between them, as well as a high degree of overlap. But at a group level, the differences are also real.

Studies show pretty consistently that boys account for the vast majority of behavior problems in school and outside of it at every age. Even boys who are well below any clinical threshold for behavioral disorders show more externalizing (what we would generally think of as "bad") behavior than girls. They are more rambunctious, indulge in more rough and tumble and aggressive play, and have lower emotional control. They mature more slowly socially, cognitively, and physically. They are about ten times more likely than girls to develop serious antisocial behavior in adolescence. Boys now lag behind their female classmates in academics by a fairly significant margin at every level of schooling and are far less likely to gain a college degree than their female peers. Gender and racial inequalities interact in complex ways, but we know that all of the gender discrepancies are exacerbated by race, with Black boys in particular—who are significantly more likely to grow up in disadvantaged homes than white boys—bearing the greatest impact.

There is almost certainly some innate element to sex differences. Brain scans show that boys' and girls' brains develop on different trajectories, with boys' generally developing more slowly and in a different order. The areas of the brain responsible for emotional self-regulation and impulse control develop up to two years more slowly in boys than in girls.[1]

Hormones also play a role. Although levels of testosterone are similar in boys and girls until puberty, male fetuses are bathed in testosterone in the womb. Manipulations of this process in rats and other mammals have shown that there is a direct line from higher levels of fetal testosterone to increased rough and tumble play in childhood and aggression in adulthood.[2]

• • •

Nothing says "It's not my fault" like fetal rat testosterone. After reading the rodent studies, every time I see a Facebook post from Hanna announcing that "The girls surprised us with French toast casserole this morning! Think we'll be skipping lunch," while my boys pummel each other on the living room rug, I whisper "rat gonads, rat gonads" to myself under my breath on repeat—a mantra of absolution.

But really, the deeper I dig into the research on hardwired gender differences, the more I notice a surprising pattern. The most consistent findings are not just that boys are more aggressive or rambunctious or anything else particularly "boyish." They are also—by almost every measure—more sensitive, fragile, and emotionally vulnerable.

It is well known that male infants are more delicate physically than same aged girls. Boys are significantly more likely to die in infancy and childhood from almost every illness and injury.[3] Baby boys born prematurely have a significantly higher risk for every adverse outcome, including long-term disability and death, than premature girls. Virtually all neurological and learning disabilities are also more prevalent in males than in females.[4] The male constitution is generally weaker and less resilient to harm.[5]

But what is less well known is that boys are more vulnerable emotionally, too. The sad irony is that while masculinity norms push boys to be tough—to squash their feelings and hide their weaknesses, right from birth and throughout childhood—young boys are actually more sensitive and emotionally fragile than young girls.

And, one of the most soul-chilling findings for parents of sons, is that almost every environmental stressor or parenting mistake has been shown to have a significantly greater impact on boys than it does on girls. The data shows repeatedly that while girls are more likely to weather everything from abusive parenting to poverty to poor teaching with relative resilience, the consequences for boys tend to be much greater.[6] The gap in resilience between boys and girls comes down to a mix of nature and nurture—both differences in the innate vulnerability of male brains versus female, and also aspects of male socialization that can damage boys' emotional and social development.

One of the leading experts on the vulnerability of boys is Dr. Allan Schore, professor of psychiatry and biobehavioral sciences at UCLA. His work combines neuroscience with psychology and psychoanalysis to study our emotional brains, with a particular focus on emotional and social development and early attachment.

"Talking about gender differences has become controversial because we tend to get hung up on the left hemisphere of the brain," Schore tells me on a Zoom call. "The left hemisphere is the part that governs our intellectual and cognitive functions—our thinking. So people get into arguments about whether men or women are smarter or better at math or whatever. But the more important differences are emotional ones."

Schore's area of expertise is the right hemisphere of the brain, the part that primarily deals with emotions and relationships and nonverbal communication. Human brains are complex and it is easy to oversimplify, but broadly speaking, the right brain is our emotional center. It's the part that allows us to feel—to experience love and fear and sadness and rage at a younger brother's stubborn refusal to stop existing. The right brain also gives us the ability to regulate these emotions, to calm down when we are agitated and to refrain from throwing a Lego spaceship at that brother's head. It is the right brain that causes baby boys to be more vulnerable and less developed than girls at birth.

"By the time they are born, a baby girl's right hemisphere is more than a month ahead of a baby boy's in development and resilience," Schore tells me. "Boys' brains are born more immature and vulnerable, and they mature more slowly throughout childhood."

The immaturity of their right brains mean that baby boys are less able to regulate their emotions than same aged girls. Multiple studies show that male infants are more easily distressed than females.[7] They cry more often and find it harder to calm down. They become more distraught by upsetting events, such as being separated from their mothers, and produce higher levels of the stress hormone cortisol in response, straining their more sensitive brains even further.[8]

Because their right brains are more mature and well-developed, baby girls are generally more emotionally robust. They are more independent, have less need for their caregivers, and are better able to calm themselves when they are upset, without help. Boys, on the other hand, have a greater need for their caregivers to comfort them and help them regulate their emotions.

"Mothers of boys need to put in more effort," says Schore, to my intense validation.

It is also the right hemisphere of a baby's brain that builds their very first attachment with their primary caregiver, usually the mother. This bond becomes the template for all future relationships and the foundation of virtually every measure of lifelong emotional well-being.

"It's impossible to overstate the importance of a secure attachment," Schore tells me. "It is the most consistent marker of emotional health throughout life. It is the attachment bond with the mother that teaches babies emotional self-regulation and how to form a relationship," he continues. "The mother and the baby communicate with each other, right brain to right brain. The mother responds to the baby's needs by comforting him and interacting with him, and in doing so, she helps him learn the skills he needs to eventually calm down by himself, to regulate his own emotions.

"All babies need secure attachment and responsive caregiving," Schore stresses, "but boys need more help with this. The relationship is more fragile, more vulnerable to disruption in the early months."

Because of this vulnerability, any kind of abuse or neglect or hurdles to early attachment, such as maternal postpartum depression or early daycare have consistently been shown to have a more severe long-term impact on boys than on girls. Schore's article in *Infant Mental Health Journal* (see note 8) contains a chilling section on the adverse impact of daycare at six weeks.

"It's one of the most important discoveries in the science," he tells me, "that how well a mother cares for her baby in his early months will literally change the structure of his brain." This is the field of epigenetics, where nature and nurture collide. Although our DNA sequences remain stable, individual genes get switched on and off—depending on our environments—activating molecular changes in our brains.

In both animals and humans, male and female, research has suggested that repeatedly separating a baby from his mother, or failing to respond to a baby's needs over a sustained period, can activate changes in the baby's brain that can lead to a range of negative long-term outcomes. These include hyperactivity, impairments in behavioral flexibility and executive function, and problems with emotional self-regulation later in life. These effects have been shown to be significantly stronger in male infants.[9]

The opposite is also true. When mothers are responsive and give their babies high levels of care, they can trigger a range of positive structural changes in their babies' brains. Studies in rats, for example, show that the most attentive rat mothers who give their pups the highest levels of licking and grooming in the first week of life activate epigenetic changes in their pups' brains that last until adulthood.[10] Throughout their lives, pups of the high-care mothers deal better with stress, are more exploratory in novel environments, and do better on cognitive tasks, such as mazes, than pups who had less nurturing mothers.[11]

As I listen to Schore, the pressure starts to feel immense. Love has always felt like an unknowable alchemy, but perhaps it's a terrifyingly exact science. My every act of care, but also every parenting mistake, could be literally reshuffling my boys' neurobiology, moment by moment, throughout their childhoods.

My thoughts flick to Solly, and I am flooded with fear and regret. When he was a baby, I became obsessed with schedules, with getting him to sleep in his own room. We tried, unsuccessfully, to sleep train him for ten long days, leaving him howling for five-minute bursts in his crib while I sat outside his door, weeping. I thought I was teaching him a valuable skill, but was I actually damaging him, rewiring his vulnerable young brain in ways that we are only just now starting to see? I had railed against attachment parenting, the guilt of it all, the absolutist tone. I had felt sorry for the exhausted mothers schlepping their thirty-pound toddlers around the park in slings. But maybe they had had it right after all. Maybe I hadn't done enough licking and grooming.

"Is this about attachment parenting?" I ask Schore. He looks confused.

"It's not a series of techniques," he replies, to my relief. "It's about forming a bond with that particular infant, responding to that particular infant's cues and needs. There are lots of ways you can do it—it's not a one size fits all."

But guilt always, always creeps around in the shadows of motherhood, and I am needy for exoneration. I want Allan Schore to issue some kind of "certificate of blamelessness," a guarantee that I didn't screw up in this, the most important project of my life, and that my boys would be okay.

"My sons have a hard time self-regulating," I confess, momentarily dropping my journalistic guard, my own left brain caving to my right. "Is that my fault?"

Schore's own right brain clicks into gear, and his face softens. "Do your sons have a good moral sense?" he asks.

I think of the time seven-year-old Solly clung to Zephy with all his might on the treacherously slippery bank of a creek, to keep him from falling in the water while I raced over from the other side of the park—even though Zephy had hit him only moments earlier. I think about how whenever each of them gets an extra chocolate or half hour of screen time, they always insist that their brother get the same to make sure things are "fair." I remember the time Solly decided not to buy the Lego set he'd been saving his allowance for at Target, because his babysitter might feel bad about the smaller Lego set she had given him a week earlier.

"Yes," I say, truthfully.

"Then you've done a good job," says Dr. Allan Schore, world expert.

• • •

Understanding the innate traits of boys more as vulnerabilities and sensitivities than any kind of hardwired destructiveness turns the nature-nurture story on its head. "Boys will be boys" has always been a kind of rationale for inaction, for doing less parenting. "They're just wired that way," we shrug, as we watch our small male humans run riot in the supermarket or bash each other with Tonka trucks, or haze their fraternity brothers until someone asphyxiates. Nature lets us off the hook for nurture.

But really, it should be the other way round. The realities of male vulnerability mean that the more nature there is in the mix, the more nurture boys actually need. Because of their innate fragility, boys need *more* parenting than girls, not less. They need more opportunities to build relationships and engage with their emotions than girls do. In their early years, boys also need more care from responsive caregivers, and they need it for longer.

Sadly, however, research shows clearly that, on all of these counts, they actually get significantly less. Even in families that wholeheartedly believe there is no difference in the way they are raising their sons and daughters, boys and girls receive surprisingly different levels of care from their parents and other caregivers. In most of the Western world, young boys as a whole receive less nurturing and positive attention than same aged girls, by a significant margin, right from birth.

I am shocked to discover that at least in the West, mothers are a staggering 80 percent more likely to suffer from postpartum depression if they give birth to a baby boy rather than a girl.[12] The reasons for this are unclear. Some experts have speculated that because male babies are bigger, they are likely to cause more traumatic births and are more depleting for mothers to feed and care for. But this wholly biological explanation doesn't seem to quite cover it. In cultures where boys are favored, such as India and China, the pattern goes the other way, with mothers of girls significantly more likely to become depressed.[13] It seems likely that there is a cultural element, too.

Whatever the reason, we know that postpartum depression, left untreated, can have long-term effects on children. A wide body of research shows that depression can make it difficult for a mother to give the kind of reciprocal, joyful attention that a young baby needs in order to thrive. Children of depressed mothers have higher rates of a wide range of problems, ranging from attachment problems to language delays to mental health and behavioral issues. And with their more vulnerable neurocircuitry, these negative outcomes are particularly likely for boys.[14]

I hate thinking about this, because I suffered from postpartum depression after my first son, Solly, was born. I had had a difficult birth, with severe tearing. Solly had inhaled meconium and was rushed to the NICU. He had stayed there for a few days as they pumped antibiotics into his tiny veins, while I was trapped upstairs, alone and in pain in a fluorescent-lit London postpartum ward which had the flavor of a Victorian asylum, surrounded by thirty other women and their babies. As I listened to these other babies wailing through the night, while my own baby lay on another floor of the hospital in a sterile plastic box being cared for by nurses, I became uncontrollably scared, existentially disturbed in a way that I had never before experienced. For the first time in my life, my own brain felt like a terrifying place.

Childbirth is violent and bloody. It can rip you apart, physically and emotionally. In the aftermath, the cascade of trauma and hormones can spin you toward euphoria or terror, overwhelming love or total disassociation. I was propelled into a state of low-level horror and also of deep shame. The only acceptable emotional response to a new baby was unadulterated joy, I believed, so I told no one how I was feeling. I didn't even acknowledge it to myself.

The sleepless dread of those early months felt like a fever dream. Breastfeeding, which had been sold to me as a calming tableau of Madonna-like serenity, rivaled childbirth in its raw savagery, ripping my nipples to bloody shreds. Solly cried and cried, and I couldn't comfort him.

As the months went on, the gaudy emotional bloodbath of the early days settled into a more domesticated depression, mundane and deflated. I felt as though my neurobiology had shifted forever.

We were lucky that my mental health never affected our bond. Solly was sparkly, precious, and I loved him deeply and frantically right from the start. But I had lost sight of who I was and who I had been, my grip on my sense of self and the future had faltered. And much as I hate to admit it, even to myself, the fact that my child was a boy and not a girl was part of this.

There's a neat story we tell about gender disappointment, a phenomenon that, if the internet forums are anything to go by, at least in the West, overwhelmingly affects mothers of boys. In this story a mother has a short burst of sadness when she realizes that she is pregnant with a son, and that her fantasies of pink dresses and mother-daughter shopping trips will not be coming true. But as soon as she holds her baby in her arms the feelings are swept away. She realizes that these things are superficial, that gender is a construct anyway.

For me the reality was more complex. I was deeply invested in that same belief system—that stereotypes were just that, and boys and girls could do or be anything they chose. But my sadness spoke to something deeper buried in my sense of self and other. Because gender might be nothing, but it is also everything. Just as our biological sex is coded into every cell in our bodies, our gender is written into every cultural story we live. At some level, a girl felt like a person I could deeply know. A boy was a stranger.

The story has faded with time as I have come to know and love my sons as real people, not just projections of my own fantasies and desires and fears, although a sense of gender-based alienation does still rear its head from time to time. More than anything, I'm left with a profound sense of guilt about my feelings during that time. I scour Solly's behavior for imprints of my early bewilderment and sadness, and torture myself with the idea that any problems he might encounter in life will be my fault.

• • •

Our stories about gender are often invisible, even to ourselves. Research shows that even non-depressed mothers give their baby boys less nurturing and positive touch than their baby girls. The subtle "masculinizing" of male infants starts young. Carefully designed studies show that adults tend to see baby boys as stronger, tougher, angrier, and less in need of care and protection than same aged girls and treat them differently as a result.

Various researchers have conducted experiments in which they cross-dress infants, putting baby boys in girls' clothes and vice versa, and then give them to unknowing adults to take care of. Consistently in these scenarios, when the adults believe that they are looking after boys, they treat them more roughly, use a less gentle tone of voice, give them stereotypical boys' toys to play with, and interpret their behavior through a more masculine lens.

In one such experiment, when the fake boys (who were really girls) cried, the adult subjects described them as angry and were less responsive to them, whereas when the fake girls cried, the adults indicated the babies were sad and gave them comfort and protection.

When they are reported by both academics and the media, these findings are usually framed in terms of their impact on girls—that we tend to underestimate girls' physical capabilities and socialize them to be compliant and docile, rather than adventurous and tough. I had read these studies myself and had felt the appropriate indignation about the ways in which girls are patronized and sold short, but I had barely even registered or questioned the impact that insufficient nurturing might have on young boys.

The same patterns show up in research that observes parents interacting with their own children. The angry baby boys phenomenon showed up in one study of mothers' perceptions of their children's emotional states. Not a single mother judged her daughter to be angry, but many of them rated their sons as such, even when the children themselves were displaying similar behaviors.[15]

A wide range of research shows that mothers react preferentially to their newborn daughters over their newborn sons. Mothers are more likely to respond to their daughter's cries, pick her up and cuddle her, talk to her spontaneously, and respond to her early sounds by chatting back.[16]

Both mothers and fathers also give their infant sons less positive touch, such as hugging, cuddling, rocking, and soothing than they give their baby daughters. Mothers especially spend more time with their girls than with their boys throughout their childhoods (fathers tend to spend more time with sons as they get older, but this time tends to be filled with roughhousing and competition-focused activities, including sports, rather than with emotional nurturing).[17]

Both mothers and fathers encourage their daughters to express their emotions more than they do their sons and talk more about feelings with girls. Fathers, in particular, use more emotional language with their girls, and more competition and winning-focused vocabulary with boys.[18]

• • •

"We have an epidemic of undercared-for boys," Dr. Darcia Narvaez, professor emerita of psychology at Notre Dame University tells me. "No wonder we are seeing all this toxic masculinity when they grow up."

Narvaez's work focuses on the links between attachment and care in early childhood and morality in later life. And she believes that we have a big problem with how we care for boys. She is one of the few researchers making the connection between this phenomenon of "undercare" for boys and its links to some of the traits associated with so-called toxic masculinity in later life. I found Narvaez via an article she wrote for *Psychology Today* entitled "Why Worry about Undercared for Males? Messed up Morals!"[19] in which she makes the case that early undercare of young boys can lead directly to male bad behavior in adulthood.

Undercare, as Narvaez describes, is different from active neglect. It's a subtle, often unconscious difference in how we treat boys. But it can have serious implications.

"Boys need more care than girls and they get less," Narvaez tells me. "People expect boys to be tough and resilient and independent so without even thinking about it mothers are less responsive to them. We push boys out."

In her book, *Neurobiology and the Development of Human Morality* (2014), Narvaez outlines research that echoes what Allan Schore had told me—that how we are cared for in our early years can have a profound long-term impact not just on our mental and physical health but also on our moral functioning. She argues that we become moral beings not by learning and applying a set of rules but by internalizing an entire moral architecture early in life via the love and empathy of our caregivers.

"It's surprising how much undercare negatively influences capacities for ethics and morality later in life," she tells me. "We have come to just expect a large number of adult males to be egoistic and aggressive but that is not the case in other cultures."

A wide body of research confirms this idea that physical affection for children in their early years is linked to healthy moral development. Research across forty-nine societies by the pioneering neuropsychologist Dr. James W. Prescott, for example, found that a culture's level of physical affection toward babies and young children strongly predicted its rates of adult violence and criminality.[20]

Although I am hesitant to write this for fear of piling yet more shame and fear onto mothers who are already struggling, multiple studies have also shown links between untreated maternal postpartum depression and insecure attachment and later increased aggression and reduced empathy in children.[21] (The solution is more support and better access to treatment for mothers, not more impossible expectations and fearmongering.)

There are several indications that more nurturing early care for boys might have a long-term positive impact on their social-emotional skills later in life. In the West we take it for granted that adolescent boys are emotionally less mature than girls. But a couple of surprising studies from India—a country in which infant boys often receive higher levels of early-years care than girls—focusing on adolescents in various regions found that, by every measure, teenage boys were significantly more emotionally mature than same-aged girls. The researchers put this down to "a patriarchal system, gender bias, family climate and traditions." These are all likely—at least in part—a proxy for better early years care.[22]

Clearly this is not all good news; studies such as this likely reveal as much about the neglect of young girls as much as anything else. But they also provide a clue that emotional, social, and moral immaturity among adolescent boys is not inevitable, but rather something we can work to change.

• • •

At a gut level, it's hard to square male privilege with male vulnerability, and a big ask for many women to muster much sympathy for boys and men. Centering harm to men seems to minimize the countless social obstacles and injustices that women and girls have always faced. It's tempting to be punitive rather than sympathetic, to try to somehow even the score and hold young boys accountable for the sins of their fathers. But operating from a place of punishment or shame or lack of empathy for boys is counterproductive in creating empathetic well-adjusted men.

For boys, vulnerability and privilege coexist in a complex relationship. Masculine norms and expectations confer countless advantages, but they also bring significant harm. The two come together in male socialization to create a contradictory and strangely destructive combination of indulgence and neglect.

Seeing my own boys' struggles as vulnerabilities rather than discipline problems helps me. An imposter brother had snatched away their mother's attention. In their most dysregulated moments, my older boys are just two fragile right brains howling in the dark, clawing each other out of the way to get to my right brain. I likely am undercaring for them simply because I am stretched thin, exhausted, constantly feeling like I am about to snap.

Seeing this for what it is helps me respond with love. More

and more, when they act out, I try to react by giving them care and attention, a moment of "licking and grooming" rather than harshness or punishment. It is a work in progress, for sure. I still lose my temper, threaten them with grievous "consequences," and then regret it and apologize. But the new approach works better most of the time. Or at least, I reason with myself in my more defeated moments, if I'm going to screw them up, I'd rather screw them up with too much love than not enough.

The one thing I know for sure is that I love them, each of them, deeply, passionately, sweetly: Solly's huge brown eyes, his earnest sense of justice, his wildly ambitious art projects, and his unfailing ability to get at least one item of clothing on back to front and inside out every time he gets dressed. Zephy's uncontainable joy, his little body's way of bursting out of life's most tedious moments into a spontaneous dance routine.

"I'm made out of atoms and fun," he told me once at the park, then bounded off to fight some imaginary enemies. Abe's solid sweetness, his belly laughs, and delight in being the cherished final baby. My right brain yearns for each of their right brains. I just have to hope this will be enough to carry us through.

• • •

Loving a child always comes with a built-in expectation of loss. What will we be to each other when you are grown up and no longer need me? But perhaps for mothers of boys, the question is darker, more socially loaded. Our cultural narrative still allows for a deep closeness between a mother and her grown-up daughter. "My mom is my best friend" is a perfectly acceptable, loving phrase for a teenage girl or grown woman to say while still maintaining her status as a well-functioning adult. But it is still a socially jarring claim for an adult man to make. Excessive intimacy between a mother and her grown son is still framed as suspect—at best, emasculating and oppressively coddling, at worst psychologically predatory and vaguely sexualized.

When #boymoms on the internet discuss gender disappointment, this is often one of the first things they mention. "I worry about when he's older," wrote one mother-to-be on finding out that she was pregnant with a boy. "I worry I just won't have the relationship that I would have with a daughter." Before a boy is even born, we already bring a series of gender-based preconceptions to the relationship, assuming that we will be less able to connect with him. It's not hard to see how this might subtly affect our behavior and become a self-fulfilling prophecy.

But the wider culture also demands a level of distance between mothers and sons. A mother craving too much emotional closeness with her boy after his early years is painted as either faintly ridiculous or downright selfish, somewhere between the butt of a mother-in-law joke and a psychoanalytic villain. For this particular pairing, intimacy is framed as harm. A good mother should put aside her own needs and emotions and instead push her son away, an act of love to help him to become independent and manly. For the son, detaching from his mother is a basic requirement of masculinity.

It's misogynistic nonsense, of course. Decades of research tells us that the strength of a man's emotional connection to his mother is actually one of the greatest markers of his well-being throughout life.[23] But it's nonsense that runs deep, and one that I fear my sons will be forced to buy into. Sometimes I wonder how it will go. How the loss will happen. Will they lose their heart-clenching sweetness or simply suppress it, spackle it over with masculine avoidance? Will it be sudden or slow? I want to intercept the process, tackle it to the ground, make it stop. But trapped inside centuries of sexist cultural reasoning, I still worry that to do this would be selfish, that it would hurt my boys socially.

I probably couldn't stop it if I tried, anyway. The more I look into it, the more I realize just how deeply the stories of masculinity snarl into the fabric of our daily lives—both what we expect from boys, and what we fail to expect from them.

CHAPTER 2

"GIRL STORIES"

WHAT WE ARE FAILING TO TEACH BOYS ABOUT BEING HUMAN

When Zephy was maybe five, our family went on a vacation. We were by the pool when he spied a group of little girl mermaids in sparkly waterproof tails, captivated by a larger, adult mermaid, who was teaching them basic merskills. Apparently, the hotel was offering a mermaid experience, complete with mermaid lesson and photoshoot.

Zephy was enchanted and begged me to sign him up. Feeling pride in my gender-norms-bucking boy, we went to the hotel's front desk to ask about availability and prices. Predictably, the package was wildly expensive, but they had a spot open in the next morning's class, and I agreed to enroll him.

But as I was filling out the forms, the receptionist spotted Zephy skulking behind me in his swimming trunks. "Ah, a boy," she said. "My mistake, sorry. Boys are sharks, not mermaids. Shall I sign you up for the shark experience instead?"

The shark experience. That could be the tagline for the entirety of boy socialization. *Boyhood. The shark experience.* Zephy's whole childhood would likely be one shark experience after another. I didn't want to pay for the shark experience.

I mumbled some excuse to Zephy about the price being higher than we could afford, and we walked away. He was disappointed. It sat badly and it still does.

I know what it's like to grow up feeling as though you are part of your mother's political project. When I was a child, in the late seventies and early eighties, my mom was a feminist, back when they called them "women's libbers," with a sneer. Her feminism was the dogmatic, second wave flavor, much more about no than yes. Lots of things were forbidden. No Barbie. No nail polish or bikinis. No Girl's World, a strange disembodied plastic head that British girls of the 1980s used to practice styling hair and putting on makeup. My mother taught my sister and me to say, with barely a hint of irony, that pink was "the color of our oppression." I spent most of the early eighties in a unisex playsuit with a bizarrely unflattering short haircut, craving objectification. For a clothes-loving, gender normative little girl, it sometimes felt like a deprivation tank.

At the beginning of one summer term, when I was eight or nine, our elementary school sent out a letter to parents. There would be some changes to the boys' school uniform—instead of the usual gray flannel, boys would now be allowed to wear denim shorts. The girls' uniform would remain the same: a blue-and-white checked dress. But, in a radical change for that time, girls could also choose to wear the denim shorts from the boys' uniform. The idea was catnip for my mother. Our family didn't have a lot of money, and new clothes were rare. But she read this letter and announced that she was going to buy me the denim shorts. The boys' shorts!

I did not want to wear the boys' shorts. The idea was horrifying. "Can I have a new summer dress instead?" I asked.

"Um, we don't really have the money for that," she replied, in much the same awkwardly defensive "don't-stand-in-the-way-of-my-ideological-mission-with-your-retrograde-personal-desires" tone that I used to nix the shark experience for Zephy.

"But you have the money for the shorts!" I wailed.

"Well, we have some money, but not very much," she hedged. I didn't get the shorts or the summer dress. This wasn't about what I wanted. It wasn't really about me at all.

The people who sniggered and called feminists women's libbers were gleeful when they saw me craving pink or sparkles.

"You see!" they gloated, "it's natural for girls to want this! If you deprive them, they'll only want it more!" People love to see a dogmatist get their comeuppance, and the joy is only sweeter when that dogmatist is a woman and a feminist. Back then, *feminist* was basically another word for "unattractive," and on some level there was nothing more repellent, more socially threatening than an unattractive woman. Whatever else she might do or achieve in life, a woman's main job was to be pretty and unthreatening, and little girls were in active training for this social duty. Pink preserved the social order. Feminism really only gained mainstream social traction when it gave in and embraced the nonthreatening pink aesthetic itself.

In one sense, the sneerers were right. What I lacked during my childhood I craved in adulthood. Now I do spend an absurd amount of money that I don't have on clothes. I love fake nails, that mean I can't type; crippling heels, that mean I can't walk. There's a small part of me that wants to be totally incapacitated by femininity.

I'm still not sure that deprivation is the best way to get a child to truly embrace an ideology. But maybe in those early years of second wave feminism, that kind of simple, bulldozing messaging was necessary. Because over the long term, I'm grateful to my mom for holding the line and understand why she did it. Her feminist project improved my own life in immeasurable ways.

Her willingness to challenge gender roles and expectations left me with an aptitude for critical thinking, as well as a deeper faith in myself, a basic knowledge that my concerns were as important as a man's. I grew up believing that I could be the main character, not the sidekick or accessory; that I could write about my opinions for a living and be the one making the jokes, as well as the one laughing at them. It's no coincidence that many of my closest friends in adulthood—women that I met and liked instantly, with no idea how they were raised—turned out to have had similar upbringings, with similar outcomes. Our mothers broke the back of the constant gendering of girlhood. Now we get to be full people, not just women.

I try to think about this when I encourage my sons to break free of the roles assigned to them, to challenge masculinity norms and embrace new possibilities. I tell myself that these things don't always go in a straight line, but instead play out in complex and unexpected ways; that my children aren't instruments of my will, and it's good that they are pushing back. That in the long run, this is worth fighting for.

There's a lot to unpack in my mother's political project, even on its own terms. In her version of feminism, girl socialization was the system that needed changing. Whatever boys were doing was to be admired and emulated. At minimum, boy socialization was default normal, not open to question. Her value system certainly reinforced the idea that masculine is aspirational, feminine is lesser.

This framing was probably necessary for the reality of the times, but it also missed something crucial. In all its dissecting and questioning of the harmful and limiting messages aimed at girls, it failed to recognize what is good and important and admirable about girl socialization, and what the culture of girlhood might have to offer boys. The longer I spend raising sons, the more I am starting to feel that there is something critical that my boys are missing out on, that the world is failing to teach them. Something that they could learn from girl culture.

• • •

One afternoon when Solly and Zephy are in elementary school, we stop in the bookstore after school. I spot a magazine on the shelf that has the kind of hypergendered pink branding that doesn't just suck in girls but also actively pushes away boys. Its hot-pink, sparkly cover screams out to them, "Look away! Even glancing in this direction will crush whatever insecure fragments of masculinity that you have so far managed to shore up!"

In between the friendship-bracelet tutorials and the "What Type of Hamster Sums Up Your Personality?" quizzes, the magazine features a story about a young girl who was invited to two birthday parties that are scheduled for the same time. Scared to disappoint either friend, she comes up with an elaborate plan to shuttle unnoticed between the parties, joining in the games at one before racing off to arrive just in time for the same games at the other, then repeating this sprint for cake at each house and so on, exhausting herself in the process. This is a tale of high-intensity emotional labor, and, as a mother of three and a woman in the world, I relate to it strongly—if not the actual scenario itself, then at least the compulsive people-pleasing impulses driving the narrative.

This birthday party stressfest is a pretty standard-issue story for girls. My sons' female peers will likely have read or watched hundreds like it—narratives centered around friendships, relationships, and social and emotional dynamics. And notably, in these stories, girls must consider and manage the feelings of others. These were my stories as a young girl, too—the movies and TV shows I watched, the books and comics I read, the values I internalized about what was important.

But flicking through the magazine now, as the mother of three boys, this type of people-driven story feels like it's from another world. I quickly realize that despite my liberal vanities about raising my sons in a relatively gender-neutral way, they have most likely never read a story like this, let alone found themselves in a similar situation in real life.

As male toddlers, my sons were quickly funneled into a vehicle-only narrative world. Preschool masculinity norms apparently stipulate that human dilemmas may only be explored through the emotional lives of bulldozers or steam trains (or the occasional precocious stegosaurus).

When they aged out of the digger demographic, the boys transitioned seamlessly into a fictional universe dominated by heroes, villains, fighting, and a whole lot of "saving the day." Virtually every story they read, TV show they watch, and video game they play is essentially a story with two men (or male-identifying nonhuman creatures) pitted against each other in some form of combat, which inevitably ends with one crowned a hero and the other brutally defeated. Almost all of them have a winner and a loser, a good guy and a bad guy.

It is within this aggressive and emotionally limited frame of reference that boys learn the early scripts of masculinity—both what is expected of them, and what has nothing to do with them. Their fictional world contains very little emotional complexity. There is no interiority or social negotiation. No friendship dilemmas or internal conflict. None of the mess of being a real human in relationship with other humans. When these concerns do make an appearance, it tends to be more as an afterthought or hurried subplot, almost never the main point.

Of course, boys are free to consume "girl stories," too. But in addition to the gendered marketing, the characters in these types of stories are almost always girls. While there are now usually at least a smattering of female characters in boys' adventure and battle stories, there are few even token role models for boys to see themselves reflected in the kinds of friendship and relational stories that girls consume as standard.

One exception to the no-people-focused-stories-for-boys rule is the small subgenre of realistic chapter books aimed at elementary and middle school boys. These are actually wildly popular. Jeff Kinney's Diary of a Wimpy Kid series, for example, has sold more than 250 million copies, while the middle school graphic novel series Big Nate has sold more than 20 million. My boys and their friends gobble up these books, hungry for something that reflects their own lives. They gain a fair amount from them, too—a jumping-off point to think about their own real-world challenges and relationships, and a way to open up discussions about the emotional dilemmas they face.

But the protagonist in this genre is almost invariably a slightly depressing antihero. This character is now familiar—a middle-school nihilist who is almost aggressively mediocre. His driving motivation tends to be a kind of contempt—for teachers, friends, annoying siblings, and nagging parents. He is often casually misogynistic, in the "stupid, dumb girls" vein, and carries around a pervasive sense of grievance. If we follow his trajectory of resentment and self-loathing to its most extreme conclusion, it's not a huge stretch to imagine him in ten years' time, elbow deep in the manosphere, trolling feminists online from his parents' basement.

In the Wimpy Kid books in particular, friendship itself is subtly pitched as effeminate. Throughout the series, Greg, the main character, sneers relentlessly at his "best friend" Rowley, almost to the point of bullying. In one scene, Rowley tries to give Greg a "best friends locket." Greg ridicules him and refuses to wear it because it is "for girls."

Obviously, there are gender-neutral books and shows that are marketed to both boys and girls and contain more relational or friendship content, book series such as Harry Potter and The Mysterious Benedict Society; TV shows such as *Gravity Falls* or *The Dragon Prince*. In recent years, in a couple of TV shows, a female or nonbinary director has reimagined traditional boy content to give it a more relational focus, sneaking emotions and relationships in through the back door. The animated hit *Steven Universe,* for example, is in many ways classic boy territory: a young boy lives with a group of magical alien warriors, develops superpowers, and then helps the aliens protect humanity from monsters. But in the hands of creator Rebecca Sugar, it became essentially a show about friendship, love, tolerance, and the importance of healthy relationships.

In a similar vein, when Zephy got into competitive Rubik's cubing (a scene that is overwhelmingly dominated by boys and young males), we watched the hit Netflix documentary *The Speed Cubers* together. Director Sue Kim takes this naturally dry and statistics-heavy subject matter, one that can easily become two mono-focused boys reciting cubing algorithms at each other, and turns it into a moving human-interest story of an unusual friendship between two male competitors, the world champion Feliks Zemdegs and his autistic rival, Max Park.

These exceptions are bright lights, but for the most part, in boys' narrative worlds, exploration of friendship or relationships, or the need to manage other peoples' emotional needs is either absent or a minor side concern.

"Girl stories" have their problems, too, of course. Historically girls were fed a diet of books and movies populated by beautiful princesses, whose value lay in their looks, and who were passive and lacked agency and needed rescuing by men. But by now, most feminists are generally aware of the harm in these tropes and have done good work in addressing them. In her bestselling book *Cinderella Ate My Daughter: Dispatches from the Front Lines of the New Girlie-Girl Culture* (2012), for example, the journalist and author Peggy Orenstein picked apart the "princessification" of girl culture and the stereotyping and sexist messaging embedded within it, about beauty, body image, self-worth, ambition, and female-versus-male agency.

Critiques like these had a measurable impact. Disney is now giving its princesses special powers and control over their own destinies, and the Barbie movie mentioned the word "patriarchy" ten times in under two hours. Meanwhile in the world of children's books, every time we see the word *girl* we can now expect to see an adjective such as *strong* or *mighty* lurking nearby, and most self-respecting progressive parents feed their daughters a steady diet of stereotype-busting role models so they can see themselves as superheroes and scientists and Supreme Court justices.

But because feminine-coded skills and priorities are so undervalued, we barely register that there is a worrying gap in boy socialization. We have hardly considered our failure to give boys role models that could help them see themselves as connected, emotionally nuanced, relational beings, or even to see these kinds of social-emotional skills as something worth prioritizing and cultivating.

In a sexist culture, we tend to trivialize young girls' preoccupation with the intricacies of relationships as "girl drama." This is the product of a corrosive gender hierarchy in which we automatically assign concerns or pastimes that are associated with girls or women a lower cultural value than those associated with boys and men. Women's interests are generally dismissed as niche or insignificant—fine for them but not worthy of the serious attention of boys or men. Fashion, say, is shallow and frivolous, whereas baseball is basically a branch of philosophy.

The association of emotional labor with women has had a fair amount of press recently, along with its cousins, people-pleasing and likability. The neoliberal girl-power iteration of feminism, with its emphasis on individual assertiveness and self-confidence, has generally tried to socialize these impulses out of girls and women, concerned that girls are taking on too much of this kind of work. But this story also misses the idea that emotional labor is fundamental to human connection and therefore beneficial for boys and men.

While girls are admired for engaging in traditionally male pursuits, for a boy or man to enjoy anything coded as feminine is still somehow shameful, and the same applies to relationship-driven stories.

Gal Beckerman, a former editor at *The New York Times Book Review*, and now senior editor for books at *The Atlantic,* remembers his secret boyhood passion for the Baby-sitters Club book series (now a Netflix show), which focuses on the friendships and emotional dynamics of a group of twelve-year-old girls.

"So deep is my remembered shame," he wrote in a confessional piece about the series for the *Times*, "that even now, sitting at my keyboard at the age of forty-three, I'm blushing.

"It seemed like the only real options for me were *The Hobbit* or the Hardy Boys or Choose Your Own Adventure books," the article continued. "Stories that as I recall all involved dragons and trap doors and motorcycle chases. Sneaking home one of Ann Martin's books . . . felt like a crime. I mean, all of the covers were pastel."

Beckerman built his career around a love of literature and credits the emotional complexity of books such as the Baby-sitters Club with giving him the tools in adulthood to understand and appreciate literary fiction.

"There was something about exploring emotions and relationships that I felt was absent from the books that were being shoved towards me," he tells me in an interview. "I think I connected with the stories because they were the questions I had about my own life and the people around me and the social situations I was finding in school."

I ask him if he thinks he would have enjoyed, as a child, a book about four boys and their social dynamics. He seems stumped, pausing to grope for what such a book might look like. Eventually he gives up. "It's hard to even imagine a book like that for boys," he admits. "It's just this assumption about what boys like and want."

After talking to Beckerman, I lightly coerce my two older boys to watch the Netflix reboot of the Baby-sitters Club with me, hoping to inspire in them a similar interest in more relational themes. But they quickly find the show alienating. It's not hard to see why. It's not just that boys are almost totally invisible in the story. The girl characters also adopt a familiar "girl power" vocabulary and tonal register, to subtly denigrate them. Within the first three minutes of the first episode, one of the girls complains to her best friend that her male teacher expects the girls in the class to be "polite and invisible," and had penalized her for calling out the sexism in Thomas Jefferson's "all men are created equal" logic, while ignoring the fact that the boys in her class are just "sticking Kleenex down their pants and wiping sweat on each other." Zephy wails that the show is "negatively stereotyping boys," perhaps oversensitive to this shtick after two hours of the Barbie movie the previous week, watching the Kens get roasted as gormless, mockable himbos.

Apart from this passing mention, boys are mainly notable by their absence in the Baby-sitters Club. One character does pay hurried lip service to the idea that "boys can take care of kids too," but this doesn't play out—none of the actual babysitters in the club are boys. It's hard to imagine Netflix adapting a 1980s book series called, say, Science Club, featuring a boy-only group, without updating it to include at least one girl. It's easy to see why my boys immediately assume that the show and its themes are not for them.

• • •

Niobe Way is a professor of developmental psychology at New York University and has been studying boys' friendships for more than twenty years. She agrees that there are very few examples of relationship-driven stories aimed at boys. Way remembers searching in a school library for a book about friendship that featured boy characters and finding nothing. She found gender-neutral books that featured friendships, usually between boys and girls, such as Harry Potter; and books that featured pairs of male friends, where the friendship was incidental to the story. She found no books for boys in which the friendship was the main point and actually drove the narrative.

"I couldn't even find one," she tells me, slightly exasperated. "They just weren't there. The only books about friendship for boys were about being friends with an animal."

Stories matter. They are our emotional and social blueprints, what we come to expect of ourselves and others and how we engage with our lives. And through the stories they are told, boys and girls are tracked into two subtly but significantly different value systems: one that centers relationships, emotions, and complex social dynamics; and another that largely ignores them, depicting human interaction as essentially oppositional and competitive.

In the narratives they consume, as well as the broader cultural landscape in which they operate, girls get a huge head start on relational skills—in the day-to-day thorniness and complexity of emotional life. Story by story, girls are given the message that other people's feelings are their concern and their responsibility. Boys are learning that these things have little to do with them.

Perhaps it's no surprise, then, that in surveys teenage girls are significantly more likely than same aged boys to report that they feel "a lot of pressure to manage other people's emotions," to "keep everybody happy," and "to put others' feelings before their own."[1]

It's an imbalance that gives boys and men permission to check out of this kind of relational work and puts exhausting pressure on girls and women to shoulder the social and emotional load of life. It seamlessly becomes a woman's job to remember the birthdays and wipe the tears and send the thank-you notes and understand that Grandma's increasingly aggressive eyebrow twitch means that she secretly hates Aunt Susan and they need to be separated before Susan tells the necklace story again.

This doesn't just place an unfair burden on girls and women. What is perhaps less visible in our cultural narrative is that it harms boys and men, too. In excess, this kind of emotional labor can be taxing, for sure, but it is also one of the fundamentals of human intimacy. Without it, boys are missing out on internalizing concepts and learning skills that are crucial to a full, connected, psychologically healthy life. Our failure to teach boys these skills and give them role models for a more intimate and emotionally focused kind of friendship has left many of them struggling to form the kinds of deep and supportive connections they need and crave.

• • •

When I interviewed boys for this book—macho jocks and lonely incels, cool kids and socially awkward ones, gay and straight—I was surprised with how emotionally open they were with me. I had half expected teenage boys to be these grunting numbskulls, but they desperately wanted to talk, to tell me all about their lives and feelings. The conversations usually went on much longer than the time I had scheduled. Seemingly starved of the social permission to open up to anyone else with this level of candor, the boys talked to me for hours about their relationships and crushes, their families, their secrets and fears.

It makes sense that it would be easier to open up to an adult interviewer than a male peer. With me, the conversation really only goes one way; they have no obligation to manage my feelings or needs or engage in any complex relational give-and-take. In this context, the boys I talked to were able to process their lives and emotions in nuanced and thoughtful ways, and they were hungry to do so. But almost without exception, they told me that they struggled to relate to their friends with anything like the same honesty or depth.

It was a theme that came up over and over again, with boys who otherwise seemed to have little in common. They were lonely. It manifested itself in different ways for each of them, but the pattern was striking. Although a handful were genuinely socially isolated, most had plenty of friends. But they felt that something was missing in those friendships. Their connections seemed shallow: they hung out, had fun, but they didn't ever quite get past the superficial. This wasn't through lack of desire. Almost without exception, the boys I spoke to all wanted deeper, more supportive, and more emotionally focused connections with friends but had no real idea how to go about it.

Marshall, nineteen, is a gentle-natured college freshman in South Carolina, studying design. He was introduced to me after I put out a call for boys of all backgrounds to interview for this book. He and I have scheduled a one-hour Zoom call, but we end up talking for nearly three hours. He tells me about his childhood, running semiferal in a pack of neighborhood kids, and about his relationship with his parents (generally good, but they don't talk much). He talks about his bout of depression in middle school and his feelings of loneliness and alienation now. Marshall shares an apartment with his older brother, Aidan, a junior at the same college. The pair also have a younger brother, who still lives at home with their parents.

My ears perk up when I hear that Marshall is one of three boys. I love hearing about families with three brothers, projecting my own fantasies onto them, secretly hoping for them to provide me with an idyllic vision for our own future. I long to hear stories of brotherly loyalty and protectiveness, of hilarious high jinks, and in more histrionic moments, maybe risking their lives for each other on the battlefield. The idea of college-aged Solly and Zephy, giant and stubbly, renting an apartment together clenches my heart in that joy-loss grip that characterizes so much of parenthood.

But Marshall and Aidan's relationship seems nothing like this fantasy. They hang out sometimes and play video games together, share some friends and a lot of childhood memories. But although they get along fine and there is no conflict, there is little emotional closeness.

"I don't talk to my brother that much," Marshall tells me. "Not about relationships or anything like that. We don't talk about anything emotional. He mainly just talks to his girlfriend."

For the most part, Marshall and Aidan both tend to stay in their rooms, each on his own device, and Marshall gets his information about his brother mainly through their parents. He knows, for example, that his brother went through a period of depression in high school. He can relate—Marshall is still scarred by his own depressive episode in middle school. But the brothers never talked about it together, never shared confidences or supported each other during the hard times.

It's not just with his brother. This inability to form close emotional bonds with his friends has been a pattern since middle school. Marshall is charming and socially skilled; he doesn't come off as awkward, and in our conversation he is beguilingly honest and vulnerable. But since he hit adolescence, his friendships with other boys have been frustratingly superficial.

"It's hard to find somebody that you can just talk to about what you're feeling," he tells me. "I think it definitely is a boy thing."

"What would happen if you tried?" I ask.

"I don't think it would be a bad thing. I think that they would probably take it well," he replies. "I mean, there's definitely certain people that would just be like, why are you like bringing this up? You're just dumping this on me. But I think that the kinds of friends that I try to have anyways, I think they would be fine with it. It's just still really hard to even get the words out in the first place."

In elementary school Marshall had a best friend, Lincoln. He and Lincoln were close, going to each other's houses and sharing their secrets and lives. But when he went to middle school, things changed. His new school was in a different district and none of his old friends were there. The school focused heavily on test scores.

Lonely and with the academic pressure piling on, Marshall fell into a depression. When he wasn't at school, he spent hours lying in his room in the dark and watching anime or playing video games.

"I don't think I had anybody that I could talk to that I felt like I was safe with," he tells me. "It's still something that's really hard to talk about with friends. I assume that girls are more emotionally open with each other."

He is almost certainly right. Although of course there is a lot of variation in male friendships as well as female, the guarded and somewhat bleak picture Marshall and other boys paint of how they relate to their friends stands in stark contrast to how girls tend to describe their friendships.

When the British magazine *The Economist* published a long essay about the lives of teenage girls, conducting dozens of interviews with girls from across America and Europe about their lives and priorities, the difference from what boys are telling me is striking.

"The intensity and closeness of girl-friendships is an experience that many women feel shapes their lives," the author wrote. "It is also one of the first things girls mention when asked what they like about being a girl."

One interviewee described how she told her best friend everything, "because she's Frankie. She's like my diary." Another high schooler described her closest friendship. "We fully understand each other, we can rely on each other. If we have a bad day, we help each other. Boys just don't do that." Across the board in the interviews, girls reported that they shared everything with their friends and knew they could count on one another when times were tough.

A local mom I talk with who has both a teenage son and daughter describes a similar contrast in their friendships. "Ben has always found it much harder than Emily to find that kind of deep connection," she tells me. "When Emily and her friends have a sleepover, six of them all cram into one bed and they stay up all night talking, going really deep. When Ben sleeps over at a friend's house, they play video games and then the friend goes to bed in his own room and Ben sleeps downstairs."

With female friendships, there seem to be two conflicting stereotypes at play. Supportive and intimate; but also catty and exclusive. People often describe the machinations of girls' social lives as inherently devious and cruel. Boys are seen, by contrast, as feral and happy-go-lucky, running wild in good-hearted packs, simpler but also somehow loftier and more noble, above the petty intrigue and histrionics of female friendships.

The "mean girl" dynamic is a misogynistic caricature, for sure, but there is also truth in it. Research does show that girls are more likely to report being verbally bullied and excluded at school (boys are more likely to report being physically bullied).[2] Many girls describe middle school and high school as a kind of social hell. But really, these apparently contradictory stereotypes are two sides of the same coin: Girls are socialized to be more invested in their relationships. As a result, their connections are deeper and the stakes are higher. Girls expect more from their friends and tend to get more in return, both good and bad.

The differences between boys and girls start early. My boys' friendships are mostly based on shared interests, rather than deep emotional connection. They become friends with another kid because he also likes *Star Wars,* or Pokémon or Legos, and that is what they talk about, often incessantly. While the girls in their classes sink deeper into ever more sophisticated social dynamics and intimate disclosures, my sons and their friends take turns delivering lengthy monologues about whatever video game they are obsessed with. They rarely process what is going on in their lives with their friends, or share secrets or confidences or comfort. If I ask one of the boys a simple question such as "Is Ari enjoying school?" or "Did Ezra have a good vacation?" they usually have no idea.

The way my boys and their peers relate to each other seems like the junior version of many adult male friendships that I see, the relentless conversations about baseball or rare vinyl records or which obscure actor was in which movie, filling the spaces and ruling out the emasculating possibility of going any deeper.

I remember once witnessing an exchange between Solly and a

teacher when he was in second grade. Solly was being too hard on himself about a failed art project, and the teacher was trying to encourage the skill of "self-compassion." The teacher asked Solly to consider how he would comfort his best friend Ezra in a similar situation. The idea was to remind Solly to give himself the same forgiveness and empathy that he would extend to a friend.

But Solly just stared back blankly. He is an empathetic kid with a kind heart, but he really did not see it as his role to comfort Ezra at all. It was as though she had asked Solly how he would go about scheduling Ezra's dentist appointment or filling out his medical forms for camp. Boys are not taught to believe they can play a role in each other's emotional lives.

As Solly has gotten older, his friendships have settled into a more bantering dynamic, with lots of elaborate in-jokes, many of them meme based. I love their emphasis on humor, the ever more creative comedy that adolescent boys at their best often generate. Their cultural aversion to earnestness can push them to be very funny. But it still stays firmly on the surface.

It's hard to know how typical my son's friendships are of boys more generally, but when I ask around, many mothers of sons describe similar dynamics. Talia, a mom of three boys aged thirteen, eleven, and nine, tells me that her sons' friendships are similarly lacking in emotional intimacy. They talk about movies, video games, occasionally things that happen at school, but never really about their feelings or personal struggles. Her oldest son, although popular with his classmates, never shares any emotional worries with his friends. Her middle son once tried to share with his friendship group his fear that his cat might be dying, but they didn't seem interested. So he gave up and never mentioned it again. Her nine-year-old got the closest to intimate conversation when a friend asked him whether he was sad about his parents' recent divorce.

"He said no, and that was it," his mom tells me.

I am sure that there are many boys who have vulnerable, emotionally open relationships with each other, but I rarely come across them. And it's hardly surprising. Boys have few role models for these types of relationships with other boys, no real cultural blueprint for how they might look.

• • •

It's hard for me to relate to how my boys connect with their friends. Female friendships have been the heartbeat of my life. My childhood friendships were hugely intimate, deeply overinvested, highly political, and occasionally brutal. We knew the ins and outs of each other's family lives, hopes, and frustrations. We cried easily and readily and comforted each other. We could also be mean. The high-octane relational contradictions were summed up in a note that was gleefully hand delivered to me by two of my best friends in third grade:

> Dear Ruth,
> We hate you. Lots of love from Ana and Suzie.

With their lack of emotional intensity and fervor, I find my sons' friendships alien. More than anything, this fundamentally different approach to human intimacy is at the heart of any grief I feel about not having a daughter. I feel worried for my sons, and at some level I fear that they are missing out on the best thing in life. And I feel the loss for myself, a sadness that I won't get to witness that particular joy unfold for my own children.

People console me with the reassurance that friendships between boys and men are not worse than the female version, just different. But this reframe sits uneasily. It's not that I can't see lots to admire in male friendships. Men and boys are often deeply loving and loyal to their friends, I tell myself, they just express it in different ways.

But my interviews with older boys suggest that they themselves also feel something is missing. Rather than defending their model of friendship, they also feel that they aren't getting the closeness and support that they need and want.

The research backs up this hunch. Academics studying gender

differences consistently find that friendships between women are more intimate and supportive and of higher quality than those between men.[3] A fair amount of evidence suggests that women find it easier to access social support and connection than men, and that this is driven by gender role expectations that are embedded from earliest childhood.[4]

• • •

Oliver is a sociable and popular nineteen-year-old with a tight-knit group of male friends, most of whom he has known since kindergarten. After graduating high school, four of them moved into a shared house together. They hang out, play guitars, and rib each other with a million long-running in-jokes. One night they accidentally broke through a partition wall in their rented house, and sheepishly slunk off to Home Depot together the next morning and rebuilt it before the landlady found out.

Oliver and his buddies are clearly close, but when I ask him to describe these friendships he replies instantly, "It's a very unsupportive support system. The world doesn't teach us to be emotionally competent. You can be best friends with someone that you treat awful."

Rather than nurturing or supportive, Oliver describes the underlying dynamic to his friendships as competitive. "I think for me it started really young," he tells me. "Because I wanted to be the best, the smartest, the funniest. I think back to elementary school. I had my best friend and during recess we would play this game called Power Game, where we would have powers and we would defeat monsters. We were working together to defeat the imaginary monsters, but we were always trying to be more powerful than one another so that we could defeat the monsters better than the other one. But introducing that competition into friendships created aggression."

This competitive dynamic in his friendships continued as Oliver got older. "I used to have a friend in high school," he remembers. "And we would be constantly competing for everything: for food or the best seats or who was faster or girls or who got better grades. Everything. We hung out together all the time and I loved him a lot, but it was really unhealthy. And it brought out that state of *I need to be better than this person*. Then that's when it becomes where you're not treating others with respect. You're manipulating and trying to win. It was very stressful."

"What was behind it all, do you think?" I ask him. He considers for a minute.

"I think it stems from insecurity and masculinity," he says eventually. "I think there's this aspect of calling the shots and owning a certain sphere."

Although girls are also often competitive with their friends, this dynamic is usually moderated by the social expectation that they should also be mutually supportive. But for Oliver, the constant competition made it hard to open up to his friends about his emotions or talk honestly with them when things weren't going so well.

"There's no way you can feel sad," he tells me. "Not only can you not talk about it but if you are sad, then you're not able to react in the way that you need to. So you can be on top. There's absolutely no room for that because you start falling behind. I'm beginning to associate it more with being a man," he continues. "Like realizing my patterns and then being like, oh, that's masculinity. Boys are taught to not feel emotions and not to validate each other's emotions. It makes it extremely hard to have deep relationships with people."

Oliver grew up in Berkeley, California, one of the most liberal communities in America. The phrase "toxic masculinity" trips lightly off his tongue—his high school even ran classes on it. In middle school his whole grade watched *The Mask You Live In,* the 2015 documentary about masculinity norms, which outlined how young boys are unable to access emotions and connection. Oliver knows the language, understands the problem, but still, he found himself falling into the same patterns.

"I see a lot of men who are good people, and they don't have the poster child toxic masculinity traits where they beat and rape," he tells me. "But they're emotionally constipated. It's about the way that you see yourself, the way that you connect with others, the way that you motivate yourself, the way that you see others."

It is perhaps not surprising that Oliver saw human relationships as essentially competitive endeavors. This was the narrative landscape that was presented to him from earliest childhood. Like most boys, Oliver never really saw a model for how friendships between boys could be emotionally open, intimate, and mutually supportive, with complex relational give and take. In the combative worldview presented to young boys, where good and evil are binary opposites slugging it out, ultimately one person must win, and another lose.

"I think that a big thing that I've really internalized when it comes to emotional stuff is this concept of good and evil," he tells me. "I think it's pretty toxic and not very healthy because, Jesus, we are such complex beings."

After bottling up his emotions for so long, Oliver went through a period of serious depression in middle school and started seeing a therapist, whom he still sees now. He tells me that it was in therapy that he started noticing the patterns and associating them with masculinity and is working hard to be more emotionally open.

Oliver is one of those people who can explain photokinesis and how tides work, who knows every obscure rule of soccer and how to make a rope swing. Listening to him talk, it's as though he has become knowledgeable about emotions in the same way—through intellectual curiosity and hard work, rather than cultural absorption. Now he's trying to change things up and introduce different dynamics to his newer friendships.

When Oliver got to college, a liberal arts school on the West Coast, he met his new roommate, Jordan. While Oliver was brought up in an almost aggressively liberal environment, in which masculine expectations snuck in through the back door, Jordan grew up with a more up-front version of masculinity.

In eighth grade, Jordan's parents told him and his twin brother,

Max, that they had to pick a sport, any sport, as long as it would help pay their way through college. They both picked tennis, and their parents packed them off to a boarding school that specialized in tennis in Southern California with eighty boys and only fifteen girls. The culture was masculine and intense.

"There was a lot of hazing and just bullying, I guess," Jordan tells me. "I never really saw it that way while I was there, though. I didn't really have that explained to me until I met Oliver. It consisted of generally getting beaten up and pranked, just thrown around and treated like—I don't know." Jordan gropes for the right word. "*Slave* doesn't really work, but like you have to do everything they tell you, even if it's nasty or gross or just impossible."

Every Wednesday night, the older boys would organize what they called Fight Night. This meant that one eighth grader would get into the ring with two senior boys and fight them, invariably resulting in the younger boy getting badly beaten up. Jordan was a regular.

"I pretty much got the shit kicked out of me," he remembers. "Everyone would be cheering, and then they would pick you up, and then everybody would leave."

"What was that like?" I ask him, expecting to hear a tale of emotional scarring.

"I thought it was awesome."

It wasn't until Jordan went to college and met Oliver that he started to question the practice.

"We got into a conversation about trauma and how all that goes down. And then I was like, 'I don't have any trauma. I had nothing traumatic happen in my life.' And then we just ended up talking about that, and Oliver was like, 'That's not normal. Older people don't just beat up younger kids and call that fun.' I'd never really met anybody that was super insightful like that. I can't explain it. He's Oliver. We just connected really well."

Jordan and his boarding school friends were very close. "They were like brothers to me," he tells me, talking openly about how much he still loves them, how they looked out for one another, protected each other.

He tells me about how one of his friends, Brett, hated Fight Night, and didn't want to join in. The other boys bullied him, calling him gay and a pussy. Although Jordan enjoyed Fight Night himself, drawing social kudos from being one of its regular "stars," he fought to get the institution removed, sending multiple emails to the director of the school about it. Not because he had a deep principled objection to Fight Night's existence—quite the opposite—but because it upset his friend. Jordan's friendships were genuine and deep. But even with this level of love and loyalty, he still found it impossible to be emotionally vulnerable with his male buddies, or even with his twin.

"I definitely didn't cry in front of my brother," he tells me, "because that seemed like a weak thing to do."

After growing up in this environment, meeting Oliver was a revelation to Jordan.

"Oliver was the first person that I could talk to like that. I've never talked to anybody or really opened up to anybody before I met him."

When Jordan started suffering from anxiety, feeling trapped and overwhelmed and developing daily panic attacks, Oliver was the one who urged him to see a therapist.

"I think I just never really showed any of my emotions and then I started to, and it sort of freaked me out a little bit," Jordan tells me. "I refused to see a therapist until like two months ago."

"So, what changed?"

"Oliver talked me into doing it."

"What is it about Oliver, do you think, that makes you feel able to do that?" I ask.

"I think he's not overly masculine. All the people that I've met in my life are supermasculine," he replies, then catches himself and stops, clearly worried that he might have insulted his friend. The irony hits me that even in the context of a conversation about how harmful masculine expectations have been for him, at some level Jordan still sees the idea of stripping his friend of the descriptor as a humiliation. "Maybe masculine's the wrong word," he backtracks quickly.

Listening to Jordan talk, it occurs to me that maybe it's actually the opposite. It's not because Oliver is not masculine that he is able to challenge these norms. Tall, sporty, and successful with girls, by most measures Oliver places high on the hierarchy of masculinity. Perhaps it is precisely because he *is* masculine, that his credentials are securely established, that he has enough social capital to allow him a little leeway.

Jordan still draws the line at crying in front of other people, but after seeing a new model for friendship with Oliver, he is now making the effort to be more emotional and vulnerable with his other friends, too.

"I think with my high school friends, recently I've been calling them, I feel like I've opened up a little bit more. It's also a little scary though, 'cause then a lot of people know stuff about me," he says.

In the absence of good early models for intimate friendships, boys have to figure all this out on their own. But most of the boys I interviewed thought their relationship patterns with their male friends were already too well established, and it would be hard to change their dynamics. When they wanted more emotional closeness and support, most of them either looked to their girlfriends to provide it or made friends with girls instead.

Cross-gender friendships have documented benefits for boys.[5] Research shows that boys derive emotional and social support from their female friends, but notably the benefits don't go the other way. The same studies show few benefits for girls from being friends with boys, which is likely another way of saying that no matter who they are friends with, girls end up taking on most relational labor.

This tendency for boys to seek out female friends to provide the emotional support and connection that is lacking in their male friendships reinforces the idea that emotional and social labor is women's work. These patterns often continue into adulthood, when girlfriends and wives can easily become their male partner's total emotional support system.

• • •

Friendships with girls have been life changing for seventeen-year-old Cameron, a junior in high school in a small town in the Midwest. When he was in elementary school, almost all of Cameron's friends were boys. "We would wrestle and have Nerf gun fights and play video games," he tells me. "It was really stereotypical."

In middle school, he got into music and played guitar in a band, continuing to hang out with mainly boys. But as he got older, he started to see the culture of male friendships as increasingly limiting, and even aggressive.

"It's so hard to get males in a group to be vulnerable with each other. It feels really, really rare," he explains. "I think in my experience, hanging out with a group of guys has just felt like one long extended comedy bit. You're just making joke after joke and you have to put on this sarcastic personality. It's more like a competitive interaction disguised as friendship."

By the time he started high school, Cameron started finding himself enjoying the company of girls more than boys, and by sophomore year, he fell in with a new group of four female friends.

"It just felt easier to talk to them and it felt like it wasn't a competition," he tells me. "I would look at groups of guys hanging out and talking and it would look like they were competing with each other, like seeing who could bench-press the most weight or bragging about how many girls they kissed last weekend. It felt hostile with a thin disguise of friendliness. And then, when I hung out with my group of female friends, it felt like a warm, welcoming, open environment and we could seriously talk about anything. I would have sleepovers with this group of girls, and we would talk for hours on end about just the world and life and death. And it felt like I could just pour out my soul."

Cameron perhaps had more of a cultural model for this type of friendship than many boys. He has two sisters, one older and one younger. Although as a young child he tells me that he watched a lot of Power Rangers and Ninja Turtles, as he got older, his sisters started taking charge of the TV remote, and Cameron found he was drawn to the emotional and relationship content of the shows they were watching. His favorite was a Disney show called

Liv and Maddie, which focused on the family relationships and friendship dramas of teenage twin girls. But watching it still felt taboo.

"I think maybe in watching these girl shows I had this tiny voice in the back of my head being like, *This is a girl show. You're a boy; you're not supposed to be watching this,*" he tells me. "I didn't really let it take any action on me, but it was there."

Cameron has recently started experimenting with they/them pronouns, though he uses he/him most of the time (and asked me to do so for this book). It's not that he feels ill at ease in the male-assigned body he was born into, he tells me. For him this is a social choice.

"I don't feel like I'm female," he says. "I'm happy being male. I don't feel like I have to transition or become something else. I just think it's nice to put myself in a different category to sort of escape being associated with males and guys and boys. I just started experimenting with different pronouns and gender identities and expressions just to see how it makes me feel, to see if there's a more comfortable position in society to put myself in."

I'm happy for Cameron that he is exploring new ways to be himself. But it makes me sad that he believes his only hope of finding the type of intimate connections he craves is to reject the category of "boy." I would love to see us make this type of intimacy socially acceptable for all boys, not just the ones who abandon boyhood altogether.

• • •

Dr. Niobe Way, of New York University, has come to believe that adolescent males are suffering from a crisis of connection. After interviewing thousands of boys over the last couple of decades, Way has become convinced that the differences in male and female friendships are socialized and not innate. In her interviews, she has noticed a pattern emerge. Boys in preschool and elementary school have similar levels of empathy and emotional intelligence to girls of the same age and form similarly emotionally connected friendships.

But as they reach adolescence, social expectations and masculinity norms get in the way and they pull back, and their friendships take on a more superficial and competitive quality.

"They're born as human, and then we basically smack it out of them as they get older," Way tells me. "They have this relational intelligence that is remarkable, but then the culture gets in the way and basically shuts them down. Then they start to disconnect from their own feelings and disconnect from each other."

Other researchers see the process of detachment starting even younger. Judy Chu, a lecturer in human biology at Stanford University and author of *When Boys Become Boys* (2014), conducted a study of four- and five-year-old boys. She found that they were as capable as girls at reading emotions and forming close friendships.[6] But by the time they reached first grade, they started to subscribe to more classic notions of masculinity and become more emotionally distant from friends. Her work showed that this newfound distance only applied when boys were with their peers. With their parents, they were still able to share how they were feeling and be connected and vulnerable.

"All of us are born needing, and being able to develop, close personal relationships," she said in an interview. "And those are essential to our health. So what does it mean that we socialize boys away from that inherent need?"

This pattern shows up in other research, too. Because of a lack of cultural role models for emotional intimacy and a lack of practice, boys often start to lose the skills of connection. Studies shows that although they start off with comparable abilities, as they get older, boys start to score lower than girls of the same age on virtually all measures of empathy and social skills, a gap that grows throughout childhood and adolescence.[7] One large longitudinal study showed not only that girls score higher than boys on all measures of social and emotional skills throughout elementary school, but also that boys' capacities in these areas actually decrease year by year between kindergarten and fifth grade, suggesting a strong socialization component.[8]

As a culture, we are just starting to buy into the idea that men need to be more emotionally vulnerable, and that emotional stoicism has been harmful for boys' and men's mental health. This work is important and we need to make way more progress on this front. But vulnerability is only one part of intimacy. Without reciprocity it can easily just become emotional dumping.

Relational skills are hugely complex. If a marketing team was trying to brand them for men in a way that would remove the trivializing stigma of femininity, they would call the skill set something along the lines of "complex live-action social data processing," or "military-grade emotional surveillance." It's not just about sharing your feelings. Strong relationships involve an intricate moment-to-moment balancing of our own needs versus another person's. We all have a built-in capacity for this, but it's also something that can be learned and nurtured.

In addition to being more open about their own emotions, boys also need to learn how to listen to other people's: to take an interest in others' lives and experiences, ask the right questions, judge the right moment for a conversation, and figure out how to respond appropriately to someone else's vulnerability. Just telling boys and men to be more vulnerable without modeling and teaching all the other complex skills of social and emotional give-and-take isn't enough, and could easily just end up generating more emotional labor for the women in their lives.

• • •

I am surprised and pleased when it's my husband, Neil, who takes the initiative on this. He is the one who starts coaching the boys on taking a deeper interest in their friends' lives and being more supportive toward them. He is the one who gets books out from the library for Solly about middle school friendship dynamics and plays Calico Critters with Abe, acting out complex woodland social dramas.

One evening at dinner, we were discussing what we would be doing over summer break. Neil asked Solly what his friends' plans were. Predictably, Solly had no idea and seemed surprised that his parents would think he might know such rarified information. Neil told him that he should be asking his friends these kinds of questions, that friendship means knowing about each other's lives and helping each other in times of trouble.

"If that's the definition, then I don't have any friends," Solly replied, completely unbothered. But the seed was planted.

Similarly, when Zephy's friend Jamar was going through a hard time in third grade after a conflict with a teacher, Neil coached Zephy before a playdate to remember to ask Jamar how he was doing, to talk to him about what happened if Jamar wanted to, and to give his friend some support. It probably wouldn't have occurred to Zephy to do this without Neil spelling it out, but he did what his dad suggested, and he and Jamar ended up having a long conversation about the incident. Jamar told Zephy about the panicky feelings he had been having ever since the incident, and Zephy did his best to comfort him.

Neil is motivated to do this because as he has gotten older, he has realized there might be something lacking in his own friendships. He sees the long heart-to-hearts I have with my friends about every aspect of our lives, the way we support each other when one of us is sick or depressed or going through a tough time. His friends are kind people, but they all seem to be locked into some version of the stereotypical male pattern: they banter, go to concerts together, jam with guitars, but have little deeper emotional intimacy. Neil wants our boys to have a different model.

In some ways it's easier for Neil to do this than for me. He has Dad Privilege: people assume that men are operating from a place of goodwill and sanity until proven otherwise. When Neil gives the boys a baby doll or reads them the Ivy and Bean books, it's because he is a great dad. But World's Best Dad equals World's Most Average and Open to Criticism Mom. When I do the same, I'm an eye roll.

But by coaching them in these types of interactions, Neil is doing our boys a great service. For all age groups, strong social connections and supportive relationships have consistently been shown to be the most significant predictor of good mental health and a happy life, while the lack of them is damaging. Social isolation carries a similar risk of premature death to smoking and is roughly twice as dangerous to our health as obesity.

Today American men are the loneliest they have ever been, and the seeds of this loneliness and emotional disconnection take root during boyhood.[9] Never mind homework and extracurriculars and sports. Prioritizing strong supportive relationships for our sons is likely the most important thing we can do for their long-term physical and mental well-being.

• • •

One of *Saturday Night Live*'s funniest moments in recent memory was a sketch called "Man Park," a pitch-perfect piece of social commentary that instantly went viral. The skit opens with a lonely looking dude-bro, sitting alone at home on his couch. "According to studies," intones the voice-over, "many men say they have no close friendships, and three in four report receiving all their emotional support from their wife or girlfriend."

The solution to this problem is a breakthrough piece of social engineering called the Man Park. "It's like a dog park, but for guys in relationships, so they can make friends and have an outlet besides their girlfriends and wives."

Cut to shots of the Man Park, where the guys fist bump and high-five each other while screaming non sequiturs in each other's faces: "How about Bo Burnham?" and "Vin Diesel has a twin brother!" while their wives sit on the benches at the side, smiling indulgently and asking each other, "Which one's yours?"

"It's not their fault masculinity makes intimacy so hard," the voice-over continues, as the men yell the word "Marvel" and slap each other on the back, parrying and deflecting and evading the core humiliation of craving intimacy from another man.

The video has had more than four million views and at one point was emailed to me by seemingly every woman I know. We all laughed in recognition, but on YouTube, the comments section felt closer to tragedy than comedy. There was an outpouring of comments from men who related—who wished they had more friends or that the ones they did have were more supportive. They shared how lonely they felt.

We talk about toxic masculinity in extremes—the #MeToo monster, the school-shooter—but it is more like a spectrum. We have normalized a kind of workaday subtoxic masculinity, which is as much about what we don't expose boys to as what we do. Young boys need to see themselves as fully relational beings, for their own sakes and for others, not least the girls and women in their lives.

The stories we hear and tell help us determine what is possible for us, how we should be showing up in the world. And in the vast majority of situations we are likely to encounter in the course of a lifetime, there is no hero and no villain, no death and no glory, but just a bunch of needy humans kvetching over who said what. Learning to navigate that with grace and skill is the beating heart of human connection.

• • •

I brush off my worries about the lack of intimacy in my own sons' friendships by reassuring myself that this is normal for boys. But my lingering fears about this are compounded by other concerns about them. I'm starting to wonder whether there might be something more going on.

Because things are not getting any easier for us at home. I had also been trying to convince myself that the older boys' wild physicality and emotional volatility was due to the shock of a new baby brother. But Abe is nearly three now and things have barely changed. If anything, they are harder than ever.

My sons are wild. Their energy and hyperactivity are off the charts. They are constantly wrestling. We call it play fighting, but that doesn't really capture it. Play fighting implies lightheartedness. The defining mood of this wresting is something I had never seen before I had sons, a kind of liminal space right on the bleeding edge between play and rage, with the careering runaway logic of a barfight.

They also don't sleep. It's not just the little one. All three of them still regularly wake up at least once a night, often more, and we haven't had a full night's rest in years. Most days, the two older boys have meltdowns that can last for an hour or more. We have started telling people euphemistically that they "struggle with emotional self-regulation." This decontaminated phrasing allows us to pretend that we have some expertise or at least basic competence in handling their behavior, but in reality, we are utterly overwhelmed.

This season of mothering feels impossibly hard. I was an approval-addicted good girl as a child, a parent-pleasing productivity machine, churning out cello practice and homework and quiet amenability. My boys' physicality shocks me. I feel like a failure for being unable to get a handle on this situation and bring them under control.

Late at night, I start googling. "Why is parenting . . ." I begin typing. Google autocompletes: "so hard?" Clearly a million exhausted mothers across the world are asking the same question. Google's answers are mainly sociological ones: Cultural expectations of motherhood have expanded beyond recognition; parenting has become more intensive and child centered; economic factors mean that both parents have to work; childcare is expensive and mothers receive little social support. All of these answers are interesting and true, but they don't seem to cut to the bone of the experience for me. The social expectations of motherhood are indeed punishing. But the really hard part is the kids.

I change tack and start googling "child meltdowns" and "hyperactive kids" and land on the diagnostic criteria for autism and ADHD. I scan them anxiously.

Do the boys have, for example, "deficits in social-emotional reciprocity, ranging . . . from abnormal social approach and failure of normal back and forth conversation" (Diagnostic and Statistical Manual of Mental Disorders V criteria A1 for autism spectrum disorder)? Does Zephy and his best friend, Ari's, incomprehensible monologuing about Nintendo or Pokémon or Rubik's cubes count as a "failure of normal back and forth conversation"? It certainly would in my social circles. But then wouldn't that make half the boys in second grade autistic?

Does Abe's blind obsession with construction vehicles count as a "highly restrictive, fixated" interest that is "abnormal in intensity or focus" (DSM V autism spectrum disorder criteria B3)? But most of the preschool boys I meet are similarly infatuated.

Popular culture tends to portray autism as either a kind of robotic self-involvement or a circus act of savantlike superhuman magic tricks. Neither of these caricatures apply to my boys. On the other hand, the official ADHD diagnostic criteria could be an extract from Zephy's future memoir.

Marked restlessness that is difficult to control? Appears to be driven by a motor? Lacks ability to play and engage in leisure activities in a quiet manner? Sidetracked by external or unimportant stimuli? Avoids or is disinclined to begin homework? Poor listening skills? Yes to all.

But then again, this list also reads like a more codified, formal version of the basic "boys will be boys" story that is so ubiquitous in the culture generally. Boys can't sit still. Boys are like dogs. Boys, eh? The diagnostic criteria just seemed to be an inventory of the baseline social expectations for male children.

At their birthday parties and playdates, most of my sons' friends seem equally hyped up and out of control. Perhaps my fear that there might be something diagnosably wrong with my boys is just me imposing the value system of a forty-something-year-old woman onto them. Am I pathologizing boyhood?

I seem to be simultaneously inhabiting two contradictory realities. In one version, something is clinically wrong with my children, and I am just in denial, deluding myself with the fantasy that they are just like other boys because I don't want it to be true. In the other, they are just regular rowdy male children, and the only problem is my parenting. I can't keep them under control and am failing to mold them into the sensitive, feminist sons that my progressive values require me to deliver. In my social media feeds, the same meme keeps popping up, succinctly reallocating responsibility in my direction: "~~PROTECT YOUR DAUGHTERS.~~ TEACH YOUR SONS." As a mother of boys, it's now on me. I wholeheartedly agree with the gender reframing, but in practice my sons seem impervious to my teaching.

Without a formal assessment, there is no way of knowing which of these realities is closer to the truth. And because the boys are doing fine at school, no one will pay for one, and private testing costs thousands of dollars. So I shove the question to the back of my mind.

• • •

Whether or not there is something diagnosable going on with my own sons, the more I think about it, the more it becomes clear just how many invisible social forces there are acting on boys as a whole to encourage this type of behavior. Cultural stories push boys away from quiet reflection and empathy, toward fighting and competition and aggression. The scripts of masculinity are everywhere, telling them who they should be in the world, and who they must never be.

Much of this is subtle, almost invisible. In some ways, at least where we live in the progressive Bay Area, people are starting to challenge gender norms for boys. Solly's male best friend in kindergarten wore a dress to school at least once a week, and while some parents suppressed sniggers, the kids barely noticed. We are starting to push back against some of the more rigid stories of what it means to be a boy.

But ours is a bubble. While the left is trying to push back against the more damaging expectations of masculinity, much of America is doubling down.

CHAPTER 3

BOY STORIES

THE SCRIPTS OF MASCULINITY

I'm at a truck stop somewhere on the Nevada-Utah border, in line to order a hamburger. In front of me a giant, mildly threatening looking man with a January 6 insurrection–style beard huffs impatiently at the wait. He looks at his phone repeatedly, as if he's merely on standby, checking Reddit and awaiting orders to storm the Capitol.

On the TV in the background a game show called *Guy's Grocery Games* is playing. Contestants compete with each other to find a list of items in a supermarket at top speed. A man named Jeremy is telling the host, the reality star Guy Fieri, that this task will be a challenge for him because he never goes grocery shopping—his wife always does it. "Ha ha ha," he adds. "Ha ha ha," confirms Guy.

I think about just how much the performance of manhood sets the tone of our daily lives, in all its rageful entitlement and controlling apathy. The space we make for it.

I've stopped here en route to Cedar City, in southern Utah, to visit Iron Gate, a new residential therapy and therapeutic housing center for adolescent boys and young men. Local social worker and entrepreneur Kade Janes opened the facility just a few months ago in response to what he sees as a growing problem among the young male population—what he calls a failure to launch.

Kade, who is now in his late forties, has worked with young

people for most of his career. Recently he has been coming across more and more boys who are reaching adulthood without ticking off any of the traditional markers of independence: heading to college or finding a job or a partner. Instead they are holed up in their parents' basements playing video games and watching porn.

Much as I hate to believe it, this cliché is supported by a worrying amount of data. While as a group girls and young women are vigorously embracing the tasks of young adulthood, their male counterparts are struggling. Girls are now significantly more likely to enroll in college than boys, and less likely to drop out when they get there. Women now receive nearly 60 percent of all bachelor's degrees and three out of five masters degrees.

Unemployment is falling among young women, but rising among young men faster than in any other demographic group. As Richard Reeves, senior fellow at the Brookings Institution, put it in his book *Of Boys and Men: Why the Modern Male Is Struggling, Why It Matters, and What to Do About It* (2022), "Girls and women have had to fight misogyny without. Boys and men are now struggling for motivation within."

No one is quite sure of the reasons why this generation of young men is floundering and avoidant. Experts have floated many social, economic, and biological explanations, from late-maturing brains to the decline of manual jobs to the rise of feminism. One group of prominent economists even claimed that the bulk of the decline in young male employment rates can be explained by the fact that video games have "gotten really good."[1] In her influential newsletter, *Culture Study,* the writer Anne Helen Petersen made the argument that this flavor of male entitlement and laziness has always existed; it has just become more obvious now that we are starting to remove the barriers to success for other groups. "Men don't need ambition. They have privilege," she wrote. "They rise unless they work hard at sucking."

Kade has his own view. He considers himself politically and socially conservative, and like many on the right, he sees the problem as the result of a steady onslaught of what he calls the "demasculinization" of society. He believes that in a feminist-indoctrinated, identity politics–obsessed America, traditional manhood is under attack. Since the left has branded masculinity as toxic, men and boys are being systematically stripped of their natural role and inheritance. Kade points to various factors—everything from moronic TV dads to gender fluidity to a lack of physical activity for boys in school—as contributing to the problem. Without an obvious place in society, he believes that boys have become neutered and adrift.

"We now have two generations' worth of young men that honestly don't really know how to be men," he told me on the phone. "And their version of manhood is pretty messed up."

Kade isn't the only one with manhood on his mind. Since Trump's presidency and the explosion of the #MeToo movement, the world has been grappling with masculinity's shady past and uncertain future. This highly charged concept hits at the heart of the values split between left and right. For the left, masculinity is part of the problem. Liberals argue that we need less aggression, less unreconstructed manhood. In response, the right is digging in. For them, masculinity is not the problem but the solution. The whole conversation speaks to a dark fear among conservatives that America itself has been emasculated.

Now right-wing politicians and commentators are turning threatened American masculinity into a major talking point and a key part of their political project. America is becoming weak and effeminate, they claim (it goes without saying that effeminate is a bad thing). The right promises to bring the tough guy back to American politics, to restore manhood itself.

Ironically, given how strongly this voting bloc ridicules the concept of identity politics when it is applied to, say, trans people or people of color, this masculinity obsession can seem like its ultimate expression. These guys are not arguing for tougher or braver women or for more heavily muscled nonbinary people. The virtues themselves only have value insofar as they are embodied by a specific demographic group: men.

Meanwhile, in popular culture, YouTubers and podcasters are also preaching the masculinity gospel, gaining huge traction with directionless adolescent boys. The phrase "alpha male" has taken on a new scope and power, and a generation of influencers has developed a mini self-help industry devoted to the promise of achieving that status, often with a side order of horrifying hate speech. Their reach is staggering. The TikTok videos of the most notorious of this group, for example, self-proclaimed "misogynist" Andrew Tate, received well more than eleven billion views before he was banned from the platform and later arrested.

Kade subscribes to a more old-school vision of masculinity—the chivalrous protector-provider and family man. He hates the boorish, ungentlemanly chest beating of Trump and his ilk, and is horrified by the idea of sexual assault, believing that violence against women is antithetical to real manliness. Kade believes a man's role is to provide the "wall around the garden, protecting the beauty inside." Motivated by his strong religious faith and traditional values, his mission is to highlight what he sees as the positive face of masculinity and bring back the values of traditional manhood.

With this in mind, Kade bought an old house in his sleepy hometown of Cedar City and transformed it into the Iron Gate center. The facility is aimed at young people, and in particular young men with mental health and minor behavioral problems or a general failure to launch. For a few thousand dollars, a parent can send their son to Kade for a three-month program that involves faith-based life coaching (Kade is Mormon, but the program is open to people of any faith or none), group and individual therapy from a model devised by Kade himself, support in finding education or a job, rigorous physical activity, and various support groups. He has invited me to come and stay for a few days to see what their approach is all about.

Kade's language and politics jangle against my feminist sensibilities, but I can't deny that his vision tugs at something in me. He and I may differ on what we see as the root causes of the problem, but I share his concerns about boys and young men. A couple of weeks before, I'd had coffee with a friend whose seventeen-year-old son was struggling with video game addiction and was not doing his homework or applying to college.

"All my friends' teen boys are a mess, too," she had told me. It was hyperbolic, of course, but it stuck, and it scared me. I have to admit there is part of me that finds something compelling in Kade's worldview—the idea of creating a generation of young men who will stand strong and step up, and, if I'm honest, take the load off women for a hot second. Besides, Kade represents what a good portion of America believes, and I want to understand more about why. I want to know whether it is possible to strip the harm out of masculinity, to rebrand it and channel it as a potential force for good.

Kade himself is very masculine. I have never met him in person, but I know this because he has told me several times. In each of our three Zoom conversations he mentioned his height (six foot three) as well as the general manliness of his presence.

"I'm tall, I'm six foot three, and I come across kind of gruff," he told me. "So if I say anything, and it doesn't even have to be aggressive, but if it's just assertive, then I've run into multiple situations where a female's like, you're just trying to oppress me. And I've actually been grateful for it because it makes me stop and go, 'Geez, is that what I'm doing?' I don't want to do that, and maybe I am. But having women who love manhood and love the idea of someone protecting and providing? If we are not doing that as men, what are we doing?"

• • •

After a long drive, I finally pull up outside the Iron Gate house and am immediately charmed by its deep nostalgia, dollhouse aesthetic. Built in 1908, with a quaint wraparound porch with white cane armchairs and floral print curtains visible at every window, it feels more like your fantasy grandmother's ancestral home than the headquarters of "Reclaiming Manhood."

Kade greets me at the door. He is pretty tall, and I guess relatively masculine, but I'm glad to say, not overwhelmingly so. Before he introduces me to the residents, we sit in the lobby and talk for a while. Kade tells me about his four daughters. He has always been surprised at how well behaved they are. He can think of only two times they have ever broken a toy, in stark contrast to Kade and his brothers growing up, who broke every toy in the house and kicked holes in the wall. "You know what it's like with boys, right?" he asks me, companionably co-opting me into his gender-essentialist worldview.

I feel the familiar conflicted knot in my stomach. The whole "boys are wild by nature" is such a central part of the reasoning of so many on the right, the starting point for so many assumptions and stereotypes and inequalities, and I hate that it is also true for my sons. Even though I have read all the research into fetal testosterone myself and know that there is something real in what Kade is saying, and even though my own boys do in fact break all the toys, a fact that does not seem to be entirely unrelated to gender, my progressive identity hinges in some way on being able to push back against people like Kade.

How much we are all prepared to admit, even to ourselves, depends heavily on who we are talking to. It makes me realize again just how much of the nature-nurture debate comes down to politicized tribalism, and how little room it leaves for nuance. I briefly consider arguing with Kade, but in the end I settle on a weirdly false, noncommittal laugh. He senses my hesitation.

"That's what women don't realize," he tells me. "If you take that away from a boy, then he really is gonna have a hard time because that's what he's wired to do."

Kade gives me a tour of the house. He shows me the bedrooms with their cottagecore bedspreads and miniature scented soaps in the bathroom. The patio, with its wrought iron rocking chairs for people to gather round an outdoor table.

As we go, Kade and I talk about masculinity—one of his favorite subjects. We have failed to distinguish between the healthy and unhealthy versions of it, he tells me. In its healthy incarnation, he believes, masculinity is the underpinning of a functioning society. "The world would fall apart without men," he explains.

He stops briefly to fill a small diffuser with lavender oil that he has selected from a wooden display box on the kitchen counter.

One of the coaches at Iron Gate is also a Blue Diamond in an aromatherapy oil selling program, Kade tells me. "Which is very high," he adds.

I ask Kade for his definition of healthy masculinity. "Someone who's accountable, who feels accountable," he replies. "Someone who understands the importance of being able to provide for themselves and other people. Someone who's mentally and emotionally balanced enough to have genuine relationships with other people."

I think about what he is saying for a moment. On the face of it, this doesn't seem to be a list of traditionally masculine traits. The only word in here that seems to be associated in any way in my mind with masculinity is "provide." Accountability is hardly a gendered virtue, and if anything, relationship building seems culturally more associated with women than men. It seems as though Kade is just talking about the basic qualities needed for adulthood in general. It makes me wonder whether masculinity as a framework actually does help boys step up to become healthy adults, or whether it hinders that process.

We end the tour in the kitchen. Kade and his team keep the fridge stocked with food, and anyone who attends a program at the center, as an inpatient or outpatient, is allowed to come in and hang out. As a result, the kitchen has become a gathering spot.

This is where I meet Bryce, the first official inpatient resident of Iron Gate. He is standing at the stove making himself an elaborate and delicious-looking grilled sandwich, intricately layering egg, cheese, and spinach and frying it section by section. He notices my hungry expression and offers to make one for me, too. Kade drifts away and Bryce and I chat over our sandwiches.

Twenty-one-year-old Bryce is instantly likable, with a flirty, breezy charisma. Despite the fact that he is legally an adult and recently married, his parents signed him up for the Iron Gate program after he got pulled over for a DUI and spent the night in jail.

Bryce's alcohol use had been escalating for the last couple of years. Alcohol is forbidden for Mormons and his habit started off small. He would down a couple of cans of beer in secret while his wife was at work or to calm himself before stressful family events and then chew gum to mask the smell. He saw it as a way to escape the difficult emotions starting to engulf him. "I just wanted something to get me away from my feelings," he tells me.

For Bryce, alcohol wasn't so much about partying as self-medicating. Newly married, far from friends and family after moving to a new state, he felt lonely and unsure of where he was headed in life. He had been feeling increasingly low, scaring himself with dark moods and intrusive thoughts, but feared it would be unmanly to tell anyone about his feelings or seek help.

"I was playing the masculinity tough guy card of 'I can push through this on my own,'" he tells me. "I was like, 'I am depressed. I do have anxiety, but I'm not gonna tell anyone until I die.' I literally thought if you took anxiety pills or had anxiety or depression, it meant you were weak."

I am briefly struck by the irony of this. Bryce is now here at Iron Gate, a facility whose unofficial mission statement according to Kade includes "restoring traditional masculinity." But from what Bryce is telling me, it seems as though the pressure to be masculine was really part of his problem in the first place.

I ask him about his relationship to masculinity.

"For most of my life I never played the masculine thing, like 'Oh, I'm tough,'" he replies. "I was more the emotional one. I would cry in class. I just got emotional about everything. Puppies, babies. All my friends were girls. I didn't like hanging out with guys and I just would go and hang out with the cheer party—fifteen, twenty girls. And I just loved being around that environment—the soft, nurturing emotion. I could be emotional without guys judging me. But then, when I got older, the shame turned me on to masculinity."

Like many men, instead of sharing his feelings, Bryce started obliterating them with alcohol. As his drinking ramped up, so did his lying.

"I was turning my back on my wife and her family. I didn't want them to know. And then it turned into my brother and my best friend, and it got to a point where I was also embarrassed to tell them. And that's when I hit rock bottom; when no one knew at all except for me.

"I had no worth in my own eyes. I literally, I was worthless. Then it was the following week that I broke down and went and found a doctor and just told them everything. And I was crying, and I was just like, 'I need to be open and raw with you and tell you I'm done hiding my feelings' and listed how I've been feeling and what I've been doing. I told him I was gonna stop drinking and everything and then I got on medication."

The antidepressants helped for a while, but then, without therapy and still feeling the pressure to hide what he was going through from his friends and family, Bryce relapsed. As he felt more and more hopeless, his drinking increased.

Then one night, at his lowest point, he drove out to a gas station off the freeway somewhere in Idaho. He bought several canned cocktails and drank them in the filthy public bathroom. Then he did something he had never done before: He got back in the car and started driving, drunk. Bryce circled the backstreets for an hour, bleak and desperate, scared to go home to his wife. Eventually, he got back on the freeway and the police pulled him over.

"They took me in that night," he tells me. "I called my wife and my mom from jail. And then my parents came down while I was in there, and they went to our house and they got all my stuff—my clothes, luggage, shoes, everything. Took all of it out of the house. My wife was basically just kicking me out."

Bryce's parents signed him up for a three-month program at Iron Gate. Now he lives at the center and does weekly therapy and daily coaching with Kade. Kade found him a job working as an assistant to a local window cleaner. He goes for bike rides and hikes, attends every group the center has to offer, and feels that it is all helping.

"I'm so much happier now, when I go and meet with Kade and have therapy, even though it's hard," he tells me. "I'm around so many people. That's awesome. And even if it's not a therapy session, I can talk to them any time I want to. The house, it's not a facility, it's not a rehab center, it's therapeutic housing. And I love the wording of that. That's exactly what it is."

• • •

In 2019 the American Psychological Association (APA) developed its first ever set of guidelines specifically for psychologists working with men and boys. This was a departure. For as long as the field had existed, male psychology *was* psychology. Whatever men were doing or feeling was the default standard for humans as a whole. It was everyone else who needed special consideration. But now, the culture was starting to recognize the specific social pressures of masculinity and realizing that they could also cause harm. The new guidelines claimed that "traditional masculine ideology, as marked by stoicism, competitiveness, dominance, and aggression," was a risk to boys' physical and mental well-being.

The criticism came from all sides. Some argued that male privilege was still so pervasive that we shouldn't be wasting our time worrying about boys and men, anyway, and should instead be focusing resources on groups with less systemic power. Others, particularly on the right, worried that the guidelines focused too much on the negative aspects of masculinity—failing to recognize the positive qualities it can foster, such as courage, strength, and self-sacrifice. They claimed the APA's new guidelines were just further evidence of a wider attack on manhood, and the creeping feminization of American society. And some branded the guidelines a conceptual mess, pointing out that the APA had lumped together four unrelated traits—stoicism, competitiveness, dominance, and aggression—and labeled them an ideology. These critics argued that those traits were not necessarily masculine; they were universally human.

The APA's definition of masculinity certainly isn't perfect, and it would probably be impossible to come up with one that was comprehensive. Masculinity as a set of social expectations for manhood is slippery and hard to pin down. The terms differ across social contexts and cultures. Depending on the group involved, masculinity's main currency could be physical strength or business success, sexual prowess or creative grandiosity, or the ability to blindly navigate an unfamiliar city without asking for directions. But although the details vary, in many ways, the similarities are more striking. Men and boys of wildly different cultural backgrounds seem to have a surprisingly similar understanding of the rules—of what is expected of them by virtue of their gender and what is off-limits. Because perhaps even more than they mandate how to behave, masculine norms prescribe how *not* to behave, what is forbidden.

Matt Englar-Carlson is a psychologist and academic who was part of the team that helped draft the APA guidelines.

"Masculinity is defined by its opposite: Don't be a woman," he tells me. "So masculinity traits are actually anti-femininity traits. Toughness is always part of it. Be strong, show courage in the face of danger, be independent, don't show emotions, don't ask for help. And essentially, it's okay to be aggressive."

Sexism is built into the foundations of the story. Masculinity is defined in opposition to femininity, but the two are not equal. Masculinity's guiding principle is not just that men must be different from women but that they must be superior. Boys' basic sense of self gets built around the belief that they must be better than girls.

It's not just women who lose out in this belief system. As Bryce was all too aware, boys are taught to see emotional vulnerability as a failing, which can make it hard to talk about or even fully recognize their own emotions. And when they fail to meet the requirements for masculinity, the cost is high. Although society loves policing women's behavior in almost any way it can, there is no real equivalent of the word *emasculation* for women, no single gendered concept that has the same power to strip a woman of her basic worth. For a woman to "act like a man" is at some level seen as aspirational, a promotion from her current lowly station. But the idea of a man acting like a woman still provokes a deep-soul squeamishness. Men work overtime to avoid emasculation, because the social price they pay for it is so high.

And, as Englar-Carlson explains to me, this is a constant, ongoing struggle. "Masculinity is a precarious social state," he tells me. "It's hard fought and easily lost. Essentially you spend your whole time trying to get on top, knowing that at any moment you can be knocked down."

But as Bryce had learned, the silent stoicism and lack of emotional openness that masculinity demands can be damaging. "If we think about all the traits that would make you more masculine, what you're going to find is that your mental health goes right down the tubes," as Englar-Carlson puts it.

A range of studies confirm this view, showing that the more closely men and boys conform to traditional masculine norms, the more likely they are to be depressed or suicidal; to perform poorly in school; and to engage in risky unhealthful behaviors—and the less likely they are to seek mental and physical healthcare.

Because society expects silent stoicism from men, mental health problems for boys often go undetected. Although anxiety, depression, and loneliness have risen sharply for all adolescents in the last decade, our cultural narrative tends to pitch teenage girls as being in the grip of a mental health crisis, whereas the so-called "boy crisis" generally gets reported as a problem of bad behavior and underachievement. We tend to view troubled boys as bad, not sad.

At one level, this makes sense. Boys do display antisocial behavior at far higher rates than girls, and recent studies do see teenage girls reporting symptoms of depression and anxiety at almost twice the rate of boys.[2] And in a sense, why wouldn't they? Patriarchy is alive and well, sexual assault is rife, the government is controlling women's bodies, and if this dataset is anything to go by, boys are pretty oblivious to the whole damn thing.

But dig a little deeper, and the studies themselves are problematic. Many researchers believe that there is a basic methodological flaw in the research, borne of the same underlying problem that is at the heart of male sadness and loneliness in the first place—the unwillingness of boys and men to be emotionally honest when asked by researchers about their emotional state.

The underreporting of male mental health problems is a well-documented phenomenon.[3] It's certainly something that I have come across again and again in my interviews with boys—the shame around admitting to what they saw as socially unacceptable weakness. Had a pollster called to question someone like Bryce at his lowest point, or presented many of the other boys I interviewed with a checklist of questions, they might well have missed their unformed, unspoken sadness.

Because boys are not given social permission to express their emotions, they often end up acting them out in other ways. As a result, depression often manifests differently in boys, with what psychologists call externalizing symptoms, rather than internalizing. So instead of showing straightforward sadness, depression in boys and men can often show up as increased aggression, behavior problems, and alcohol or substance abuse.

This can turn into a vicious cycle. Because of this differing manifestation, parents and teachers are more likely to see boys' problems as behavioral, rather than emotional. Parents and teachers often miss the underlying pain, and instead of listening to boys or empathizing with them or providing them with appropriate mental healthcare, they discipline them for their bad behavior, further compounding their sense of alienation.

This unacknowledged male sadness can be deadly. Boys often fail to recognize or report their own depression until it is so severe that they can no longer cope, with tragic results. Adolescent boys die by suicide nearly four times as often as girls.[4]

• • •

For Black boys, the pressure to not appear weak is perhaps even more extreme. In surveys, around three times as many Black men as white men say that being seen as masculine is "very important to them."[5] Research suggests that a hypermasculine, aggressive stance can be a coping mechanism for Black adolescent males, who are at a far greater risk of violence and threat than white boys.[6]

This was true for Jayden, who grew up in East Oakland in a low-income neighborhood. Shootings and other forms of violent crime were common, and as a young boy, he quickly learned to maintain a posture of rigid invulnerability.

When I meet Jayden for breakfast at his favorite bagel place, he is warm and emotionally astute, eager to analyze and discuss his own feelings and motivations. But this hasn't always been the case.

"Where I'm from, I can't be comfortable with fear," he tells me. "I can't be scared. 'Cause with me that fear, it could have meant death. Or it could have meant me being in a situation. It's better to be feared than loved in the hood. Because with that love people will use you. You have to toughen up."

"What does it mean to toughen up?" I ask him.

"No emotion," he replies. He draws his hand across his face to reveal a fixed stare and rigidly impassive expression. "Blank, cold face, no emotion. I could show anger, but nothing else," he tells me. "Nothing that's a little bit soft. At least not in public. I told my dad, 'I'll tell you I love you when it's just me and you, Dad,' but otherwise, blank." He makes the face again.

"I feel like girls get away with showing more emotions. But for guys, you have to have that anger. You're trying to be menacing a little bit. You know, to kind of get your point across—don't mess with me."

The more Jayden tried to appear angry and menacing to the outside world, the more he started to feel that way on the inside, too. Instead of sadness or fear, Jayden increasingly channeled all his emotions into rage. He started getting into fights, getting in trouble at school and in the neighborhood.

"Anger was the emotion that I understood the best," he tells me. "So, a lot of times we go with things that we're most comfortable with. I was choosing anger because I didn't want to be seen as weak or soft."

Matt Englar-Carlson believes that this is a common trap for boys. "The one thing that boys are allowed to express is anger," he says. "It's something we teach men to do; to code everything as anger. So anger and upset comes out in a lot of ways. It comes out in anger towards oneself, which can be something such as depression or even suicide. But if all you have is anger and aggression, it can come out as abuse or violence or controlling behaviors."

It wasn't until Jayden went to college that he was able to express, and even to fully experience, other emotions.

"I took a college course on psychology, and they told us that anger was a secondary emotion," he tells me. "And once I understood that, it broke my whole mentality of things. So I was just like, 'Okay, what was I angry about? Was I sad? Where was the anger coming from? What was the primary emotion?' Because for so long, I've gotten used to just going with the anger, that I would never go deeper into the source. Because anger's like a fire. It can warm the whole house up, bring something to light. Or it can burn the whole thing down and be really destructive."

• • •

The pressures and expectations of masculinity still loom large in boys' lives, and if anything, despite the right's fears about the "feminization of society," in many ways they have actually ramped up. In recent years, the masculine ideal has become ever more cartoonish and extreme. As a culture, we are moving away from the gentler, family-orientated "provider and protector" model that Kade idealizes, toward a pumped-up action-hero version of fantasy manhood—all muscles and guns and hand-to-hand combat.

Over the last couple of decades, the cultural trappings of boyhood have become increasingly focused on violence and aggression. This is part of a wider process of the gender segregation of childhood, in which late-capitalist marketers realized that by treating boys and girls as two entirely separate sets of consumers, they could double sales. As a result, movies, TV shows, and games and toy store aisles have been pushed further to gendered extremes. In almost every toy store now, there is a neon pink girls' section filled with a mix of sparkle-studded objectification in the form of princess dresses, kid makeup, and heavily sexualized dolls; miniaturized domestic drudgery in tiny irons and mops and vacuums, and baby dolls to fulfill caregiving responsibilities. The khaki and camo-hued boys' section is devoted in large part to mass slaughter (with a few emergency vehicles to mop up the bloodshed).

Most of the feminist critique about the intensification of gendered marketing has focused on the "pink washing" of girl culture, a kind of hostile takeover of girls' brains by princess-fronted corporate masterminds. Less attention has been paid to the increasing "battle-fication" and aggression of boy culture.

Lego is perhaps a good example of both the heightening of gender segregation and the blindspot in the wider critique when it comes to boys. Historically gender neutral, in 2012 the company attempted to attract more girl customers by launching the Friends line, with pink packaging and all-female minifigures. (It is notable that "Friends" was the branding they chose for a female-only line, as if friendship itself is a feminized state.)

Feminist parents and pressure groups pushed back, pointing out the sexism in the new Friends sets. They complained that they were easier to build, meaning that girls missed out on learning STEM (science, technology, engineering, and mathematics) and construction skills, and that the roles and scenarios depicted were stereotypically girlie: beautician, hairdresser, slumber party guest. (It was understood, without question, that *girlie* meant lesser.) Little attention was paid by critics either to the lack of representation for boys in relational roles in the new girls' sets, or to what was happening during the same time period to the sets marketed to boys.

Because while girls got Friends, boys got enemies. When a group of researchers from the University of Canterbury surveyed the content and marketing of Lego sets since the late 1970s, they found that as the brand became more gender segregated, the sets aimed at boys became steadily more violent.[7]

Whereas in 1978, only a tiny fraction of the sets contained weapons, and those were mainly obscure medieval ones, now nearly a third of the sets do, nearly all of them guns. Close to 40 percent of the images in the Lego catalog now contain some sort of violence, and increasingly, they depict shooting.

Lego is not alone in the boy-toy universe in ramping up the aggression. Toronto-based writer Crystal Smith, author of *The Achilles Effect: What Pop Culture Is Teaching Young Boys About Masculinity* (2011), tracked the language used in toy commercials targeting boys and girls, turning the results into an infographic in which the most common words appear in the biggest letters.

In the girls' graphic, the biggest word was *love,* with *friendship, friends,* and *fun* also prominent. For boys, the biggest word by a huge margin, dominating the entire page and dwarfing every other word in the cloud, was *battle.* Almost every word in the boys' graphic, including *ultimate, weapon, stealth, attack,* and *enemy* related to fighting in some form, with the only obvious exception being *vehicles.*[8]

It's hard to know how much of an effect growing up in the shadow of this aggressive, caricatured vision of manhood has on boys' development, but the little research that does exist suggests that these choices matter, and the toys that boys—and girls—play with can have a lasting impact on their value systems.

One group of researchers found that boys who had played mostly with stereotypically boys' toys as children were significantly more likely to hold a range of sexist views as adults than boys who had played with more gender-neutral toys.[9] The adolescents in their survey who had played mostly with boys' toys were less likely to want to see equal numbers of men and women in the workplace or to identify as feminists. They were more likely than boys who had played with more gender-neutral toys to think "more about girls' bodies and how they look than their thoughts and personalities." They also considered themselves more likely to punch someone if provoked, and were less likely to read or enjoy English as a school subject.

It's hard to unpack how much of this effect is down to the toys themselves and how much has to do with parenting values more generally. After all, parents who make the effort to give their sons gender-neutral toys are usually the same parents who hold more progressive values around gender as a whole, something that is likely to be reflected in all kinds of parenting and lifestyle choices. But toys are important symbols of those value systems and the messages we send to boys about who and what they should be in the world.

• • •

The only problem is that my boys love this stuff.

Just as I tortured my 1970s feminist mother with my cravings for Barbies and strawberry lip gloss, my boys love battles and fighting and weapons. Despite my best efforts, our lives are dominated by minimurder. My powerlessness in the face of my sons' passions has been such a defining part of my parenting experience that it's sometimes hard to believe these differences are socialized, rather than innate. It feels like I spend my entire life trying to socialize them *away* from these preferences, not toward them. It's hard to summon any kind of conviction that some unseen forces of culture, let alone my own flimsy, conflicted parenting, could go head-to-head with something as robust and ancient as biology and win.

But maybe the nature-nurture question misses the point anyway. Gender is culture. Regardless of what I do or don't do as a parent, my sons operate in a cultural system that is different from my own, and one that sometimes leaves me cold. It's hard to admit, even to myself, but a fair amount of the time I find their "boyness" alienating. I don't like battles or wrestling or *Star Wars* or sword fighting or Nerf guns or morally binary stories. I feel much more at home with "Let's analyze this minor emotional slight for three hours in painstaking detail" than "Bang bang, you're dead." These differences may be superficial, but life is made up of many superficial moments and choices. This stuff can feel pervasive enough that it can sometimes make it hard to connect with the boys.

I'm torn about what to do about it. When I try to steer them away from Nerf battles and toward books about feelings, it's hard to know whether this is a political project or a psychological one. I wonder how much this is just my own personal baggage—me trying to coerce my children into meeting my own needs. After all, good parents cultivate their children's natural interests, follow their lead, and don't try to mold them according to their own desires and agenda. When I try to challenge gender norms with the boys, is what I'm doing closer to teaching my children to say please and thank you (good), or more like being a tightly wound baseball dad with a child who hates baseball (bad)?

I don't want to turn my sons into a political project that tramples all over their own preferences and passions. But then again, the world is heavily gendered. If I sit back and do nothing, my boys are already a political project, just not mine.

My mother simply forbade the toys she found problematic. Maybe I am too lazy for that approach, or my children are less obliging. Weary of all the arguments, I have uneasily settled on a philosophy of expansion rather than deprivation, attempting to add in rather than take away. They can have the Nerf guns and the battle movies, but I try to inject some critical thinking, to call out the stereotypes when I see them and add in other things, too: books about emotions and relationships, TV shows about middle school friendship dramas, dollhouses, and My Little Pony toys. Some of it takes. Most of it doesn't.

But I keep telling myself that, as in my own childhood, it's a long game. They are young, trying things out, searching for their place in the world, and trying to fit in. I just keep hoping that at some level it is all sinking in.

• • •

It's not just toys. This vision of hyped-up, aggressive masculinity, which we are increasingly selling to boys and men, shows up across popular culture. Take body shape: On screen and off it, we are fetishizing an ever more ultra-muscled physique for men. Hollywood movies, and in particular the wildly popular superhero epics that dominate the box office, now routinely use CGI technology to add muscle mass to their male stars. The 1960s version of Batman looks positively weedy compared to Ben Affleck's ultra-ripped 2016 model.

While over time the idealized body for women has been shrinking to unhealthy and sometimes dangerous proportions, the ideal for men has been growing to an unattainably jacked state. On social media, actors post about their #fitnessjourneys to bulk up for the roles. But no actual human fitness journey could ever achieve the muscle mass of the modern CGI-enhanced superhero.

Even toys have become more muscular over time. In the 1960s, G.I. Joe didn't even have defined abs. Now, if he were scaled up to human size, he would have bigger muscles than even the top performing bodybuilders. Meanwhile, online influencers and YouTubers push punishing fitness, diet, and weight training regimens, promising adolescent boys that with the right amount of effort, they, too, can achieve the same muscleman build.

The pressure on boys to emulate this body shape can be intense. As nineteen-year-old Ryan put it, "Every time I flip on a superhero movie, I'm seeing this crazy physique, and then suddenly I'm expecting myself to be like that? There is a feeling of just never being enough. And then on social media, the algorithm's showing you this absolutely yoked dude doing pull ups with chains around his neck, and they're like, oh, you can get this physique in two weeks or whatever. Trying to shape your mentality of what it means to be a man."

Ryan recently graduated from a large state college in the South, after majoring in oceanography. He is handsome and articulate, with a sweet, nerdy love of fish that reminds me of my son Solly, whose devotion to the minutiae of marine life started in preschool and shows no sign of letting up as he approaches puberty.

Ryan confides in me that at one point in college, he had trained so hard trying to achieve this impossible body shape, putting in hours at the gym lifting weights that were too heavy for him, that he actually shattered a vertebra. He is not alone in his dissatisfaction with his body. Most of the research in this area focuses on girls and women, but the few studies that do exist about boys' relationships to their bodies show that they are also becoming increasingly self-loathing. In one study, around a third of the boys surveyed said they were unhappy with their body shapes, with the vast majority wanting to be more muscular.[10]

Meanwhile, in part as a backlash to the feminist resurgence following the #MeToo movement, an entire "masculinity industry" of YouTubers, TikTokers, podcasters, and other social media stars, has emerged selling young guys a similar vision of testosterone-heavy fantasy-manhood. Many boys are barely out of the Lego battles stage when the TikTok and YouTube algorithms start showing them masculinity content, and the reach of these influencers is vast. Masculinity guru Joe Rogan's podcast, for example, averages an audience of eleven million per episode (for comparison, CNN's primetime news program pulls in less than a million). One 2023 survey by the advocacy group Hope Not Hate found that a staggering eight out of ten British boys aged sixteen to seventeen had consumed misogynistic influencer Andrew Tate's content, and that same demographic was more likely to have heard of Tate than of the British prime minister.[11]

Drawing on a strange mashup of evolutionary psychology, bodybuilding tips, fast cars, and right-wing politicking, these influencers trade in an action-hero reverie of manly self-improvement. The masculinity advice ranges from the bizarre but relatively innocuous (meat-only diets, never masturbate) to the horrifying (beating women). These wildly popular influencers offer a twisted promise to every lost, insecure teenage boy that if he simply follows an intense regimen of weight training, protein ingesting, and oddly manipulative dating tips, he, too, can achieve coveted alpha status. For something that is supposed to be so innate, masculinity sure seems to take a lot of hard work.

In an odd way, these influencers have identified the same general problem with young men as policymakers and parents, the same failure to launch issue that Kade is trying to tackle in Utah. These influencers are, for the most part, targeting the eternal adolescent playing *Fortnite* in his childhood bedroom.

"Women don't want a guy who sits around and plays video games and eats Cheetos," YouTuber Casey Zander tells his viewers, which briefly aligns my agenda and his. Zander offers classes in "Masculine Behavioral Therapy" which includes modules on things such as Mastering the Masculine Mindset to Get Her Addicted and Steps to Brainwash Her and Get the Upper Hand. In his videos Zander tells us that he used to be a shy mama's boy before he embarked on his own masculinity journey. Now he is a chiseled alpha who believes that "every man on planet Earth should strive to be free of all social barriers."

Andrew Tate, one of the most influential and also one of the darkest forces in the online masculinity industry, took the logic further. Although much of Tate's content is the same insecure ramblings as the rest of the manliness crew—the pseudo evo-psychology and wolf pack analogies; the same fragile reaching for the same predictable status markers—his hate speech is more chillingly up-front. "I'm absolutely a misogynist," he boasted in one interview.

At various times Tate's videos have talked about hitting women and choking them, stopping them from leaving the house, and throwing their possessions out a window.

"It's bang out the machete, boom in her face, and grip her by the neck. Shut up, bitch," he says in one now notorious video, describing how he would react if a woman accused him of cheating.

Tate and his cohort scare me and almost every other mom I know. It's obvious how their slick promises and twisted logic prey on young boys, already primed from birth to believe that masculinity is the basic marker of worth, and that emasculation is a fate to be feared. Tate knows his audience, pulling out all of the key tropes of boyhood to suck them in—the sports cars and battle metaphors and superhero analogies. And his formula works.

Like any concerned parent, I am desperate to come up with some definitive script to use with my sons to talk to them about Tate and the rest of the influencers, some perfect killer argument that will convince my boys definitively that their claims are nonsensical and toxic, that patriarchy is a system that harms not just women but men and boys, too. That even if they like the cars, the misogyny should be a dealbreaker. That these guys are not the answer to any sadness or insecurity or alienation that they may be experiencing. But up against their Bugattis and sleek production, a middle-aged woman spouting feminist theory barely stands a chance. I suspect that this is not a battle I will win with logic, but one I will need to fight on a different front.

• • •

I've been staying at the Iron Gate residential therapy center in Utah for a few days now and am starting to feel strangely at home. The house is a social hub, with a constant stream of people coming and going—inpatients, outpatients, and coaches—hanging out and chatting in the kitchen or on the sofas in the entryway or attending coaching or therapy sessions.

It's a quirky mix of people. There's Logan, a young plumbing apprentice who is worried that his porn use is escalating out of control; and Spencer, a twenty-two-year-old student with a bodybuilder physique and a slightly lost expression, whose mom keeps sending him masculinity YouTube videos.

There's Aaron, who, playing out Kade's failure to launch cliché to the letter, literally lives in his grandma's basement, down the road from the center. Before finding Iron Gate, he was desperately lonely and depressed. Having dropped out of college, he was spending his days playing video games and hanging out on internet chat forums. Now he comes to every group the center has to offer and spends as much of his time here as he can. He's always busy helping out, refilling the pen jar; flattening pizza boxes and taking them out to the trash; and setting up the chairs for the next meeting. The center has given him a sense of community and a place where he belongs.

I've sat in on a few therapy groups and coaching sessions now. Without exception, the young guys are all exceptionally polite and respectful. For the most part, in the group sessions, they sit and listen to Kade talk.

Kade likes to talk, often in gnomic aphorisms. He doesn't like consumption, but he does like "creativity, capacity, and connection." He likes flow charts, often drawing them on the whiteboard to illustrate his points. He doesn't like gender fluidity. He's fine with you being gay, or trans, but you need to "think about the consequences of your choice."

He also tells a lot of stories that start with a puffed up, "So I told the guy . . ." and end with a mic drop: "and everyone was just like . . . '*Wow!*' " In most of them, he casts himself as the big guy, the hero. There's something about this "I'm the strongest and the biggest and the best" posturing that feels a little childlike, reminiscent of my own boys in their fighting contests. It's as though he always has something to prove, his masculinity never quite a settled question in his own mind.

It reminds me of what Matt Englar-Carlson told me a while back: "masculinity is a precarious social state." Listening to Kade's stories, I wonder if this might be one of the built-in fault lines of the entire masculine project. The constant proving and re-proving comes across as so fragile, so thin-skinned, that it is itself emasculating.

But the more time I spend with Kade, the more I realize that he also possesses real wisdom. He tells the group of young men that if they don't understand their own worth, they will never be able to understand anyone else's worth. That they need to stop being perfectionists, and that it is corrosive to feel they have to be perfect in order to have self-esteem. He reminds them that they need to be trustworthy and be "impeccable with their word." That they should stop being critical, both of others and of themselves, and assume the best about people. The platitudes feel a little folksy, but also profound.

"The two things we are trying to achieve are that people feel safe and they feel heard," Kade tells me after one session. It seems to be working. Without exception, when I ask them, all of the boys and young men, both inpatients and outpatients, say they have loved their time at Iron Gate, and they think the work has changed them, helped them grow.

The only thing missing seems to be the masculinity. It's an odd disconnect. For all Kade's talk about the need to restore traditional manhood and the importance of masculine values, there actually seems to be very little of that kind of thing here. Since I arrived there has been almost nothing that I have seen in the program that seems identifiably masculine. No feats of physical strength or toughness, no advice to man up, be more stoic, or suppress their emotions. No aggression. In many ways masculinity seems to be the opposite of what Kade is offering.

The parts of the program that seem to be helping these young men the most, if we can label them as gendered rather than simply human, seem not to be traditionally masculine at all, but instead drawn directly from the playbook of female cultural norms: relationship building, emotional openness and vulnerability, a sense of community. If anything, the vibe at Iron Gate, with everyone gathered in the kitchen or around the dining room table, sharing snacks and feelings, reminds me more of a girls' slumber party.

Kade is convinced that restoring masculine values will help boys step up and become adults. But really it seems like the opposite might be the case. Decades of research show us that what promotes healthy adulthood is not emotional stoicism and toughness, and certainly not aggression, but healthy relationships—a sense of connection and belonging.

The famous Harvard Grant Study, and its companion, the Glueck Study, followed a cohort of hundreds of men through their lives, from young adulthood onward, starting in 1938. The aim was to try to understand over time the factors that make for a good life, the social and personal ingredients that help men thrive. For decades, researchers collected a wealth of data about all aspects of these men's lives—their relationships, jobs, lifestyles, and emotional states, as well as their mental and physical health.

The results were surprisingly simple. More than anything else, for these men, the key to a happy, healthy, well-adjusted adulthood was good relationships. Strong connections to friends, family, and community were associated with every marker of mental and physical health and well-being and all measures of life satisfaction, and even with income and career success.

Strong relationships may be the key to a healthy adulthood, but contrary to what Kade had initially argued, and as so many boys have told me, masculinity norms actively get in the way of intimacy and relationship building. The stories we tell boys about what it means to be a man—that life is a series of battles to fight, that relationships are about competing rather than cooperating, that they must be stoic and tough and not share their emotions or validate other people's—all work against building strong relationships. Masculine norms don't help boys become healthy adults. They stand in the way.

And ultimately it is those relationships with friends, family, and community that are the best inoculation for boys against the pull of the misogynistic influencers online. The more connected and loved boys feel, the more community they have in their own lives, and the more empathy they feel from their loved ones, the less need they have to search for belonging in these spaces.

I had been looking for a perfect script to use with my sons to counteract the message of the masculinity influencers, some killer argument that I could use that would dismantle patriarchy in their minds and convince them that what Andrew Tate and his ilk are saying is idiotic and harmful. But I am beginning to realize that there is no script. The only script is, in Kade's words, feeling "safe and heard" elsewhere.

• • •

So why is it so important to Kade to advertise what he offers as masculinity? In some ways it feels like a branding exercise—a sneaky way to get boys and men to open up and share their emotions, like blending your toddler's broccoli into his mac and cheese.

And why do I feel myself pushing back on it? After all, if Kade chooses to label emotional vulnerability or accountability or healthy relationships as masculine in order to let himself and his clients embrace them, then what is the problem with that? Surely anything that gets boys and men to buy into these behaviors has to be a good thing.

But I can't help feeling that the whole framing is reinforcing many of the underlying problems rather than challenging them. Somehow this attempt to fold traditionally feminine norms into the definition of masculinity doesn't just render the whole concept meaningless. It has a whiff of sexism about it, too. If we have to attach the label "masculine" to a behavior before it can have value to men, we are still buying into the basic gender hierarchy in which male is superior, female is lesser, and giving weight to the idea that a man embracing anything feminine is a humiliation.

It also paradoxically keeps boys locked in a box. The constant need to validate every conceivable choice as masculine only reinforces the importance of masculinity, sending boys a clear message that being masculine is so fundamental to their worth that they must never reject it altogether.

It's not just Kade. Many experts who work with boys are starting to use terms such as "healthy masculinity" or "positive masculinity" to distinguish it from the unhealthy or toxic variety. The former football player Don McPherson, for example, uses the branding "aspirational masculinity" for a series of programs for boys and young men that focus on violence prevention and emotional vulnerability.

Similarly, when three psychologists from the APA's Society for the Psychological Study of Men and Masculinities set up their program for middle and high school boys, they were careful to retain the masculinity framework and not challenge the idea at any more fundamental level. Their stated goal was to "preserve the positive in traditional masculinity while jettisoning the bad parts."

They explained, "While keeping men strong, we want to remove the aspects of strength that get us in trouble." They were not quite able to get on board with any conception of manhood that did not involve strength at all.

If the APA were to sponsor a program for girls under the

branding "aspirational femininity," that aimed to "keep women pretty," or that reassured them that they could be a scientist or a CEO and "still be feminine and sexy," we would immediately flag the sexism as either laughably quaint or tradwife-style regressive. But we still see masculinity itself as a non-negotiable, and are still threatened by the idea of jettisoning it altogether, unable to conceive of any real vision for maleness outside of it.

Perhaps this is because we see masculinity as rooted in biology rather than socialization. Psychologists still talk about adolescent boys needing to "develop their sense of masculinity" as though it's some kind of preprogrammed universal stage of child development, like crawling or separation anxiety, rather than a social construct. Meanwhile, it would be a rare psychologist who would argue that a teenage girl's key developmental task is to "come into her sense of femininity."

Of course, there is nothing wrong with many of the traits associated with either femininity or masculinity. Although they are obviously not exclusive to men, masculine-associated attributes such as bravery, strength, physical toughness, and even emotional stoicism in the right contexts, can all be wonderful qualities, even lifesaving ones. No one is trying to take these away or minimize their value.

But "healthy masculinity" does not quite cut it as the answer for boys who are trying to develop a well-rounded sense of self, any more than "healthy femininity" would be a reasonable alternative to feminism for any girl trying to break free of gender stereotypes and claim full personhood.

If we really want to challenge the oppressive pressures that masculine norms place on boys, we need to question the basic terms at a more fundamental level. I would prefer to see a world in which a boy can identify as a boy but feel no pressure to be masculine at all. A world in which boys have the critical thinking skills and social permission to call out and challenge society's expectations around masculinity in the same way that girls are learning to challenge the idea that femininity should be the key measure of worth for a woman. I want to work toward giving boys the same kind of consciousness-raising that women have had around the oppressive expectations of femininity and submissiveness.

• • •

My fantasy that all boys might one day be freed from the masculinity trap altogether, is a long way off for twenty-two-year-old Spencer, a regular at the weekly men's therapy group at Iron Gate. Spencer's mom, Wendy, is a big believer in masculinity. She feels that traditional manly values are under attack in our culture, and Spencer agrees. His mom is the one who introduced him to a lot of the masculinity content he consumes online, including YouTuber Casey Zander and his "masculine behavioral therapy."

It's not just the stuff his mom sends him. Spencer seeks out a lot of masculinity content himself, reads books about the topic, searches for videos and listens to podcasts. Coming across as masculine is very important to him. He believes that feminism, or at least as it is "currently defined," is "not raising women up, but putting men down below." These views are unpopular with his classmates and teachers at the nearby university where Spencer is a student. He wrote a paper recently about why the world should be seeing masculine values in a more positive light, and he got a bad grade. He believes this was unfair, especially given that a female classmate wrote a paper about Barbie from a feminist perspective and was universally praised.

Spencer was initially reluctant to come to the men's group at Iron Gate. "In my mind, when I hear 'support group,' it sounds weak," he tells me. "But really, if I humble myself, this is pretty much a support group. But it's strong. Right? Like I've just come to realize support groups can be strong when they're done the right way."

While Spencer and I are talking, the theme of weakness and strength comes up several times. He seems to evaluate his every thought and action on the basis of whether it is strong or weak—at school, in his relationship with his girlfriend, and in couples therapy. Even about whether it's okay to masturbate (masturbation is weak, apparently, according to YouTuber Casey Zander and Spencer's mom).

"What does being weak mean to you?" I ask him.

"When I'm weak, it makes me feel less of a man."

"So you feel like being a man is really important to you?"

"Oh, it is. It's extremely important," he replies.

"What values would you associate with being a man?" I ask.

"Strength," he replies, instantly.

Stuck inside this circular logic, it seems that before Spencer can accept any quality in himself, or take any action, he first needs it to be officially validated as strong or masculine. Almost anything can qualify, as long as it is branded that way.

When sharing emotions and being vulnerable is sold to him as a manly virtue, for example, Spencer is able to accept it. He needs to understand himself as masculine in order to understand himself as worthy. Masculinity is, in his view, the key marker of value.

But this preoccupation with his own masculinity doesn't quite seem to be making Spencer feel strong and powerful. If anything, the basic terms seem to be leaving him ever more nervous and insecure, unable to trust his own choices or preferences without external validation. I realize that so many of the boys that I have talked to seem, at least to some extent, to be trapped in this same oppressive paradigm. Spencer suddenly seems achingly fragile, and I feel a stab of protectiveness toward him.

He starts telling me about one of his favorite masculinity books, the bestselling *Wild at Heart: Discovering the Secret of a Man's Soul* (2001), by the evangelical Christian author John Eldredge, which has sold well over a million copies. In the book Eldredge pinpoints what he sees as the three basic desires of the "masculine heart," all of which Spencer identifies with strongly: a battle to fight, an adventure to live, and a beauty to rescue.

I wince particularly hard at "a beauty to rescue." The idea that a woman is not a full human in her own right but a kind of narrative MacGuffin in some dude's overblown hero fantasy makes me feel mildly enraged. In the actual book, Eldredge answers this critique by tying himself in knots to convince the reader that the beauty in question might not necessarily be a woman and could also be the allure found in, say, nature or poetry or art (it is unclear how the rescuing part fits into this). Somehow, thinking of women as an item on this bucket list of beautiful experiences to be enjoyed by men on their journeys of spiritual growth only seems to make the sexism worse, not better.

On the face of it, the whole thing sounds ludicrous. Do grown men really still think this way? But the more I mentally run through the stories that my boys and their peers actually consume—in books, movies, TV shows, and video games—the more I realize that Eldredge's hokey sexism might not actually be the ramblings of a relatively obscure evangelical Christian author, but rather an efficient description of the basic foundation of the male narrative universe.

• • •

Glory-seeking heroes have dominated boys' fictional worlds since humans started telling stories. In the classic narrative, the superheroes, fantasy warriors, and video game avatars tend to be one man, working alone, often with some kind of superhuman power or at the very least hypermasculine strength and abilities, who slays the villain, saves the day in a blaze of glory, and usually "gets the girl" as a result. Women are generally secondary characters, essentially objects that men either rescue or acquire as prizes for their bravery and heroism.

The hero's journey is the basis for the majority of Hollywood movies. Marvel superhero epics alone dominate the modern cinematic landscape, drawing in close to a third of all box office revenue for all movies in a given year. Hero narratives in various forms are also the foundation of a significant number of the video games boys love, and the majority of the books and TV shows marketed to them, everything from Harry Potter to Percy Jackson, Spider-Man to Paw Patrol. As such, the hero's journey has become, in some crucial way, an organizing principle for men's inner lives.

So compelling is the idea of the hero's journey to the male psyche that research by the U.S. Department of Defense found that ISIS recruiters had studied this narrative formula and replicated it in recruitment videos to target adolescent boys, whom they saw as particularly susceptible to this kind of heroic fantasy.[12]

At their best, these narratives can provide enticing imaginative worlds and valuable lessons about morality, bravery, and self-sacrifice. Clearly, the vast majority of young boys consume them and go on to live happy, productive lives. But there are invisible harms to this impossible vision of manhood, and boys can easily internalize damaging expectations from them about masculinity and their own place in the world.

Boys are socialized to see themselves as the hero on his journey and the main character in any story, and to see everyone else, and especially women, as minor characters or narrative foils. As such, boys subtly absorb the idea that women and girls are not quite actual people with their own true agency or interiority, but rather abstractions that exist to further a man's narrative.

Stories in which men and boys star as glory-studded main characters send strong messages to boys about their own specialness and centrality to the world, about what is owed to them simply by virtue of their being male, and the level of adulation they can expect as their birthright.

But this sense of specialness and superiority comes at a price. Taken together, the messages about individual heroism contained in these stories can end up breeding an odd combination in boys of both entitlement and inadequacy.

The hero's story creates impossibly punishing expectations for boys of what a man should be: physically invulnerable, emotionally bulletproof, and ideally, superhuman. Actual boys and men, with human flaws and vulnerabilities, will always fall short. Failure is built into the project. Bryce and Jayden and Spencer had all, in their own ways, fallen prey to these expectations, internalizing a low-level shame at their inability to live up to the impossible demands of the masculine ideal.

It's a message that has always troubled Joel Christensen, a professor of classical studies at Brandeis University. His work focuses on the ways in which the stories we are exposed to shape our sense of self. Christensen has a particular interest in hero narratives and their impact on the male psyche and the construction of masculinity.

"The stories that we hear from a young age shape what we think is possible in the world and what we think is true for ourselves," Christensen tells me. "And so for me it's a simple question. How do we socialize men and women differently? How do we tell them different stories to give them basic scripts about how to behave in the world?"

I think about the friendship and relationship narratives we give to girls, that help them absorb the idea that they are part of a relational system, a community that everyone contributes to and draws from, while boys are socialized to think they need to be unique and special.

Christensen writes about the ancient Greek concept of *kleos,* a kind of fame and glory or "eternal renown" that a hero earned through his great deeds. This was the basic reward system for the classical hero, his motivating drive. And at some level, that hunger for specialness and glory has endured as a kind of baseline expectation in the modern male psyche.

"I think it's about innate ability. You believe that you're innately better and good," Christensen explains.

With all this in the background, it makes sense that men might avoid the boring tasks of adulthood. If you are shooting for eternal renown, doing the laundry or studying for your social studies test might well feel a little beneath you. The model of quiet diligence and cooperation that girls are encouraged to emulate can easily read as emasculating when compared to the glorious feats of the hero.

But in most situations that life throws at us, quiet diligence is more important to success than splashy acts or a feeling that you are special. It's not innate genius or superpowers or once-in-a-lifetime feats of bravery that get you into college or land you a job or force you out of your childhood bedroom. Mostly it's tedious, incremental drudgery. It's perhaps not surprising that boys are spending so much time playing video games—they provide the only arenas in which they can play out their hero fantasies and expectations of glory, instead of fulfilling the tedious tasks of the real world.

The pressure to be masculine might have helped boys launch into adulthood when it was an economic requirement, when men were the sole breadwinners and had to provide financially for a family. But now, with most women working and less expectation that men will be the main wage earners, masculinity has been stripped of the only part of the story that really promoted adulthood. Without the breadwinning, what's left are just toxic scraps—a grab bag of childish vanities and impossible pressures.

When boys and men fail to meet the wildly unrealistic expectations of heroic manhood, it can lead to a deep sense of inadequacy, according to Matt Englar-Carlson.

"Shame is the core emotion for men," he tells me. "Men are pretty aware when they don't meet gender expectations. Then there's a shame cycle that occurs, that remains internal."

In its most extreme manifestation, this pervasive sense of shame and inadequacy is reflected in the psychological profiles of the high-school shooter or misogynistic incel. Manifestos written by these young men show just how deeply they are tortured by the gap between their internalized entitlement to glory and heroism, and the crushing reality of being an unspectacular adolescent boy, ignored and rejected by the women that he has been led to believe are his birthright.

• • •

In late 2022, the Romanian police caught up with masculinity influencer Andrew Tate and arrested him on grounds of sex trafficking and rape. Tate's misogynistic arrogance may well have been his downfall. A few days earlier he had trolled teenage climate activist Greta Thunberg on Twitter with a picture of himself posing with his Bugatti and boasting about his collection of thirty-three cars and the toxic emissions they produced. She tweeted straight back, asking him to email her directly with more details at smalldickenergy@getalife.com.

Tate responded in a video with some toxic emissions of his own, rambling on about how Greta had been brainwashed by the government to encourage us all to tax ourselves into poverty. Unfortunately for him, he failed to notice that a pizza box in view bore the logo of a Romanian pizza company, an oversight that legal experts claimed gave police the confirmation they needed that Tate was in the country, and the ability to track him down.

Whether or not this story is apocryphal, it captured something about our cultural moment regarding gender. The whole thing read like a girl-power superhero reboot from the "mighty girls" section of the bookstore. The tiny underdog Greta defeating the filthy rich supervillain and saving the planet. She was the triumphant, clever girl, embodying all of society's hopes for the future. Tate represented the absolute worst of men: oafish, idiotic, menacing. That should have been the end of the story, a resounding defeat for a beast of the past. But this is a series that will keep running. Perhaps not with these two individuals, but these two wildly influential cultural tropes continue to battle it out for control of the narrative, for our hearts and minds.

"I realized yesterday that nothing is stopping me from becoming Batman," Tate once boasted. "I have a Batcave. I have an Alfred. I have a Batmobile, a Bugatti. I can fight. I'm rich as fuck. I'm charismatic. There's nothing stopping me putting on a suit and being Batman."

He told an audience of lost, insecure teenage boys, "The masculine perspective you have to understand is that life is war. It's a war for the female you want. It's a war for the car you want. It's a war for the money you want. It's a war for the status. Masculine life is war."

In a million subtle ways it was a message that his audience had been primed from birth to receive. This is, at heart, exactly the story our culture sells to young boys. Masculine life is war. You are a superhero, and life is a series of enemies for you to defeat. Succeed, and the world is yours. Fail, and you are a pussy.

• • •

On my last night in Utah, I stay up late, snuggled under the flowery bedspread in my room, thinking about masculinity—Kade's version of it and Andrew Tate's version. I watch a few Casey Zander videos on YouTube. "Don't use this for evil," Zander makes sure to clarify, before dispensing his advice on how to brainwash women into wanting to have sex with you.

Of course, there is a meaningful difference between benevolent sexism and its darker, more violent face. Andrew Tate is a bad man, by almost any reasonable definition. Kade is a good man, providing a genuinely helpful service. With a few obvious blips, Casey Zander seems like a nice enough kid. But in essence, the systems they are working with are similar. They all cast women not as equal humans in their own right but as objects reliant on men's benevolence. "I love women" and "I hate women" are really two sides of the same coin.

Whether men are providing the wall around the garden for women or locking them in the house, they are still viewing them not as equals but as dependents, essentially at the mercy of men's moods and goodwill. Benevolent sexism still bears risks and indignities for women.

And ultimately it also bears risks for boys, pushing them into patterns of behavior that keep them unhealthy and disconnected and scared. However prettily they are dressed up, the stories of masculinity don't just hurt women, they also harm boys and men.

• • •

I had enjoyed my time in Utah and thought Kade was offering something of real value. Without a doubt, he is helping his clients.

But perhaps more for reasons that are the opposite of the ones he is advertising. Boys don't need more masculinity, but freedom from that paradigm; they need permission to be fully human without the pressure to conform to oppressive masculine norms.

Kade is offering boys community, attention, warmth, and the opportunity to be vulnerable. And it is working. We could quibble about the details, but I wish that all boys could draw on a similar sense of belonging and connection.

My flight home is early, and I set off from the house when it's still pitch-dark. Bryce has gotten up to wave goodbye, helping me to load my suitcase into the rental car. I drive off, realizing that I will miss this place. The warmth and generosity of this quirky, offbeat community.

I'm driving along the freeway mulling it all over when I feel the steering wheel pull ominously to the right and the car flail out of control. My tire is flat, and I don't know how to change it. I pull over and call Triple A, resigning myself to a wait of several hours and to missing my flight home. But within ten minutes, a truck shows up.

A man gets out holding a jack. He asks me what brings me to town, and we talk a little. It turns out he's an old schoolmate of Kade's. He changes the wheel in minutes and I'm on my way again.

"The world would fall apart without men," Kade had told me in one of our many masculinity conversations. I had bristled. Of course, I could have learned how to change a tire. Of course, it could have been a woman who showed up with a jack on Highway 15. But despite my feminist upbringing, I never did, and it almost never is. We sort ourselves into these gender roles as much as we are sorted into them. And I was sure happy to see Clint from Cedar City Towing Service.

CHAPTER 4

"FEMINIZING THE CLASSROOM"

BOYS AND SCHOOL

The seventh graders in Ms. Ryan's Modern Masculinities class are crackling around the edges of puberty, a handful with deep voices, most still squeaky, some retaining their boyish wiggliness, others newly languid.

This is the Browning School, in New York City, a sixty-thousand-dollars-a-year, K through 12, all-boys incubator of power, which counts three Rockefellers among its alumni as well as numerous captains of industry, media barons, judges, secretaries of state, and at least one governor. The boys at Browning wear compulsory coats and ties, each pulling the dress code off slightly differently. Some sport navy power blazers with gold buttons, hair slicked back, ties knotted into plump half windsors. Others slouch in old-world tweeds and cords, and a few style out their formalwear as tiny poppet Mick Jaggers. The overall effect is strangely adorable. In these minimen I can see the future contours of my tax adviser, the banker refusing my loan application, the guy with the guitar who shattered my heart in college.

As much as it was about sex, #MeToo was about unchecked male power, about entitlement and moral immunity for a certain type of man. For the most part, at least in its public face, the movement exposed not disenfranchised or poor men, but those at the top of the ladder, at the place where class and gender privilege come together in a kind of gilded, rotten untouchability. Historically, elite all-boys schools have played an outsize role in creating these concentrations of male privilege and unaccountability.

The American all-boys schools tend to ape a British aesthetic and tradition, and having grown up in the UK, the culture is familiar to me. As a teenager I briefly dated a boy from one of the fancier London schools and got to know his friends. Their version of masculinity was foppish and floppy-haired, likely laughably fey to an American locker-room sensibility. But in substance their codes of manhood were every bit as rigid and unforgiving. They were clever and funny and misogynistic as hell. I remember one of their female teachers taking some time off work due to a miscarriage. For the rest of the school year, the boys referred to her as Miss Carriage.

Right in the heart of New York's unfathomably monied Upper East Side, Browning caters to a similar demographic, but its current administration has taken a radical approach to shifting that culture. Browning's principal, Dr. John Botti, joined the school in 2016, right before Trump was elected president and the #MeToo movement propelled the country into its major reckoning around toxic masculinity. Botti prefers not to use the phrase, as he thinks it often alienates boys and shuts down conversations, but he is committed to tackling the underlying issues.

"I think there's a real dangerous propensity for boys to fall into stereotypes, scripts, and schemas about who they're supposed to be in the world," he tells me. "I wanted to make sure we're not a place that's just reifying gender privilege."

Concerned that adolescent boys often shut down emotionally and feel under pressure to perform a kind of bulletproof, strutting masculinity in front of their peers, Botti was determined to transform Browning into an environment that questioned toxic norms and behaviors, prioritized relationships, and encouraged emotional vulnerability and expression.

He and his staff have remade the curriculum and approach to learning at Browning, in consultation with Dr. Niobe Way, the New York University psychology professor who studies how masculinity norms affect boys' friendships and ability to connect with others. They have also drawn on the work of several other experts in boys' development and have now redirected the school's approach to be relationally based, focusing on connection and relationships as the foundation of learning, something historically lacking in boys' education.

The school has also started a new curriculum for fifth to twelfth grade called Modern Masculinities, with compulsory weekly classes for all students. The classes aim to challenge problematic masculine biases and beliefs such as homophobia and misogyny, and to promote critical thinking about these norms and the part the boys themselves play in upholding them. The boys also learn about empathy and emotional openness. The aim is to turn out boys who are emotionally healthier, more attuned citizens, and freed from the pressure to adhere to rigid masculine norms in the classroom—better, more diligent students.

• • •

Today the seventh graders are discussing a handout featuring a news story from the *Daily Mail*. The picture shows two teenage boys sitting on chairs in a schoolyard, holding hands, their heads hanging low. Surrounding them is a circle of onlookers. The headline reads "Humiliation for two male high school students as they are forced to hold hands as a punishment for fighting."

"Why do you think it is humiliating for these boys to hold hands?" Ms. Ryan asks the class. "Why would that be a punishment for boys in particular?"

"It's bringing them down," says a slick-haired boy in a bow tie. "It's degrading."

"Never in my life have I thought of holding hands as humiliating or degrading," Ms. Ryan replies. "I think of it as a gesture of love and affection. What do you think is going on here? Do you think they would have done the same punishment for girls?"

"No way," says an earnest-looking boy in wire-framed glasses. "This revolves around the stereotype that boys shouldn't show their feelings."

Another boy cuts in. "It's the hard truth to say this, but I think it's basically because people think it's gay. Most of us have felt that."

"Yeah, if you're gay you are acting like a girl," chimes in a boy in a checked shirt, tipping his chair back.

"If you show a lot of vulnerable feelings as a boy, what does that make you?" Ms. Ryan asks.

"A woman," a few boys reply in unison.

Ms. Ryan steps in. "So, if you are gay, you are like a woman. Well, what is wrong with being a woman?"

The class goes silent, perhaps processing the awkward realization that Ms. Ryan is herself a woman. She turns to the whiteboard and writes BOYS WILL BE BOYS in large capital letters, then taps each word in turn with her pen.

"Some people believe that boys are wired this way," she tells the class. "Not to show their feelings, for example, or to behave in certain ways. Why is that harmful?"

"It's stereotyping," replies the boy in the checked shirt.

"Yes," says Ms. Ryan. "I want you to think about stereotypes—how do you think stereotypes affect what we see?"

"When you see stereotypes, you see things through a scope, a tube—it blocks off the outside world," the boy replies.

"That's right," says Ms. Ryan. "You are seeing things, but you are seeing them through a set of assumptions. What we want you to do at Browning is to stop yourself when this happens and to move directly to wondering and asking yourself, 'Why do I think this?' "

• • •

Browning's attempt to challenge masculinity norms and gender stereotypes in the classroom runs counter to many of the main currents in contemporary thinking around boys' education. The question of what to do about the problem of boys and school has become highly charged, tapping into our deepest divisions and anxieties around gender politics.

Over the last twenty years or so, perhaps the word most commonly used by journalists and policy makers to describe the academic performance of boys is *underachievement*. Across the United States, boys are falling behind their female peers at school. Academically, by almost every measure, girls now outperform boys at all levels of education, from kindergarten through college.

In reading, as a group, girls do significantly better than boys in every school district in the country. Boys are, on average, three-quarters of a grade level behind girls in reading by their first year of school, and the gap widens as time goes on. Historically, boys have done better in math than girls overall, but in most parts of the country girls have now closed that gap (although boys still outperform girls at the very upper end of the math scores scale). Overall girls now get better grades in high school across all subjects, including math and science, traditionally seen as "boy" subjects.[1]

Boys, on the other hand, account for close to 90 percent of school discipline violations. They are suspended more than twice as often and expelled more than three times as often as girls.[2] They take fewer advanced placement classes and participate in fewer extracurriculars. One of the biggest factors in the whole male failure-to-launch phenomenon is that boys are now about 20 percent less likely to enroll in college than same aged girls.[3] And if they do get there, they are significantly more likely to drop out than their female classmates.[4]

Historically, there has always been a wide racial gap in educational achievement, particularly between white and Black students. This is because Black students have always been at a major social and economic disadvantage compared with their white peers, for a wide variety of reasons stemming from deeply rooted systemic racism in the United States. This includes not just outright discrimination but also higher poverty rates, lower incomes, housing inequity, poorly funded schools, and fewer resources across the board for Black students as well as the experience of growing up in a country that prioritizes whiteness.

But the racial achievement gap in education is heavily complicated by gender. When it comes to educational outcomes, Black boys are one of the worst off groups in the country. Just 13 percent of eighth-grade Black boys are considered proficient in reading, compared to 34 percent of white boys.[5] Black boys make up only 18 percent of students in American schools, but they account for two-thirds of all school suspensions. As a group, Black boys also have the worst test scores, the worst discipline records, and the highest dropout rates of all demographic groups in the United States.

But the same is not true for Black girls. Despite suffering the same compounded and entrenched racial injustice as Black boys, Black girls now actually do better than white boys on a wide variety of educational outcomes. Black girls are now more likely to graduate from high school than white boys.[6] More Black women aged eighteen to twenty-four are enrolled in college than white males of the same age, and Black women in their late twenties are more likely than their white male peers to hold a master's degree.[7]

In many ways, these numbers turn everything about how we understand systems of racial and gender privilege on its head, at least when it comes to education. Black girls have the same economic and social disadvantages as Black boys. They grow up in the same families and attend the same poorly funded schools. They both come up against the same racist systems. The fact that young Black girls are able to overcome multiple compounded injustices to overtake *white boys*—the recipients of every type of systemic privilege America has to offer—is hugely impressive on their part. It also suggests that gender itself is a major factor, and that there is something deeply problematic in the way that we are socializing boys of all races.

Across all racial groups, the quality of the pool of male applicants for universities in the United States is now so low overall that admissions directors at private colleges (which are not bound by Title IX rules) routinely bump up mediocre applications from high school boys while rejecting girls with better grades, test scores, and extracurriculars in an attempt to achieve an equal gender balance on campus.

In a 2017 op-ed for the *Washington Post* entitled "Who's Benefiting from Affirmative Action? White Men," the University of Pennsylvania professor Jonathan Zimmerman wrote that sixty-four elite colleges, including Brown and Wesleyan, had admitted making it easier for boys to get in than girls, and noted that a male applicant is now 14 percent more likely to get accepted to college than a comparable female applicant. "Benefiting the white male over a superior Asian American or female candidate makes no sense," he wrote. "Indeed, it makes a mockery of affirmative action itself."

Fears about boys' underachievement are almost certainly overblown. In reality, the gap between girls' and boys' academic achievement is only a relative discrepancy. In absolute terms, both boys' and girls' test scores have been improving overall over the last two decades; it's just that girls' performance has been improving more quickly. The anxiety about boys' underperformance probably stems in part from a deep-seated unease about women's gains in power at the perceived expense of men. But the disparity has become large enough—and made people uncomfortable enough—to prompt talk of a "boy crisis," or, in more overwrought circles, a "war on boys" in schools.

The question is what is causing this discrepancy. It's not intelligence. Boys and girls have similar IQ scores. And, much as the feminist in me hates to admit it, on various other tests that aim to measure raw aptitude rather than knowledge or study, boys often actually do better than girls. On the SAT college entrance test, boys still score around 13 points higher than girls overall. This is mainly due to significantly higher math scores (girls do a little better than boys on the combined reading and writing section, but not enough to counter boys' math performance). And surprisingly, given gender stereotypes about boys and reading, before 2016, when the reading and writing portions of the SAT were separate rather than lumped in together, boys actually scored higher than girls on the reading section. There are many in-built flaws and biases in these tests that some argue still favor boys, but it seems unlikely, given these results, that boys are innately less intelligent than girls.

As a group, boys don't lag behind girls at school because they are less smart. They trail them because they are less conscientious—less willing or able to study and listen and behave themselves. The stereotypes of the anxiously perfectionist high school girl and the unmotivated slacker teen boy are grounded in real data.

Adolescent girls spend nearly an hour and a half more per week on homework than same aged boys. In a study on middle schoolers conducted by Angela Duckworth, the author of *Grit: The Power of Passion and Perseverance* (2016), girls left boys in the dust on every measure of self-discipline including study habits, impulse control, classroom behavior, and goal setting, and their grades were significantly higher as a result, even though the boys in the study actually scored five points higher on an IQ test that Duckworth administered.[8]

This difference in diligence and behavior starts from an early age. Five-year-old girls are significantly more likely to be judged kindergarten ready than same aged boys, due, for the most part, to a difference not in academic capability but in their ability to sit still, listen, and use their quiet indoor voices.

Those on the right tend to argue that these differences in boys' and girls' school-related behaviors are innate rather than socialized, and that boys are biologically hardwired to behave in certain ways. This story is a version of the "boys will be boys" narrative, often drawing on gender science (of varying degrees of validity) to make the case that boys' brains and hormones are inherently different, and that schools are failing to accommodate their natural boyness and instead are forcing them to behave like girls.

Boys' advocates on the right are co-opting boys' underachievement in school into a larger men's rights movement. Boys are the real victims, they claim, in a narrative they call "the feminizing of the classroom," arguing that we have transformed schools into spaces that are at best unsuited for boys and at worst downright hostile toward them. In this belief system, boys' failures are the result of feminism.

One of the more prominent of these voices is Christina Hoff Sommers. In her book *The War Against Boys: How Misguided*

Policies Are Harming Our Young Men (2013), she argues that schools have increasingly become natural environments for girls, who enjoy sitting still and being "good," while boys' innate behaviors and interests are devalued and squashed.

"As our schools have become more feelings-centered, risk-averse, collaboration-oriented and sedentary, they have moved further and further from boys' characteristic sensibilities," Sommers wrote in an op-ed in *The New York Times*. She pointed to the fact that the vast majority of teachers are women, and claims that "girlie" interests and concerns are prioritized in the classroom, and that boys are often forbidden from writing about the violent topics that might spark their interest such as war and weapons.

By way of example, she cited a school in Lexington, Massachusetts, that taught women's history, encouraged boys and girls to cooperate on a quilt-making project, and chastised a boy for handing out invitations to his birthday party in class because he was inviting only boys. (This school doesn't serve as particularly convincing evidence for her argument about underachievement. It actually performs way above the state average across all subjects, and its student body is more than 50 percent male.)

But it's not just those on the right who are centering biologically essentialist explanations for boys' underperformance. Progressive parents and policy makers also tend to frame the so-called boy crisis as one of innate biological limitations and hardwired interests, rather than socialization.

One of the more influential liberal voices on boys' education in recent years has been Richard Reeves, aforementioned author of *Of Boys and Men: Why the Modern Male Is Struggling, Why It Matters, and What to Do About It*. In the book, Reeves points to the neuroscience that suggests that boys' brains develop more slowly than those of girls. The prefrontal cortex, for example—the part of the brain that is primarily responsible for impulse control, emotional self-regulation, and various aspects of executive function—develops a full two years later in boys.

In response to this delay in brain maturation, Reeves comes up with what on the face of it looks like a simple, elegant, and uncontroversial solution. He suggests that we redshirt all boys, a college athletics term that Reeves uses to mean holding boys back a year to start kindergarten. This is something that many parents with sons already do informally, but in Reeves's proposal, it would happen across the board, and the official kindergarten starting age would be a year older for all boys than it is for girls. This would mean that throughout their school careers, boys would always be a year older than girls in their same grade.

Reeves's big idea made a splash, and he went on CBS News and NPR, and an array of other radio shows and podcasts of all kinds, to talk about nationwide redshirting and how it could provide the magic answer to the issue of boys' underachievement.

As with many magic solutions that purport to solve complex problems, there are some serious issues with Reeves's idea. The most obvious of these is that it would leave parents of boys paying for an extra year of childcare. (Reeves suggests that the proposal would need to be introduced in tandem with new childcare funding, but this seems a little unrealistic, given that no American administration in history has managed to come up with comprehensively funded federal childcare for any age group.)

Even if the childcare issues could be solved, there is a range of evidence to suggest that this proposal would not actually lead to better outcomes for boys, and probably would have quite the opposite effect. A number of studies show that, counterintuitively, children who start school at an older age actually fare worse on a number of measures longer term than those who start at younger ages, and that this effect is particularly strong for boys.

Researchers from Harvard found that contrary to popular myth, children, and especially boys, who start kindergarten when older are significantly more likely to end up dropping out of high school, have lower rates of college completion, and even have decreased lifetime earnings than children who start kindergarten at age five. Their data shows that in recent years, the unofficial redshirting by parents of boys has actually helped *increase* the gender gap in school rather than decrease it.[9]

Other research has shown various disadvantages for children who are old for their grade, compared with children who are at the younger end. The older children are more likely to be held back a grade at all points throughout their school career; are less likely to take a college admissions exam, such as the SAT; have lower lifetime earnings; and even, according to one study, score significantly lower on an IQ test at age eighteen than same aged children who started kindergarten as the youngest in their grade.[10]

Researchers aren't quite sure why this is the case, but speculate that younger children learn from their older peers and are more likely to develop vital skills of hard work and persistence to keep up with them. So it would seem that by making boys a year older than their female classmates, we might actually be putting them at a disadvantage.

Whether or not his redshirting idea has merit, Richard Reeves's thinking is motivated by a more sophisticated, but ultimately similar kind of biological essentialism to the right's "boys will be boys, it's all hardwired" narrative. In Reeves's view, the differences between boys and girls are rooted not in socialization or in some combination of nature and nurture but wholly in biology. Instead of digging into the ways in which boys are socialized in their early years, working to give them the social permission to explore a wider range of interests, or telling them a less restrictive story about their own possibilities, we just need to find a way to accommodate their innate limitations.

This is a common theme in the discourse, even among the left. The same scrupulously liberal parents who wouldn't dream of making any overly deterministic statements about the fixed capacities of girls, who would never casually declare that girls were biologically incapable of doing math, or temperamentally docile, or hormonally primed for housework, still happily throw around phrases like "boys can't sit still," "boys are immature/aggressive/reluctant readers" or just a shrugging catchall, "*Boys!*" when they sprint around the classroom in circles during quiet reading time.

It's an odd dissonance. Whatever they may have done wrong, it's hard to deny that men, formerly boys, built much of our civilization—not just the buildings and bridges and roads, but also modern democracy, the justice system, most of Western and Eastern philosophy, the scientific method, and modern medicine, as well as a major part of the literary canon. Until relatively recently, boys and men were the only people who were allowed to study at all. This body of achievement is hard to square with the idea that boys are biologically incapable of sitting still on the rug or writing a sentence without a "movement break" in the middle or reading anything other than Dog Man on repeat.

It's not that the biologically essentialist narrative is wrong, exactly. There *are* genuine differences in self-control and behavior and executive function between girls and boys throughout childhood that are rooted in biology. Boys' brains do develop later than girls' brains and this difference persists well into adolescence. We do need to take this into account when we talk about the structures and expectations of school.

But the whole biologically hardwired narrative is also reductive, leaving little room for a nuanced and rigorous conversation about the way we socialize boys, the constant invisible messages we send them about who and what they should be in the world, and the effect this might be having on their behavior and performance. If anything, the biological differences mean that boys need *more* focus on nurture and socialization, not less.

Dr. Juliet Williams, a professor of gender studies at UCLA, has become concerned about the increasingly essentializing ways in which parents and educators are talking about young boys.

"As a progressive feminist, we know what the rules are with girls," she tells me. "You should be socializing your daughter that the sky's the limit. If you want to be an astronaut, if you want to be a stay-at-home mom, wherever your sense of self leads, with the presumption being that if you give girls the opportunity, they can excel. But then for the boys, there's this essentialism. In the areas where we see boys not thriving—in social and emotional development, in reading and language arts and other arts fields, the attitude is 'Boys just don't like that stuff; boys aren't good at that.'

"But," she continues, "when we say to boys, 'This is how boys are,' we're basically saying, 'Your best hope is to always be a very limited human being.' And I don't know why we would ever do that. We're certainly not doing that for girls."

• • •

It's not that Williams is denying the existence of any innate differences between boys and girls. But she believes that we are focusing too much on biology. In doing so, we are shutting down a more important conversation about the different ways that we socialize boys and girls, and the messages we give them about their capabilities, interests, and how they should behave. Williams believes that by failing to look critically at socialization and come up with interventions to address it, we are missing a large piece of the puzzle as to why boys are falling behind.

What she is saying resonates with me. Over the last decade or so, the discourse around girls' prospects has become almost aggressively inspirational: "Girl power!" "You can do anything!" The future is female!" In any areas in which girls do still underperform when compared with boys, it has always been a feminist principle to reach for social explanations, rather than biological ones. In math, for example, until recently, boys consistently performed better than girls at all grade levels. While a few cranks claimed that this was because boys were innately smarter or more mathematically minded, for the most part, the serious narrative from the feminist left around closing the math gap focused on differences in socialization, and ways to address that.

Parents and teachers scrutinized the subtle ways they inadvertently communicated to girls that math is for boys. Psychologists studied *stereotype threat,* the psychological phenomenon whereby people tend to perform worse at a task after being reminded that a negative stereotype exists about their group's abilities in that area. Various studies showed that when girls were reminded that math is a "boy subject" right before a test, they performed worse than girls who were primed to believe that boys and girls had equal mathematical capabilities.[11] In the quest to close the math gap, educators dug into the influence of role models, and policy makers studied teacher bias and discrimination in math and other STEM fields.[12] Meanwhile, commentators noted that we give boys construction toys that flex their emerging spatial awareness skills, while girls get Barbies programmed to say in an electronic falsetto, "*Math class is tough! Want to go shopping*?"

The soul-searching around the gender gap in math and the interventions it generated have been successful. For the most part, girls have caught up with boys in math scores, and in many school districts, they have actually overtaken them.

But we have failed to do the same critical thinking around the way we socialize boys when it comes to their school performance. Rather than questioning the messages we send to boys about who they should be in the world or exposing them to a wider range of human experiences and interests, or a more optimistic story about their potential and capabilities, it's as though at some level we have written them off. We assume their interests and limitations are hardwired; the best we can do is shrug our shoulders and work around them.

• • •

In actuality, a fair amount of evidence shows that the ways in which we socialize boys does have an impact on both their attitudes toward school, and their performance and behavior in the classroom. A wide-scale study across the United States, Canada, and the United Kingdom found that in each of the three countries studied, parents spent significantly more time in the early years with their girls than with their boys on reading, telling stories, singing songs, drawing, and teaching letters.[13] After controlling for other factors, the researchers estimated that the extra time parents spend with girls accounts for between a quarter and a third of the gender differences in school readiness and test scores in kindergarten.

Other studies have shown similar results, and the discrepancy in how much time parents spend teaching these preacademic skills with daughters versus sons is particularly wide for single mothers.[14] There is likely an overlap between nature and nurture as to why parents do this: both a higher likelihood that girls will sit still for this kind of activity, and an unconscious assumption about what male and female children should be doing or might enjoy.

But although it can occasionally feel soul annihilating, the hours we spend chanting "A A A ahhh pul" make a big difference. It's not just because of the skills themselves, but also because of the messages we are sending to children about the value of these skills, and how much importance they should be placing on them. When we spend more time teaching preacademic skills to our daughters, we are subtly communicating the idea to *all* children that these activities are for girls.

At the same time, the messages we give boys about masculinity—"Be active and physical and tough!"; "You are a glorious action hero who is above the quiet tedium of writing a book report!"—often get in the way of the reflection and slow, careful diligence needed to be a good student.

These early messages are powerful. By the time boys reach school age, research shows they have already internalized the idea that school is for girls. One study of elementary school–aged children from the University of Kent found that both boys and girls believed that boys were academically inferior to girls and thought that adults would agree with them. The same study also hints that these low expectations for boys can easily become a self-fulfilling prophecy.[15]

The researchers gave the children a test in reading, writing, and math, telling half of the children in advance that boys tend to do worse on the test, and the other half that girls and boys were expected to perform similarly. Both statements came true. In the group where boys were told they were likely to do badly, that is exactly what happened (the girls' performance was unaffected). In the group told that the two sexes were likely to perform similarly, the boys' performance improved, while the girls' stayed the same.

Stereotype threat is a phenomenon that is significantly more studied and discussed when it comes to girls and math, but research suggests that it is even more prevalent for boys when it comes to reading and language arts.[16] In another study, when boys were told that a task was a reading exercise, they performed worse than girls, but when they were told the same task was a game, they actually performed better.

The main academic gap between boys and girls now is in reading (boys still generally hold their own in math and science). The conventional wisdom is that girls are just naturally better readers, with a higher innate verbal ability. But research such as this suggests that the reading gap might be driven as much by the social messages we give boys, that reading is a feminized activity.

"If you teach boys that activity and aggression are good and passivity and quietness are bad, they're not gonna read," Juliet Williams tells me. "And a student who doesn't read is not going to be a good student."

While listening to Williams, I realize just how common the trope of the school-hating boy is in the chapter books my sons consume. Diary of a Wimpy Kid, Big Nate, Captain Underpants, and My Weird School—these series all have a male protagonist (or two) whose driving narrative motivation is his contempt for school. I remember reading Solly the wonderful Land of Stories series, which stars sixth grader boy-girl twins: Alex, a studious, teacher-pleasing bookworm sister and Connor, a school-despising, always-in-trouble brother who struggles to concentrate in class. I hadn't even considered the stereotyping at the time. But had the books featured, say, a brave, strong boy and fearful, timid girl, or a sister who struggled with math and her computer genius brother, I would have called out the sexism in a heartbeat. As happens so often, the boy stereotypes fly below the radar.

In Williams's view, the social messages we are sending boys are setting them up to fail. "Boys are given an impossible set of expectations that they have to be tough and defy authority, and show leadership and also be learners, which is a feminized positionality," she tells me. "But rather than go the route of defeminizing learning, I would rather that we destigmatized femininity for boys in the same way that we have destigmatized masculinity for girls."

Studies confirm the idea that the stories that boys internalize about what it means to be masculine do get in the way of them succeeding in school, particularly in subjects generally coded as feminine, such as reading and the humanities. When a group of sociologists surveyed boys from fifty-two middle schools and eighty high schools across the country to understand how their relationship to masculinity affected their school performance, they found that overall, the more closely a boy subscribed to traditional masculine norms, the worse his grades were. But tellingly, this effect did not apply to math, only to English and their overall GPA.[17] The researchers speculated that this was because math is traditionally seen as a "boy subject," so achieving in math did not undermine a boy's masculine status, whereas excelling in English came at a social cost to boys. This was even more true for boys of color, particularly Latino and Black boys.

• • •

The idea that feminism—or its sneaky misogynistic proxy, "feminizing"—is to blame for boys' underachievement is based on a faulty premise. Far from feminism being the cause of boys' struggles, it looks as though it might be part of the solution. Girls outperform boys in reading tests in every state in the country, but research shows that when boys are raised in more gender-progressive states, the gap is much smaller. In one study in 2010, researchers compared boys' and girls' test scores in math and reading from across the country against a couple of measures of gender attitudes in the communities in which they lived.[18] The main one was how strongly the adults in that community agreed with the statement "It is much better for everyone involved if the man is the achiever outside the home and the woman takes care of the home and family."

A strong correlation emerged. The higher the percentage of

people who strongly agreed with this statement, indicating a community with a more conservative attitude toward gender, the worse boys in that community performed in relation to girls in reading. (Tellingly, in those same, more traditional communities, girls also performed worse in math relative to boys.) In communities with more progressive attitudes toward gender, boys did better in reading, and although they didn't catch up with girls completely, the gaps were much smaller.

A similar effect is clear at Browning. Gene Campbell, an English teacher, has seen how questioning and challenging masculinity norms in the classroom can have positive effects on boys' reading engagement.

"Boys can come in, and there's a freedom from having to perform their masculinity," he tells me. "I always tell this story about having taught *Pride and Prejudice* at a coed school and only the girls spoke the whole time—none of the boys ever wanted any part of it. And then I went to teach at a boy's school, and they were deeply invested in caring about every page, and it wasn't a 'girls' text.' Those boys defended Darcy. One of them threatened to not speak in class for the rest of the year if Darcy and Lizzy didn't end up together. And it was the most incredible change from what I had lived before."

"What do you think made it different?" I ask.

"The freedom to own it. There was no expectation that to speak up and be engaged in a romantic plot would label them as anything other than intelligent and engaged."

• • •

Today in Modern Masculinities class, the Browning fifth graders have a visit from Bo, a towering and gentle twelfth grader, one of only a handful of Black boys I have seen around the building so far. He has come to talk to the younger boys about suppressing emotions. "You might have seen me around the hallways here," he tells the boys as he introduces himself. "I'm a very busy person."

Bo tells the boys a story about how he sustained a serious injury to his leg on the football field in middle school. He was in terrible pain, but with a crowd of other students looking on, he felt as though he had to hold back the tears.

"I'd always been told by friends, coaches, and my father that I had to man up," says Bo. "That I had to make sure that I didn't show I was weak or vulnerable. So I couldn't cry."

"Do you cry sometimes?" Ms. Ryan asks him.

"Yes, but not publicly."

"What does it feel like to stop yourself from crying?"

"It's a burden—of physical pain and mental pain."

"Which is worse?"

"Mental pain," Bo answers unequivocally.

"What would you tell your son one day if the same thing happened to him? Would you tell him to man up?"

"No, I'd say let out your emotions. That's when you are free."

"Is there anyone in your life that you can be vulnerable with and cry?"

"Yeah, my mom. She's the one that allows me these emotions."

A blond boy in a bow tie raises his hand. "How did you *do* it?" he asks, admiration clear in his voice. "I broke my leg last year and I didn't want to look weak either, but I was *bawling*."

Another boy breaks in to advise. "When you feel that burning in the back of your throat like you're going to cry, you should breathe and try to think of positive things."

"Why does it lead to bad things to not express your feelings?" Ms. Ryan redirects.

"If you have so much inside of you it then explodes. If you have all these things inside of you and you have no way of peacefully getting it out, then you can become violent," says the blond boy.

• • •

Megan Ryan is middle school dean of student life at Browning, and the mother of two sons herself, so the mission of addressing some of the more harmful aspects of masculinity is important to her.

"I thought about my experience with boys and men and I'm thinking this is something we're doing culturally that's pushing them away from wanting to feel connected to other men," she tells me after class. "I was watching men that I knew lose friendships and dunk all of their emotional world into their [romantic] relationships."

Ryan helped devise the Modern Masculinities curriculum in conjunction with experts and other staff. She was keen to put empathy and relationships at the center.

"Boys need a more deliberate conversation about caring for others, putting yourself in the shoes of someone else, and fundamentally understanding another person," she tells me. "Naming what it is to be empathic and how that should guide how you move through the world."

It wasn't easy at first. Ryan remembers walking into the classroom to teach the first ever Modern Masculinities class. Someone had scrawled on the whiteboard in giant letters MEN BAD. MEN VERY VERY BAD.

But instead of disciplining them, she used it to open a conversation. It turned out that several of the boys thought the class was going to be an attack on them. They were well aware of the wider conversations about toxic masculinity and were feeling defensive—the hashtag #KillAllMen had been trending on TikTok not long before. But they quickly settled into the classes, and now, for the most part, the boys feel that the curriculum has become an important and freeing experience.

When I catch up with Bo and a group of his twelfth-grade classmates over lunch, he tells me the class has made him reevaluate a lot of things he had previously taken for granted.

"It's made me more aware of myself, but also of others," he says. "It's helped me think about microaggressions, for example. These things that I would say and never realize the implications."

I ask for an example. He thinks for a minute then tells me about how he and his peers used to say the word "pause" a lot after they said anything that could potentially be interpreted as gay. The phrase comes from hip-hop culture and is used interchangeably with another hip-hop derived expression, "no homo," to distance the speaker from appearing in any way effeminate, or to diffuse the possibility that any expression of affection from one man to another might be interpreted as a homosexual advance.

The Modern Masculinities classes made Bo realize the homophobic implications of "pause," and now he and his peers have stopped saying it. When I ask them whether they think that Browning is a homophobic environment more generally, it seems as though homophobia and misogyny are deeply intertwined in their logic of masculinity.

"It's complicated. It's okay to be gay, but it's not okay to be 'gay-*ish*,'" one of them tells me. "Like you can like guys, but you can't be flamboyant or feminine. There's a standardized idea of what it means to be a man."

More than anything, the classes have prompted the Browning boys to name problems that are often invisible, and to think critically about them.

"I've started noticing the patterns a lot more since the classes," another twelfth grader says. "Like you go through something tough, and as a guy you want to suppress your emotion and bury it, because showing it would make you look weak. And so I've noticed that as a habit in myself and other people around me. It's something we do out of fear. I think it's important to have these conversations when you're a teenager as that's when you're most sensitive to other people's judgments."

• • •

Clearly Browning is an outlier—they have the resources to do what very few other schools can. The students are hugely privileged, majority white, high income, and high achieving (the school is academically selective). The word *underachievement* will rarely be used to describe these future power-hoarders.

But Browning is right in thinking that unpacking masculinity norms and prioritizing relationships and social-emotional learning might play a key role in improving outcomes for boys more generally. We know that the discrepancy in grades and academic performance between boys and girls is not related to their intelligence. The differences between boys and girls that impact their school performance are largely social-emotional and behavioral ones.

Strong social-emotional skills aren't just important for general well-being. They are also a huge factor in academic performance. Despite the stereotype of the socially awkward and friendless nerd-genius, social-emotional intelligence is actually heavily associated with academic success. Research shows that strong social-emotional skills are a strong predictor of academic performance,[19] and at least one study shows that emotional intelligence is actually a better predictor of grades than standardized test scores.[20]

Right from birth, we know that the ways in which we socialize boys put them at a disadvantage in acquiring these types of skills. Boys receive less nurturing and positive touch in babyhood, something that is necessary for good emotional self-regulation. We use less emotion-based language with boys throughout childhood and spend less time talking about their feelings from their earliest years onward.

From the start, we funnel boys into a narrative universe that centers defeating enemies over connecting with friends; fighting instead of cooperating. Meanwhile their female peers get a comprehensive grounding in friendship and other relationships, and the expression of emotions. And as boys grow older, in a million subtle ways we tell them both to hide their own emotions, and not to engage with other people's, selling them the story that to be a man is to be tough and physical and stoic, rather than self-reflective and emotional and communitarian.

It is no surprise that boys start kindergarten behind girls on social-emotional skills, and that the gap persists throughout childhood and adolescence. Some of this is biology, sure, but a huge piece of it is the masculine socialization that is staring us right in the face.

Schools perpetuate the problem in the way they engage with boys. Because of the ways in which we subtly encourage boys either to suppress their feelings or limit them to anger, boys' emotional issues often look more like behavioral problems, and schools tend to respond to them as such. In a culture in which boys are cast from an early age as action heroes, rather than full emotional beings, we tend to view troubled boys as needing discipline, rather than care.

It is something that concerns psychologist Matt Englar-Carlson. "A lot of what we consider being behavioral difficulties in school with boys actually might be more about emotional regulation," he tells me. "What looks like a behavioral outburst can actually be emotional dysregulation."

This often means that rather than engaging and connecting with boys and trying to understand what is going on with them, or referring them for mental health support, teachers tend to funnel them into disciplinary systems. Male students are significantly more likely to be disciplined harshly than their female classmates and this problem is particularly acute for boys of color, especially Black boys.

Boys in general are more than twice as likely to be suspended from school than girls, and around three times more likely to be expelled.[21] Black students are four times as likely to be suspended than white students. We know that suspension and expulsion are punishments that don't work; they have been shown repeatedly to harm students' academic progress and engagement with school, with long-term consequences. One study found that if a student was suspended once, their odds of dropping out of high school doubled, and for every additional suspension, their odds of graduating from high school plummeted even further.[22]

Many of these students are also suffering from multiple traumas at home, including poor living conditions, violence, and the effects of poverty. Meanwhile, schools are cutting back on mental health services. According to the Center for American Progress, less than a quarter of high schoolers in the United States have access to a school psychologist, and the school psychologists that do exist tend to be more focused on academic testing than on students' emotions.

Only around 60 percent of U.S. students have access to a counselor, and in predominantly Black schools, that figure is even lower. School counselors are horribly overworked. Instead of offering counseling, schools are increasingly turning to disciplinary action to deal with what are essentially emotional problems.

This cycle of discipline and disengagement is one that Jayden remembers all too well from his time in his underfunded, majority Black schools in Oakland, California. His school career didn't start off badly. One of Jayden's earliest memories is a misunderstanding over reciting the alphabet to the class in second grade, and the gratitude he still feels toward his teacher for handling the incident with kindness and understanding, rather than punishment.

"I said my ABCs, but he thought I didn't say nothing," Jayden remembers. "He called me out in front of the whole class. He said I didn't say them, when I did. I felt the need to assert myself because I felt embarrassed in front of so many people. It's humiliating. 'Cause where I'm from, if you humiliate me, I'm gonna get at you. That was my mentality.

"So I got out my chair and I walked up to the front of the class and I pushed the teacher. But the teacher was so cool. I got mad love for Mr. L, so much respect for him 'cause he could have got me expelled. But his understanding of the situation was like, no, this boy just needs help on his emotions and handling his anger. I'm always in deep gratitude for that from him."

Rather than disciplining him, his teacher signed Jayden up for an anger management class. But things started to deteriorate from there. In Jayden's view, the anger management classes were badly designed and inadequate, and instead of using the classes as an alternative to punishment, the school continued to discipline bad behavior in addition. As he got older, Jayden started to get into fights with classmates, and the school responded by repeatedly suspending him.

"I feel like if you are gonna put somebody in an anger management class and they get into a fight, then that person shouldn't get suspended," Jayden tells me. "You have him in a special class for his anger. What is suspending him gonna do? You're gonna penalize him for being angry?"

What the punishments failed to take into account was that in Jayden's community, for a boy to fail to hit back when someone hit him first was seen as weak and humiliating. No amount of punishment from the school could change that basic requirement for masculinity.

Eventually the school called in a therapist. But Jayden felt the person they chose didn't understand him or his situation.

"She was a nice lady. She was trying. But the problem was that you have these white people. These people come from a different cultural background. So we're living in two completely different worlds. You had this middle-aged white woman trying to talk to an eight-year-old boy from Oakland. I felt like instead of trying to break into my head, how about you come to the community and go take some experiences for yourself and see how it makes you feel? Then maybe you can relate."

Jayden got suspended nine times over the course of his school career, almost always for fighting. The more school Jayden missed, the further behind he got with his schoolwork and the more anxious and angry he became. The stress made him get into more fights, and the cycle continued.

"I didn't really learn nothing from suspension," he tells me. "I mean, they made me miss my work and I had to catch it back up. I feel like they were just fucking up my education. They suspend me for two days and I have to catch up on two days of things that I missed plus the new lesson."

• • •

Rather than removing boys from the classroom when they act out, centering social-emotional learning and connection and changing school culture to encourage strong relationships between students and teachers can make a big difference.

Several studies show that, when they are done well, social-emotional learning programs are effective, not just for students' well-being, but also for improving academic performance. A meta-analysis of more than two hundred different social-emotional learning programs across the United States showed improvements in a wide range of outcomes, including a significant jump in academic achievement.[23]

And perhaps because they are getting less of this kind of education in life more generally, research shows that these types of programs are particularly effective for boys. One large-scale multiyear program for first through third grade students across the United States, for example, introduced a social-emotional curriculum that taught self-control, emotional understanding, and communication along with various other social skills. Researchers compared boys and girls who went through the program with children in control schools in the same districts. They found that the program had significant effects on a wide range of outcomes, including reducing aggression and hyperactivity among students, improving student friendships, and increasing academic engagement. But, notably, the effects were only present for boys.[24]

These kinds of programs still have a long way to go. Schools are underfunded and teachers are already under huge pressure, overworked and lacking in resources. At their worst the programs can be just a few mindful breathing exercises shoved into a day overstuffed with standardized test preparation. Some programs have started to consider issues of race and equity, and to build these concerns into the curriculum, but they are in their infancy and for the most part, need much wider application and deeper thought.

Even less work has been done to expand these programs to include any content for either teachers or students about gender, and particularly about how expectations and pressures to be masculine affect boys' social-emotional well-being as well as their academic engagement and performance. Few schools are doing the kind of critical thinking about masculinity that Browning is doing. Of course, the Browning School has resources that almost no other school has. But any steps in this direction might make these programs even more effective.

We also urgently need to change classroom culture more generally. Parents can help campaign for schools to pull back on the harsh discipline and suspensions for boys, in particular, and instead try to listen to boys' underlying emotions and offer them empathy and understanding. Schools should do their best to become warm, supportive places that foster thoughtful relationships between teachers and students, and emphasize social skills and emotional connection.

You might even call it "feminizing the classroom."

CHAPTER 5

HYPERCONNECTION AND DISCONNECTION

BOYS ONLINE

If guilt is our internal police force, then for me, motherhood has been like living in a police state. Before I had children, the voice of my conscience was a mostly benevolent little chirrup in the background. But since becoming a mother, it has turned from Jiminy Cricket to abusive sociopath.

I have the ability to feel guilty about almost any parenting choice but also about its exact opposite. I veer wildly between feeling guilty for not making the boys do enough chores, meaning they might grow up to be entitled, sexist men; and feeling guilty for being too strict about chores, and turning my relationship with them into a constant nagfest. I feel guilty for not signing them up for enough improving extracurriculars and thereby failing to prepare them for America's cutthroat college applications marketplace, but also for overscheduling them and not allowing them a joyous and untethered childhood. For spending too little time with them and also for hovering too closely, suffocating them. In the depths of this state, every mental pathway leads to my being a Bad Mother.

I'm exhausted by this conviction that every minor choice I make today carries such high stakes—how easily any small misstep or oversight could end up as heartache or bad character or dysfunctionality for my sons when they are adults. (Oddly, it doesn't work the other way round. Any parenting successes or things I might be doing right are far less psychologically compelling to me.)

It's probably a form of narcissism, this obsessive self-reproach, a delusion that allows me to believe that my own role is central, and that I have a high degree of control over how my children will turn out. A psychoanalyst would probably argue that that is exactly why my subconscious keeps churning the guilt out—as a psychological hack to subdue the chaotic howl of motherhood and force it into something neat and controllable.

Or perhaps it's because our culture does its best to encourage maternal self-flagellation. For a certain type of privileged American parent (and for parent, read "mother"), the pressure is on to make every moment enriching, every interaction with our children pitch-perfect. The norm for upper-middle-class parenting has become what sociologists call concerted cultivation, running an intense program of cultural enrichment, emotional validation, and educational optimization. The average college-educated mother now spends an additional *nine hours* a week with her children than her 1960s counterpart, despite being far more likely to also work outside of the home. She should, ideally, be spending the remainder of her time feeling guilty.

Meanwhile, the American parenting industry is highly incentivized to emphasize the link between a mother's moment to moment performance and a child's life outcomes. Big Parenting has taken most mothers' tendency for self-criticism and run with it, making millions out of our insecurities, hubris, and terror that our every tiny action will have long-term consequences.

But although they are easy to parody, these expectations are hard to dismiss. Guilt tends to draw its evidence from half-truths rather than outright lies, and half-truths are often the most alluring stories, with just enough reality to make them plausible and just enough distortion to make them seductive. The "you need to do all this to be a good mother" story is both patently false and, in some twisted sense, kind of true.

Of course, what we do and don't do as parents matters, at least in aggregate. The hours we put in, baking cupcakes and pointing out fire trucks and breaking up fights and confirming, bleary-eyed, that the Wheels on the Bus do indeed go round and round, make a big difference to a wide range of outcomes for our children. And on the flip side, even minor slights and lapses can sink into our children's psyches and turn them into insecure or aggrieved or maladjusted adults.

For many parents, nowhere are the half-truths and the guilt more compelling than when it comes to screens. The screen time debate has become central in the wider parenting conversation. And too often, it manages to turn us into our most judgmental, self-critical, and fearful selves.

We tend to frame the discussion over how much screen time is appropriate as a battle we have with our kids, but at least for me, it is as much a battle I have with myself. We're parenting in a society in which up to a quarter of parents are experiencing clinical symptoms of burnout, and articles with headlines such as "There is No Break Coming for Parents—Ever" are a staple. Childcare is unsubsidized, and barely affordable for anyone but the richest. Many of us are raising our children in atomized nuclear families, without a "village" to rely on, or any substantive support from government or family or anyone else. In their absence, screen time has become our federal childcare system, our social safety net.

In our family, at least, screens are the only thing that guarantees us a break, a real break—not a child tentatively trying to play by our side and getting bored and whining and asking us where his Baby Yoda minifigure isssss ("No, not *that* Baby Yoda!"). Screens give us a rock-solid, guaranteed moment of respite from the overstimulation and demands and noise and from the constant feeling of being one "boyish roughhousing" flailing limb away from a concussion.

But the calculation is a complicated one. It quickly becomes a vicious cycle—the more screen time our boys have, the less able they are to amuse themselves without their devices, and the more dependent they (and we) become on their screens. The key, clearly, is moderation. But moderation is hard both to enforce and to quantify—one parent's healthy moderation is another's spiral of self-loathing.

On any given day, it is probably fine that Abe has spent an entire morning making seventy-five digital milkshakes for Peppa Pig, or that Zephy is glassy-eyed and twitching from three hours of Roblox. But if I let this happen every day, while I lived my own fully self-actualized life outside of parenting, it would obviously be a problem. I'm not really sure what to believe, whether my guilt about screens is actually a useful internal system of checks and balances, or whether it is selling me a lie. I hold on to the hope that all the cultural noise about screen time is just another moral panic, like the ones our foremothers had about TV or the movie theater or excessive use of the papyrus scroll.

But deep down, I am pretty sure that screens do affect my kids badly. For them, the slide into addiction is swift and thorough. I watch them change as the dopamine floods their tiny neurons. I see that the more screen time they have, the more skittish and ratty and unfocused they become—how between one hit of permitted screen time and the next they become idle and cranky, jonesing for the next fix. I see how easily they sink into a default mode, where all they can think or talk about, all that seems to spark their interest or bring them joy is video games.

Andy Crouch, author of *The Tech-Wise Family: Everyday Steps for Putting Technology in Its Proper Place* (2017), is not a person I naturally identify with on most issues. He is an evangelical Christian, a homeschooler, and a political conservative who raised his children completely screen free until the age of ten. But I find myself relating uncomfortably to a quote he gave in an interview for Vox about bringing up his kids without screens.

"As near as I can tell, elementary school boys don't know anything to do together except play video games," he said. "My son's classmates just did not want to come to his house because they did not know what to do. I don't think it was too strong to say it was painful to watch the occasional friend of his who would come over and how poorly it went most times, how bored those boys were, how little engaged they were and how my son felt that on behalf of his friends and didn't quite know what to do to help."

I prefer to see myself as a less alarmist parent, but this scene sounds painfully familiar. I remember one excruciating summer night when Solly and Zephy each had a friend over for a sleepover. It was a beautiful evening, and these are privileged kids. We have a houseful of toys and games and art supplies, a backyard, a nearby park, a cupboard full of bats and balls. Four young creative brains with infinite, untapped imaginative capacities. And yet they could find nothing to do. Every five minutes my sons came to me, begging for more screen time. In between the four of them would just kind of stare at each other or wander round aimlessly, seemingly unable to talk or play or enjoy each other's company.

When we do enforce longer periods of low or no screen time for the boys—limit screens to a couple of hours on weekends, say, or take a couple of weeks off all together—after some initial grumbling, the boys do find new ways to entertain themselves. They start drawing, playing outside, knocking soccer balls around, and inventing rowdy games. Their moods improve and so do their relationships with each other.

But before long, without the screens, I am back to being exhausted and overwhelmed. The noise, the fighting, the tantrums, the goddamn "playfighting." I have no one to call to ask if they would take the kids to the park for an hour so that I can finish the work I need to do to meet my deadline, let alone take a nap or just a moment to myself. And after-school care averages six hundred dollars per child per month. So back on the screens they go.

I try to convince myself that this is temporary, that as they get older and easier to care for, we will back away from the screens a little. But I worry that the opposite is likely to be true. These are the crucial years in which they are developing social skills, focus, and concentration. Things will likely only get worse unless we do something drastic about the amount of screen time they get. I lie awake at night worrying about it.

• • •

I am deep in this period of fear and self-loathing when I first connect with Kent Toussaint, the director of the Teen Therapy Center, in Los Angeles. Kent, a soft-spoken therapist with a long, gray, Middle Earth–style beard, has been running the center for more than a decade, offering individual and family therapy to adolescents and their caregivers from across the LA area. Every Wednesday night, he runs a therapy and social group for teenage boys called the Guys' Group.

Kent and I talk on the phone a few times. I am keen to hear from him about the issues that come up in the group, and each time we speak, I go through my mental checklist with him. I ask him about masculinity norms and vulnerability, about family conflict and alcohol and drugs and sex and porn. Kent answers my questions thoughtfully and discusses all these topics briefly, but when he is in full flow, talking about what he really thinks is ailing teenage boys and their families right now, he keeps coming back to the same single issue: screens. He notes the sheer amount of time that teenage boys are spending online and how this is contributing to a growing culture of disconnection from family, isolation from friends, and loneliness.

The Guys' Group has been running for nearly ten years now, with different boys coming and going, some staying for a few weeks, others for a couple of years. Over the last two or three years, Kent has noticed a change in the group dynamics. Previously, although the boys would often start off full of bluster and bro-ing, when given the social permission of the therapeutic setting, they would usually settle relatively quickly into deeper sharing and emotional intimacy.

But in more recent iterations of the group, Kent says he is finding it increasingly hard to get past the superficial banter and chaos. The boys are lacking the focus, the ability to listen and reflect—the basic skills required for the give and take of this form of deeper connection. Some of this change obviously comes down to different kids and personalities over the years, different group dynamics. But Kent believes that screens are playing a large part.

This is in contrast to the girls' groups the center also runs, he tells me. In the weekly all-female group for adolescents, the girls are focused and able to listen, are able to be vulnerable and to comfort each other, and often end up running well over the allotted time, discussing their emotions. Obviously, girls use screens, too, but for various reasons, the screens don't seem to be having the same effect.

Kent puts the change in the Guys' Group over time down to an increasing retreat among adolescent boys away from real-world friendships and connections and toward virtual ones. Every year, the boys Kent sees in therapy and at the Guys' Group are spending more and more of their lives online gaming, watching YouTube, and on social media and communication platforms such as Discord, and spending less and less time with friends in real life. In their online lives they play video games, form social networks, find new friends and girlfriends, and even have some virtual version of sex. But in real life, they are increasingly isolated. The pandemic made all this much worse, of course. But it was already happening before then, too.

"A lot of times parents will be reaching out or the kids will reach out because there's no one to hang out with after school or on weekends," Kent tells me. "They don't have a social circle. I mean, in person, they don't have a social circle. They have an online social circle. That's not the same, even though they have a hard time differentiating the two."

Kent is concerned that screens are starting to impact boys' ability to make and maintain relationships in real life. According to him, many boys are starting to use online spaces as a way of avoiding the awkwardness and social anxiety and potential rejection in the real world. And it has become a vicious circle. The more they avoid these social challenges, the more their social-emotional skills decline, and the harder they find it to make the kind of sustained and deep connections that real intimacy thrives on.

This was not what my fearful, screen guilt–addled brain wanted to hear. But Kent encourages me to fly down to LA to sit in on a session of the Guys' Group and talk to the guys and their parents so I can decide for myself.

• • •

Six lanky teenage boys hunch awkwardly on the plush couches in the lobby, waiting for the group to begin, knees almost touching their chins. Their bodies are too big for the cutesy corporate space, or perhaps for any indoor space. It occurs to me that there is something inherently mildly humiliating about the state of teenage boyhood, in its not-quite-manhood, and knuckle-cracking ineptitude; a loss of dignity just from existing in a series of situations all too confining for your giant limbs and outsized desires. The boys all stare at their phones and ignore each other. They certainly don't acknowledge me, an anonymous middle-aged woman, perhaps the least relevant category of human in their world.

At seven o'clock, Kent calls them, and they shuffle into a largeish meeting room and sprawl across sofas and beanbag chairs.

"Brady, you're a pussy," sixteen-year-old Lucas says randomly to the boy next to him.

"Why don't you go fuck yourself, faggot?" retorts Brady.

"That's just masturbating," Lucas fires back, then sinks into his beanbag, satisfied with his comeback.

"Girls, girls, cool it," cuts in Kevin, a fine-featured boy with a sleek ponytail. "You're both pretty."

"Shut up, Kevin, how retarded are you?" Lucas shoots back.

They carry on in this vein for a while. Listening to them, I'm genuinely surprised that this kind of casual homophobia and misogyny still flies among teenagers, especially in one of the bluest states in the country, given the prevailing narrative on the right that we are all living in some kind of woke, trigger warnings–fueled tyranny. The slurs almost seem like a formality at this point, a cultural ritual on autopilot, like a Japanese bow-ing exchange or a British person compulsively apologizing to the guy who just stepped on her toe. Kent had explained to me earlier that far from becoming socially obsolete, this type of misogynistic trash talk has had a resurgence in gamer culture online.

"It's all about who can throw the worst insult at someone else," he told me. "But it keeps it on the surface, keeps them from going deeper. And so part of the group is getting them to lower their defenses, be more open and honest with each other."

But in practice, this seems almost impossible to do. "Quiet down," Kent now pleads with the boys. They ignore him.

Brady starts singing a show tune. He takes a picture of a pretty girl with long hair out of his wallet and holds it up to the group. "I'm better than you fuckers because I have a girlfriend," he announces. Then sighs, momentarily losing his bravado. "Shame she's asexual."

"Does anyone have anything they want to share?" Kent tries again.

"Let's all kill Lucas," says Kevin, seemingly out of nowhere. "Then everything will be better."

After half an hour or so, I start to tune out a little. I am starting to see what Kent means. The atmosphere is chaotic, not unlike an average hour on the internet: trash talk, rapid-fire memes, incomprehensible jokes. It's Trump's locker room crossed with 4chan crossed with that TikTok trend you missed that briefly became the only way people under twenty-five were allowed to talk to each other.

Is this the future of male communication, I wonder? Just shouting memes into the void?

• • •

Sixteen-year-old Lucas has been a member of the Guys' Group longer than anyone else, and is probably its loudest presence, the first one to throw an insult or to ratchet the trash talk up a notch.

Lucas's parents contacted Kent a couple of years ago, when they became concerned that their son was spending most of his time online, had little social life in the real world, and was complaining about feeling lonely.

Apart from the occasional game of basketball and the weekly bowling league they had encouraged him to join, Lucas never really seemed to go anywhere or hang out with anyone. Online, he had a large social network from all over the world, including people he knew from real life and others he had never met. He would spend hours talking to them over Discord or while gaming online. But in the real world, there was almost nothing. No parties or movies or visits to friends' houses on the weekends. And what seemed more odd to his parents, was that in his peer group this seemed to be pretty normal.

"I have a bunch of friends who have kids, and they're all saying the same thing," his dad tells me. "It's like, all they do is sit on the internet. They have no interest in going to a show, no interest in going to a concert, no interest in anything else. Everything they do is on their devices."

His mom cuts in. "I've heard of kids that are worse than Lucas—that literally don't leave their room."

"Oh, correct," says his dad. "And he actually will take a walk or go to the park and play basketball. So he's a little bit more active than some."

Lucas's parents worry that this withdrawal into a virtual world is becoming a self-perpetuating problem for him and his peers.

"I think that this is having a huge impact on their ability to socialize," his dad tells me. "So the whole idea of isolation, loneliness, it's this catch-22, this cycle. They don't realize that the things that they're complaining about, they're actually fueling themselves by not going out and doing other things."

Lucas's parents adopted him when they were in their forties, and it's easy to dismiss them as older parents, clinging to a Gen X nostalgiascape of movie theaters and prom dates while the world moves on. After all, online interaction is still interaction. It might be taking place in a different format, but it's still connection.

Maybe Lucas prefers it this way. But when I speak to Lucas alone, after the group, it seems as though the situation doesn't seem to be making him particularly happy, either.

One on one, Lucas is calmer and more considered than the combative teen I saw in the group setting. He is immediately warm and open and thoughtful. I start by asking him what he likes about coming to the Guys' Group, and am surprised when he tells me that the trash talk is at the top of the list.

"It's gonna sound weird," he tells me tentatively, feeling out the terrain, "but I like it because it's very toxic. We insult each other. We say a bunch of very repulsive things that we probably wouldn't say anywhere else. A lot of things that I say here, I would not say outside or I'd get lambasted."

"Like what?" I ask.

"Like faggot," he replies. I wince.

"What do you mean by it when you say it?" I ask.

"Absolutely nothing. It's just like if you can't think of anything else to say, you just say 'faggot.'" He pauses. "I mean I'm bi [sexual], but it's like, it's just fun."

"What's fun about it to you?" I ask.

"Because in modern society, you can't say anything without someone getting offended, someone getting angry, you getting in trouble. You just kind of have to restrain yourself in society. You have to be a girl, basically, in school. So it's a place where boys can be boys, I guess."

Boys can be boys. Here we were again. Lucas had been sold the story that unchecked masculinity was a way of being true to your essential nature, your authentic self. But seeing how much more open and self-reflective he becomes away from the defensive bro-ing of the group setting, I'm struck again by just how much it really seems like the opposite is true. If anything, this type of trash talk seems more like an easy way for boys to *avoid* the vulnerability of authenticity.

I ask Lucas about his online life. He tells me that his parents don't put any limits on his screen time. "Because I'm not addicted to it. It's just like my parents are working, and I'm not gonna sit here and read a book for three hours. So what else am I gonna do? It's either sleep or play video games."

Lucas complains that when he does actually want to go out and socialize, there isn't actually anything much going on with his friends. He agrees with his parents' characterization of his peer group's social life, that things are different now. Everyone is just online all the time, and no one is really getting together much in the real world.

"No one in my friend group has parties," he tells me. "I don't know where to go to parties. I want to, but I don't know where they are. Our school doesn't have parties, or at least that I know of. And I don't know how to ask to find those parties."

Lucas's main social hub is Discord, an online communication platform and social network where people can talk to each other over voice, text, or video, either in groups or privately. Founded originally as a site for gamers, it has now expanded to include private and semiprivate communities dedicated to all kinds of interests and hobbies, ranging from totally innocuous to utterly horrifying. Unlike Instagram, which has a female-dominated user base, Discord skews heavily male—more than 65 percent of users are boys and men.

"My real-world life is a completely different thing than my online life," Lucas tells me. "It's like I'm two different people. Because I have such little success in my real life. It's easy to get success online. So I do that."

By success, Lucas means romantic success. What he really, deeply wants is a girlfriend. But in real life he's had no luck.

"I've tried," he tells me. "I've gotten rejected fifteen times. I've only felt rejection, I've never felt acceptance. I've tried all different approaches. I've tried waiting. I've thought a girl was attracted to me after three years of being friends. I asked her out. She said no. And that story is repeated quite often."

So Lucas has taken his search online. Because many of the groups are private, and users generally operate anonymously, Discord is sometimes a safe haven for darker impulses: extremist politics, violent content, and of course, sex and porn of all kinds.

But unlike most other porn sites, users can actually participate themselves, sharing and soliciting videos and pictures and having virtual sex with people from all over the world.

Lucas seems anxious telling me about this, shifting around on the sofa as he talks. "I'm doing things that could get me in trouble," he eventually confides.

"When I'm very, very sexually repressed and very, very horny, I'm like a completely different person," he admits. "I will do anything to get that release. And I don't really think about other people. I have done some things and I'm doing things now that I know are wrong and get me in pretty deep, but I don't have any other outlets to do them."

"What are you actually doing on there?" I ask.

"Nude sharing, video calls, that type of stuff. It's pretty easy to find on Discord. But it's not good and it's not healthy and it's honestly borderline manipulative. And I feel awful about it afterwards."

"Why do you think it's manipulative?" I ask.

"The manipulative part is I've had people who say they love me. They want to date me. And I say yes, because I can't just say I use these girls for sex. And then I get stuck."

Lucas tells me that he is involved in relationships with a few girls on Discord; most of them live thousands of miles away, and they have never met in real life. He isn't always honest about how he presents himself; he sometimes lies about his age, where he lives, who he is. And now the dishonesty is piling up and getting to him.

"I'm in very deep and I'm trying to push myself out," he tells me. "It's getting more and more difficult, and that's why I'm getting more and more desperate.

"I want to end it, but I can't end it because they have gotten attached to me. And eventually I just have to delete everything. I delete the apps and block people, and then I think okay, that's it. I'll never do it again. But I always come back when I'm in that sexually repressed, sexually frustrated mood. And then I end up making a new account and doing it all again. It's a cycle that I hate. It ruins me and it's probably gonna ruin me in the future even more, but there is nothing I could do about it because I don't have any other outlet. I'm only doing it because I have nobody. This isn't what I want."

He thinks for a minute. "It's sometimes even more painful online than having nothing because you can't touch them. You can't hug them. I'm very touch starved. I like feeling, I like hugging. I like snuggling. I love all that stuff."

"I'm lonely," he confides. "Romantically lonely. I have plenty of friends, but I've had no true romance in my life and that is, it's like an anchor on my heart. I'm so desperate at this point. And I can't show that desperation. It's like, I'm just pretending to be okay all the time."

• • •

"It's hard to be a real person," my friend Bonnie says sometimes, and she's right. The problem here is not that a sixteen-year-old can't get laid, that he's horny and desperate and stinging from rejection. Those problems have always existed. Adolescence has always been a mess of awkwardness and desire and shame and chaos. That's the whole point. We all need to go through it and learn from it to emerge as a full human on the other side. And in previous generations we didn't have much choice. A Lucas thirty years ago would have had the same feelings of sexual frustration and rejection, but he would have just had to wait it out, slog out the lonely hours until he found a real-life relationship. He would have forced himself to go to parties, to make connections, and to experience the real, flawed world of humanity.

But now there are options to bypass the system, to live out an entire adolescence in a kind of parallel universe of dazzling options, where we get to be whoever we want to be, present ourselves however we choose, and sidestep some of the sickening awkwardness of being a real-life human. In many ways this can open up new options for lonely teens, give them new ways to connect. But having this option doesn't seem to be making Lucas any happier. He is getting into situations he is not really equipped to handle, with no one to help guide him through it. His online world is dehumanizing and objectifying not just for the girls he is meeting but also for himself. In bypassing real life, he is also foreclosing on intimacy.

• • •

Lucas is an extreme case, and the guys from the therapy center are obviously a self-selecting group who have sought out Kent at least in part because they were lacking connection in real life. I'm concerned that talking to them might be giving me a pretty skewed perspective on what is going on more generally with boys and screens. But when I reach out to my own network of local moms, I get a flood of replies describing remarkably similar issues.

"It's been awful," says one mom with a boy in ninth grade and another in sixth. "Truly the worst part of parenting for us, by far. They can't think about anything else, can't talk about anything else. They regularly lie and cheat to get screen time. My eldest son broke a window because we wouldn't let him play *Fortnite* after he was mean to his brother. And he's not normally a rageful child. They do see friends on the weekend, but only because we push them to. If we left them to it, they would never do anything except be on a screen."

"My son is online almost constantly," a mom of a seventeen-year-old texts me. "It's had a big impact on his development and on our family life. I think loneliness is the headline for me. He barely sees his friends in real life and is lonely. I have a lot of my own sadness about this."

Several speak of sons whose social lives have moved almost entirely online, who barely get together with friends apart from at school and in structured extracurriculars.

"It's hard to know which way it's going," a friend of a friend tells me during a long, sad phone call one evening. "Ben uses screens to retreat from all those bad feelings of discomfort and loneliness and social anxiety. But then it creates a feedback loop.

If you have social anxiety, you need to do the scary thing in person to get over it. And now there's this option to be on the screen all the time. So he never does the scary thing."

It would seem that these stories are not outliers. A wide body of research shows that American adolescents are spending more time online and less time with friends in real life than any cohort of teens in the last fifty years. These trends were accelerated by the Covid pandemic, but they predate it by a good decade or so.

According to data analyzed by Dr. Jean Twenge, professor of psychology at San Diego State University, high school seniors are spending an average of seven hours less a week socializing than seniors in the late 1980s. (This research was carried out before the pandemic; the number of hours has likely dropped even further since.)

Teenagers are spending less time on every type of in-person social activity my wilting Gen X brain can come up with. They are going to fewer parties and movies, spending less time at friends' houses or just hanging out with each other than any teenagers since the 1970s, when researchers started tracking.

The drop in socializing has been particularly steep in the last ten years. An average eighth grader now gets together with friends on around forty-one fewer occasions per year than an eighth grader in 2010. A high school senior hangs out with peers twenty-five fewer times per year than his 2010 counterpart, and the numbers are going down every year.

For the most part, the time teenagers have freed up by not hanging out with their friends, they are spending on screens. Since 2012, when smartphones became widely available, and social media, online gaming, and other online communities exploded, the amount of time teenagers are spending online has increased exponentially. A full 95 percent of teenagers now have their own smartphone. By 2017, the average high school senior spent more than six hours a day online or texting. Now close to half of American teenagers report that they are online "almost constantly."

It's hard to fully get a handle on what the effects of this increase might be on kids. Obviously screen time is not all bad, and there are countless positive uses for screens. People of all ages find community and support online, connect with like-minded people they might not have access to in real life, find information, engage in hobbies, and learn new skills. Video games are fun and often social. Teenagers with mental health issues find support and belonging, and LGBTQ kids find community without stigma. A huge amount of creativity and innovation lives on the internet. Online life can open up new worlds and perspectives that might otherwise be closed off to them.

Screen time is a huge and amorphous concept. It is not one thing, but a potentially infinite number of different activities encompassing everything from stalking your ex on Instagram, to murdering your best friend in a *Fortnite* battle, to soliciting nudes on Discord, to doing your math homework. This variability makes it hard to study.

Along with a number of other confounding factors, this has meant that research into the harms of screen time has been confusing and inconclusive. When researchers look at averages across a population, the benefits of a gay teen finding lifesaving community in an online support group and the harms of a Discord addict failing to leave his bedroom for three weeks might cancel each other out, showing up for the data as nothing much going on.

So it is perhaps not surprising that the research that does exist is often wildly contradictory. Different researchers have come to very differing conclusions, even using the same basic data. For instance, two separate camps of academics studied datasets from the widescale Monitoring the Future Survey using different statistical models. One group concluded that smartphones were destroying a generation,[1] while the other, using the *exact same data* but applying different methodology, concluded that social media was no more harmful to teens than eating potatoes.[2]

There are studies that show that playing video games is linked to depression, obesity, and poor mental health; studies that show that it has little impact at all; and a handful that show that it even improves mood and cognitive abilities.[3] There are studies that conclude that social media use has little serious effect on teens, and others showing that it causes anxiety, depression, and suicidal impulses. Depending on the methodology used and what exactly the researchers are measuring, the conclusions of the research are inconsistent and confusing. Academics seem as divided as parents, locked into their own positions of alarmism or defensiveness or denial.

I spend a while trying to make sense of this body of research, hoping to find a clear answer and be able to come down on one side or the other. Screen time is harmless! Carry on! Or screen time is going to destroy my children—this is a battle worth picking, even through my exhaustion. I slog through a 269-page Google Doc compiled by the researchers Jean Twenge and Jonathan Haidt, which includes all the studies showing benefits, harms, and null effects in one place. Instead of gaining clarity, I end up bleary-eyed and little closer to any kind of truth about what any of this might mean for my kids or anyone else's.[4]

After a while, picking through the mountains of research starts to feel like a fool's errand. These large-scale population studies don't seem to be doing a great job of capturing teenagers' or parents' lived experiences or getting to the heart of what it means to grow up in this world of simultaneous hyperconnectedness and disconnection.

Generally, when researchers look at the negative effects of screen time, they focus on two separate areas of potential concern: The first comes under the general heading of "content." This is the idea that the actual substance of what teenagers are seeing and doing online is harmful in and of itself—that violent video games make kids violent, for example, or that scrolling through their friends' perfect lives and bikini bodies on Instagram makes them feel terrible about their own lives and bodies. Much of the research into social media focuses on this problem.

The second potential area of harm that researchers look at comes under the heading of "displacement." This is the idea that screens are so compelling to teens that they suck up time that would otherwise be spent on other, more beneficial activities, such as sleeping, exercising, or, crucially, socializing in person.

What I was shocked to find is that buried in the research around displacement, a significant and surprising point has gone almost completely unremarked. Displacement is a heavily gendered issue and has by far the greatest impact on boys. The phenomenon of replacing real-life activities with screen-based ones is a much worse problem for boys than for girls. Boys are spending significantly more time on screens than their female peers, and less time socializing. According to Pew Research, teenage boys spend *seven hours* a week more on screens than same aged girls, much of it spent online gaming.[5]

Meanwhile, adolescent boys are socializing far less in person than their female peers. Pew categorizes sports under the heading of "socializing." But when you take sports out of the equation, the average teenage boy spends less than an hour a week socializing face-to-face with peers (about forty-two minutes) while same aged girls spend nearly *six hours* a week hanging out with friends.[6]

Girls have, of course, also increased their screen time exponentially from previous generations, but they are still making time for real-life socializing. Meanwhile, teenage boy culture is increasingly migrating online. Large cooperative video games, such as *Fortnite*, and discussion forums, such as Discord, have become the new male social spaces.

When they are online, the way teens interact with each other also tends to follow the same gendered patterns of friendship that exist in real life. Although there is a fair amount of overlap, girls tend to use more social media, texting, and instant messaging, whereas boys do a significant amount more online gaming. Although cyberbullying and self-comparison are rife among teen girls, research also shows that the ways that girls use social media can often promote deeper connections—they validate each other, celebrate each other's successes, share personal information about their lives, and provide emotional support for each other online, much as girls do in real life.

Although boys also use social media, their time on screens is mostly dominated by video games. The vast majority of teen boys (nearly 90 percent) now game online with others, and see gaming as a source of connection and a key part of their social lives. Many of them wear headsets, and voice talk with fellow players as they go, and claim that this makes the game a social experience that promotes friendship. But when researchers dig into the actual substance of these conversations, they find that for the most part they are either strategizing about the game or trash talking.

When researchers from Pew took an in-depth look at the content of boys' conversations while playing multiplayer online video games, they occasionally noticed some brief, relatively mundane back-and-forths about what was going on in each other's lives, but more personal or deeper conversations were very rare. One teenage boy described this culture as "No hi's, no byes, no hellos."[7]

Perhaps these differences in the ways that girls and boys interact online are not that surprising, given the gendered patterns of socializing in real life. We know that friendships between boys are often less emotionally intense and more reliant on shared activities and side-by-side interaction, rather than the more face-to-face, talk-centered relationships girls often share. We also know that we put boys at a social disadvantage from their earliest years, failing to model more intimate friendships and teach them the relational and social skills required to maintain them. It would make sense that given the chance, boys might opt for the less emotionally and socially taxing option of playing video games with peers, rather than intense conversation. Gaming gives boys an easy escape from real-world social interactions.

According to Kent, this retreat to online spaces is becoming a vicious cycle. Their time online gives boys the illusion of fulfilling their social needs, but it is not giving them the real benefits. He tells me that the boys he sees in the Guys' Group and in his therapy practice are literally losing the attention span and social muscle to interact in the real world, a skill set that includes the ability to parse verbal and nonverbal social cues, tolerate and overcome moments of boredom and awkwardness, cope with rejection, and sustain a more involved conversation that goes deeper than the immediate and superficial rewards of a video game or meme.

"If you always have a screen, you always have some kind of stimulation. You never have to go down that road," Kent explains. "You don't have to connect because you always have this thing. And I think a lot of these kids aren't getting that experience because there's always a screen. There's always an Xbox, always an iPad, something."

This idea of the screen as a social crutch for boys resonates for me when I think about my own kids. It's not that the video games they play and YouTube videos they watch are in themselves so problematic—in fact they often seem relatively harmless and fun. It's more that the whole experience is so compelling to them, so dopamine rich, so eclipsing of any other pleasure or interest, that it can easily take over.

Connecting with other people in real life takes work and focus. The skills in maintaining a conversation, inventing a game, or playing with another kid are hugely complex, involving cooperation, creativity, listening, and sensitivity to the other person's ideas and feelings. This is an intricate system of give-and-take, of real-time balancing of your own needs against another person's. My boys and their friends already seem behind most of their female peers on many of these skills. Screens fill the gaps, smooth the rough edges. But they also stop boys from developing the social muscle to handle or ride out the potential awkwardness of real-world interaction.

• • •

Sixteen-year-old Sam is one of the quieter members of the Guys' Group. During the session, he mainly withdrew from the slurs and insults, instead focusing on an intricate pencil drawing he was working on in his notebook. Sam is handsome in a classic Hollywood way, tall and blond and tan. He is polite and poised, and also oddly detached. His good looks make this aloofness present as "too cool for school," but in a less handsome package, it could also read as "painfully shy."

Sam is the youngest of three boys, and his parents have

watched the cultural shift toward online socializing happen in real time. Sam's oldest brother, Josh, is now in his early twenties; his middle brother, Liam, graduated high school last year. Josh and Liam are not much older than Sam, but according to their parents, when they were teenagers, just a few years ago, things were very different.

"We didn't have the same type of internet there is now," his mom tells me. "We always had a video game console, but it was much more restricted when the older ones were younger."

Growing up, Sam's older brothers also had a more active in-person social life.

"Ours was the neighborhood house where I encouraged the kids to just come hang out in the backyard all day. Have some popsicles, come, be social in that way. Now our middle kid, Liam, has a group of friends that, every week or every two weeks, he'll go out with one or two of them, or meet at the mall. They do a game night once or twice a week at a friend's house. But with Sam, it has been 100 percent online. It is a social world online, but it's a very isolated social world."

Some of this disparity is due to the pandemic. Sam was in ninth grade when Covid hit, and his middle brother was already a senior in high school. But the patterns were in place before that. As early as middle school, Sam's social life was mainly conducted online, while his brothers were still regularly getting together with friends.

"Do you think that's more to do with their different personalities?" I ask his mom. "Or do you see it as a wider cultural change?"

"I think it's a culture shift in this very short period of time, because of how significantly the internet world has changed in the last very few years. It's logarithmic, almost, how much the kids are adapting to it."

Even by the standards of the Guys' Group, Sam does spend an awful lot of time online, mostly playing video games. His parents both work long hours outside of their home, and juggling work and other stressors has made it hard for them to monitor his screen time and set limits. Sam is supposed to be taking tenth grade online, but with his parents out of the house, instead he spends most of his time gaming.

"I play pretty much from when I wake up to when my dad gets home," he tells me. "I wake up around eight, nine-ish. My dad gets home around five or six-ish."

And now Sam's social life is almost exclusively screen based. He has a group of friends from school, but they rarely get together in person, instead choosing to meet up online and game. When I push him gently to remember the last time they hung out in real life, he can only remember one trip to the mall in the last year or so. This was partly a Covid thing, but it had started to happen prepandemic.

"We all talk over Instagram or Discord, but we never really get together that often," he tells me.

"And is that kind of just how people your age and in your community are?" I ask him. "Or is that specific to your friends?"

"It's people in general," he replies. "We don't really go out as much. 'Cuz we have online platforms that we can meet up in and talk there."

"Can you talk about the real stuff that's happening in your life with them?" I press. "Like how you are feeling, what's important to you? Or is it more just like memes and jokes and things?"

"It's really just, 'Hey Ben. You alright? Cool. Want to team up? Sure.' Then we play a couple games, talk about what we did. I never really have anything to share 'cuz it's really just the same thing every day. It's just wake up, get some school done, play some games for the rest of the day."

"Do you like it that way?" I ask. "Or would you like to see people in person more?"

"I do like physically meeting up with people," he replies. "I like actually seeing them. But just no one else feels the same way. No one else actually wants to go anywhere." His face drops a little. "I like people. Having other people around is good. Having friends is good. Just when you can't be with those friends, it starts to get to you."

"Are you lonely?" I ask.

"Yeah," he replies, without hesitation.

• • •

Which way is the causation going? Are these guys spending all their time online because they are already lonely, and this is one way to find connection? Or is their excessive screen time actually driving their loneliness, making them avoidant and destroying the wider culture of socializing? It's likely a combination of both, a feedback loop of solitude and retreat.

It seems that we are missing something about the phenomenon of young male loneliness, and how it lives online. How easily boys who are already socially anxious or isolated or awkward can use screens as a way to avoid the social challenges of the world. And how then the screens themselves become the problem. How this could so easily turn into a generation of lonely, superonline boys and young men.

I think back to one of the boys I had met on my trip to Utah and the Iron Gate therapy center a few months earlier, eighteen-year-old Aaron, one of the outpatients who was living in his grandma's basement down the road, but spending most of his time at the center. After a couple of years in a deep depression, during which he spent the majority of his life online, he was on a mission to get off the internet and start making connections in the real world.

Before he found the Iron Gate center, Aaron had been the moderator for a Discord server dedicated to gaming. At first this role had mainly involved sorting out technical problems and trying to weed out trolls. But he soon realized that he had tapped into a huge and largely invisible wellspring of male loneliness, of deeply unhappy boys and young men. A significant number of the young guys on the server were in crisis, experiencing suicidal thoughts or feelings of extreme desperation, but with nowhere to go and no outside help.

"Discord is not a place for healthy individuals," Aaron told me. "Because it's a place where you can interact without needing to feel like you're worth anything. So if you've been rejected by everyone else in your life, there's always a Discord for you."

Over time, Aaron got the reputation as the guy for people to go to if they were struggling with particularly difficult emotions, a kind of unofficial counselor and therapist.

"I'd just talk to them for however long they needed," he told me.

Without any formal training, Aaron would speak to these strangers over voice or video chat, talking them down from the ledge, trying to give them hope.

"The most helpful thing for any young guy is to talk," he said. "That's all that a lot of these guys needed. They needed someone to sit down and say, hey, by the way, you're a human being who has worth."

Aaron believes that the anonymity Discord offered and the safety of a screen to hide behind gave boys an opportunity to open up in a way that they didn't feel able to in real life.

"With women, when you get sad, you call your friend and you talk about it," he told me. "With men, there is a huge thing about mental health and shame because you're not supposed to be weak. You're not supposed to be broken."

By the time Aaron left Discord, he had had more than two hundred conversations with different people contemplating suicide. He still has the call logs. A male mental health crisis was flying completely under the radar. Aaron's work online almost certainly saved lives. But these boys and young men need real professional mental health help, not another depressed and untrained teenager winging it.

"My whole goal when I was on Discord was to get other people off Discord," Aaron told me. "For me, the mark of becoming a healthy person was when you could make that transition from needing a screen to feeling comfortable talking, to feeling comfortable opening up in the real world."

The experience also made Aaron realize that he needed to get off the platform himself.

"Leaving Discord was the best thing that happened in my life. I deleted my Discord account. I lay back on my bed in my dark room and I told myself, I need to talk to someone. Yeah. I need to talk to someone."

• • •

Sam's parents have also been trying to get him and his brothers off the screens.

"We go camping sometimes on very big trips where we take the phones and the games away from them," his mom tells me. "We say, 'You can bring a book, go back to the 1980s when I was a kid. Look outside, there's things out there.' And they're grumpy pus buckets for the first couple of days. But the moment they've had three or four days of that detoxifying, they open up and look around the rest of the world and become the little children they were when they were five years old. The change is almost overnight. Sam finally gets rid of the grump and the 'I want my phone' and looks outside and sees the beauty of everything. And all of a sudden the phone isn't needed the rest of the trip. He is all 'What are we doing today? What are we seeing today? Let's go skip rocks down at the river.' He is a completely different kid."

• • •

"Pick your battles with your children" was once standard advice, but in our absolutist, high stakes parenting culture, the default message is that every battle is one that urgently requires picking. I often wish some Silicon Valley start-up would make an app to help me decide. They could call it Battle Picker, perhaps. You type in your current parenting battle and some big data–driven algorithm decides whether or not you should be picking it.

In the absence of that, I am starting to think the screen time battle is one worth picking, at least for our family, one worth summoning my limited emotional resources to enforce now, while they are still relatively young.

But maybe I'm framing it in the wrong way. Perhaps it's not so much about cutting out screens. Even if I did want to remove my children from modern life, that ship has sailed. Maybe rather than see it as a battle to limit time online, we should all be trying to see this fight as one to increase connections and time spent engaging in the real world. Such strong cultural forces are working against social connection for boys and young men, we need to be actively pushing for it, helping boys build their social muscles, and making screen-free social time a non-negotiable, in the same way that we do for homework or toothbrushing or eating at least a few vegetables.

. . .

At the Guys' Group, Kent is willing to put in the work to get to a place of deeper connection. To keep pushing past the trash talking and banter to get to some more meaty interaction. He has been gently persisting for more than an hour, redirecting the boys, urging them to open up. Eventually, it pays off.

"Anyone want to share?" Kent asks the group again, hopefully.

And finally, they do. Brady admits that he has been fighting with his mom. He thinks she has a problem with alcohol, drinking too much hard seltzer in the evenings, then getting angry and taking it out on him. Brady is living at his dad's place and feeling overwhelmed by it all. He loves his mom, and just wants her to be the best person she is capable of being, he says.

Sam shares that his mom sometimes drinks too much, too. It doesn't happen often, but when it does, it's very noticeable; she slurs her speech, and it scares him.

Lucas offers to go with Brady to talk to his mom, to act as a mediator. The group comes up with ideas of what they might say. Austin tells Lucas he should become a therapist when he grows up. Lucas looks pleased and says he has considered it.

The conversation goes on for a good ten or fifteen minutes before it's time for group to end. The boys are focused, generous, calm. Before they leave, Brady says he feels better for knowing that he is not alone.

It's imperfect, brief, scattered, sure. But it is real intimacy. It would have been so easy to give up, to let the guys get lost in their meme-based chaos, their posturing and slurs. It took effort and skill on Kent's part. But for a moment, at least, they have connected, been vulnerable, helped each other.

It was worth pushing through to the other side.

• • •

I come back from LA newly energized and ready to change things up at home. But in practice it is not so simple. Our screen time battles are only part of the problem.

Neil and I are finally coming to the conclusion that we need to get the boys formally assessed. We have gone back and forth many times. On the one hand, they are wild and dysregulated. Their ways of relating to each other and their friends often seem alien, and their physicality is out of control. It feels as though this level of chaos can't possibly be normal. But then, on the other hand, the wider cultural narrative about boys keeps telling us that normal is exactly what it is. Ever since I walked out of the ultrasound room, people have been informing me in various ways that boys are wild animals until they become screen-addicted social recluses. I even had pages of my own research and footnotes to prove it.

But the pandemic had tipped us over the edge. While the boys had coped pretty well when they had the structured environment of school, in lockdown, everything falls apart. Our house is a roiling cauldron of tantrums and dysregulation. They have regular meltdowns at the slightest provocation, and their hyperactivity is overwhelming. We are struggling to cope.

Eventually, I track down Dr. A, a neuropsychologist who specializes in boys. We have several lengthy phone calls, in which I tell him all about the boys, pouring out all my fears in an incoherent torrent. He listens sympathetically and agrees that it would be a good idea to do some formal testing. Abe is still too young for most parts of the assessment, but he schedules each of the two older boys in for a full workup.

Before meeting them in person, Dr. A gives me a thick stack of checkbox questionnaires to fill out. They list hundreds and hundreds of major and minor tasks that my sons should be able to do, developmental milestones that they should have reached. I have to check the box for Sometimes, Rarely, or Never. Does your child respect the right to privacy for self and others? Is he careful around hot objects? Does he put his wet towel in the correct place after use? Are you a Bad Parent? Sometimes? Rarely? Never?

Solly and Zephy then go individually to Dr. A's office for three days of intensive in-person testing. How quickly can they respond to a moving letter X on a screen? Can they predict what a person is feeling from a photograph of their face? Balance a scale with square blocks on one side and triangle shaped on the other? Define an apple? These seemingly random tasks will apparently access some deeper truth about my sons, either confirm that we are being paranoid or give us a definitive label on which to hang our fears.

Dr. A takes a couple of weeks to compute all the data; I picture him with a Willy Wonka–style grand machine, inputting a wild and complex human in one end, in all his contradictions and flaws and gifts, then waiting for the machine to smoke and chug and thunder, and eventually spit out a small gray slip of paper with a one-word verdict.

A few weeks later we get the verdict. It isn't one word, but two. Dr. A diagnoses both Solly and Zephy with ADHD, which is not much of a surprise. More shocking to us, he also diagnoses them both with mild autism.

And because autism has a strong genetic component, Dr. A recommends that we have Abe tested, too, by a specialist in younger children. (He is still too young to test for ADHD.) Less than a month later, at the age of three, after a one-hour assessment over Zoom, Abe has the same diagnosis. Apparently, we have three autistic sons.

I feel like a fraud. In so many ways, my boys seem so similar to their peers. The differences are so marginal—squint, and they often disappear. I still half suspect that I must have some neurodiversity version of Munchausen syndrome by proxy. So many of the parents I talk to describe similar struggles with their neurotypical sons. The skeptical boomer voice that I carry in my head, courtesy of my parents' generation, still tells me that I'm just not being strict enough, that what the boys really need is less indulgence, more discipline.

I had been compulsively searching for answers and now I have them, but I am still unsettled. I am still not entirely convinced that we are not just diagnosing them with boyhood, with immaturity, with the wild rumpus of having three children constantly whipping each other up into a frenzy. But it is hard to argue with the machine. Maybe I am resisting the diagnoses because I just don't want them to be true.

Most of all I am scared. What does this all mean for the future?

CHAPTER 6

ANGRY LONELY BOYS

CONVERSATIONS WITH INCELS

After the diagnoses, I sink into a depression. The pandemic has seen us stuck in the house for more than a year, ADHD energy trapped and fizzing, our mental health unraveling. Isolated and frustrated, the boys have lost virtually all remaining traces of emotional self-regulation and are taking turns melting down into fits of savage despair.

On the plus side, I now have a twenty-page psychologist's report for each of them, outlining the neurobiological reasons behind this catalog of parenting failures. On one level, this feels deeply validating. The diagnoses have transformed me overnight from an ineffective, enabling mother of boys who allows male bad behavior to flourish in her home, to a heroic caregiver of three autistic children, valiantly holding her family together under impossible pressures. That mother is blameless, the subject of a heartrending GoFundMe perhaps, or the recipient of some kind of award from the Rotary Club. That mother—unlike her previous incarnation—deserves help, not judgment. Officially absolved, I start leaning hard into this new identity.

But deep down I feel bleak. Although there is validation in it, having my fears officially confirmed also feels like a scary finality, no longer a passing phase or something the boys will grow out of. My hopelessness starts to take on a self-righteous, aggressive edge, almost an ideological position. I adopt a posture of rigid pessimism, scanning the facts for confirmation of my own darkest stories, marinating in my own morbid half-truths. Despair feels coherent, secure, predictable. Hope seems a little too spiky and chaotic, too ripe for disappointment.

A while back, one of the many schemes and therapies I tried in order to get out in front of the chaos that engulfed our home was a course of one-on-one parent coaching with a cognitive behavioral therapist named Emily. The idea was to teach me some parenting techniques to deal with the children's anxiety and emotional spirals, but often the most helpful parts of the course were the times that we ended up focusing on my own.

In one of our early sessions, I went into Emily's office, sat down on the couch, and burst into tears. It was all too much. I was too exhausted, too frightened, too consumed by anxiety as to how all this would turn out, all the terrible ways it could go. Emily started with a classic cognitive behavioral therapy (CBT) technique. She asked me to follow my anxieties all the way down the track to their absolute worst conclusion, my secret darkest fear. The thinking behind this approach is that if we can really stare our personal worst-case scenario in the face, often we can expose it for the delusion it really is. If not, we can at least make peace with the idea that worrying about it will not help prevent it, and that—despite its strange illusion of control—anxious hypervigilance doesn't actually give us any additional agency over the outcome.

Sitting there on Emily's couch, I followed my fears all the way to the end of the road, to that dark, secret place at the end of the anxiety track. And there staring back at me was an incel. Incels, or involuntary celibates, have been on my radar for a while now. A group of lonely, superonline young men, they are somehow both the most pathetic and the deadliest manifestation of the threatened and enraged masculinity of the online manosphere.

The manosphere is the sprawling, online presence of various right-leaning and alt-right men's groups, including incels, masculinity influencers, men's rights activists, so-called pickup artists, a handful of hard-line men's separatist groups, and the alt-right-leaning communities of 4chan, 8chan, and other explicitly and occasionally violently misogynistic online forums.

Theirs is a worldview borne of grievance and self-victimization that positions men as the real victims in society and feminism as the enemy. Its chief target for hate is generally women, although in its bitter origin story about the unique suffering of the white male, race also features heavily. There is a notorious overlap between misogyny, white supremacy, homophobia, and antisemitism in online spaces.

But while much of the manosphere is populated by disgruntled middle-aged white men, brimming with resentment at the prospect of handing over the teensiest smidge of their power, incels are often barely out of adolescence. Many of them are essentially boys, whose deep loneliness and online overexposure have radicalized them into supporting ideologies of hate.

The word *incel* was actually originally coined by a woman, a Canadian student who started a website in the early nineties as a supportive space for people of all genders who struggled to find romantic relationships. But it was swiftly co-opted by a group of lonely young men, many of whom transformed their own inability to get laid into a comprehensive, pseudoideology of misogyny and rage.

The typical incel is at the same time both toxically entitled and profoundly depressed. He believes at some deep level that he is the natural inheritor of power but in his own life feels utterly powerless. He has been raised to feel entitled to women's bodies, and then feels deeply wronged by the harsh reality that women might actually be allowed some say in the matter.

The group is also heavily associated with mass murder. Self-identified incels, or "incel-adjacent" men have been responsible for close to one hundred violent deaths in the last few years, and countless more injuries. They are behind several prominent school shootings.

In 2014, twenty-two-year-old student Elliot Rodger uploaded a video to YouTube outlining his plans for revenge against the attractive women who had consistently rejected him and the more masculine-looking men they chose to sleep with instead. "On the Day of Retribution I am going to enter the hottest sorority house at UCSB and I will slaughter every single spoiled, stuck-up, blond slut I see inside there," he intones with the eerily affectless grandiosity of a comic book supervillain. "They have all rejected me . . . as an inferior man. . . . You will finally see that I am, in truth, the superior one, the true alpha male." That afternoon Rodger reclaimed his threatened masculinity by murdering six people, injuring fourteen more, and then shooting himself. The Southern Poverty Law Center named him the first terrorist of the alt-right. Incel message boards hailed him as a hero.

Over the next several years, various murderous incels cited Rodger as their inspiration, including Alek Minassian, who killed ten pedestrians in the busy downtown area of Toronto by ramming his van onto the sidewalk; and nineteen-year-old Nikolas Cruz, a regular poster on incel forums, who returned to his former high school, Marjory Stoneman Douglas High School in Parkland, Florida, with an AR-15 and killed seventeen people.

School shootings are a horrifyingly totemic part of American life. But in the decade since I have been a parent to boys, and particularly since Trump's presidency normalized a dark strain of misogyny and racism in public life, they seem to have taken on a more explicitly ideological flavor, to have become more rooted in a wider cultural narrative of resentment and hate. According to the nonpartisan group the Violence Project, mass shootings are becoming both more common and more ideologically motivated. Since 2015, shootings motivated explicitly by misogyny, for example, have tripled.

Emboldened by a growing right-wing culture that echoes many of their main talking points, these former misfits are no longer on the fringe of public discourse. In some ways it all seems like the logical conclusion of the deranged nihilism and normalized hate speech of the Trump years. Incels are the collective id of an America that has become lonely and individualistic, hypersexualized, and furious.

It is easy to see these deeply troubled young men as evil freaks or tragic one-offs. But perhaps the dividing lines aren't quite as bright as I like to imagine. At least on the face of it, so many of the boys I have talked to in the course of my research are struggling with issues that don't seem so very far from the forces driving the incel phenomenon, in a world that is both hyperconnected and deeply isolating. So many of them have told me about their loneliness and excessive time online, their wish for deeper real-world friendships and connection. Their parents have talked about their atrophying social lives and the alarmingly easy availability of hateful online content. Incels are an extreme manifestation, but the roots of their pain are starting to feel uncomfortably mainstream.

There have been many articles and think pieces written about the incel problem in the abstract, but I can find surprisingly few interviews with incels themselves about their own perspectives and experiences, about what led them down this path. In two recently published books that look at the phenomenon, for example, the authors didn't talk to any incels directly, but instead chose to pose online as incels themselves, peruse their forums and online spaces, and then make suppositions about their psychology and motivations from there.

On one level this lack of direct interviews is not surprising—incels are notoriously suspicious of journalists, and journalists are understandably nervous about diving too deeply into a world that at its fringes is violent and unpredictable. But many writers and commentators also have a more political objection to engaging directly with these boys.

"Incels are not a community of sad men that reflect a societal problem with loneliness," wrote the feminist author Jessica Valenti. "They're a community of violent misogynists that reflect a societal problem with sexism and sexual entitlement."

And researchers from the Institute for Research on Male Supremacism argued, "Countering these narratives requires journalists to surmount the instinct to sympathize with these men. Aggrieved male sexual entitlement is not a mental health issue but rather an ideological one."

Feminists often make the case that white men have had way more than their fair share of our tender empathy and careful understanding already, a phenomenon philosopher Kate Manne calls himpathy. (She originally conceived of the concept to refer to powerful men, particularly in cases of sexual violence, but has also used it in relation to incels.)

In an era of identity politics, male pain, and in particular, white male pain, has been politicized. As a society, we are deeply divided on whether we should even be engaging with it at all, whether we should frame incel violence as personal agony or domestic terrorism. And the distinction itself has become highly politically charged.

If an Arab Muslim commits a targeted act of mass murder, many on the left point out, the media wouldn't hesitate to label him a terrorist. But if an aggrieved white guy goes on a misogynistic killing spree, the same press reports that he has mental health problems. Now many feminists demand consistency as justice. (Although there seems to be a far greater political appetite in many online feminist communities for dehumanizing the white guy than for humanizing the brown one.)

Within this logic, humanizing incels at all feels like a political statement, empathizing with them, a betrayal of feminism.

The few interviews that do exist online with a handful of media-friendly "spokesincels" tend to be combative in tone. Journalists or YouTubers take the incels' ideological posturing at face value, and then lock themselves into faux debates about whether or not rape or mass shootings are, in fact, "wrong."

This type of interview does not seem to be getting us any further in understanding the roots of the incel problem. Without speaking directly with these young men about what is really going on in their lives, what pain pushed them toward these ideologies, how can we possibly understand what led them here and prevent anyone else from going down this path?

So, I start trawling the manosphere for incels who might be willing to talk to me.

• • •

The FAQ page of incels.co, the flagship incel website, has a surprisingly perky, antiseptic tone.

"One does not need to share any particular belief at all to be an incel. Incels can be liberal or conservative. They can be feminists or Men's Rights Activists," it reads. "Many who seek to attack incels wish to smear all incels by trying to associate us with fringe ideologies. Just like Muslims, who suffered similar broad slurs in the early 21st century, we would ask that you consider us as individual people, because that is what we are, each with our own life history and perspective."

This stylistic nod to the left, to multiculturalism, or a human resources department diversity policy is belied by the actual content of the message boards. This is a slightly deranged mix of woman hating, race-baiting, suicidal ideation, incomprehensible memes, pseudoscience, raw anguish, and tender brotherhood.

Incels have their own founding doctrine, a philosophy they call the Blackpill, derived from a wider manosphere ideology known as the Redpill. The Redpill is a reference to a scene in the film *The Matrix,* in which Keanu Reeves's character gets to choose between two pills—a blue one, which would keep him in a dream-based existence, or a red one, which would awaken him to the harsher truths of the "real world."

In the manosphere, taking the Redpill refers to the moment when a man awakens to the reality that he has been sold a lie, that it is not men who hold the privilege and power in society, but women, and specifically, feminists. The incels' Blackpill philosophy builds on this worldview, with the addendum that women are capricious and shallow creatures who are only interested in men's looks, and a man's level of sexual success is predetermined by his genes. In their view, male desirability is a strict hierarchy with incels at the bottom.

In the Blackpill schema, genetically blessed and sexually successful men are called Chads—they are tall, square-jawed, and masculine. The attractive women they sleep with are Stacys. Women in general are "femoids" or "foids" for short. Incels generally see themselves as short or overweight or otherwise failing to live up to male beauty ideals.

As they see it, their genetically bleak prospects force the incels to choose between a few basic options: One is to *looksmax,* which can mean anything from lifting weights to dangerous leg lengthening or facial masculinization surgery. Another is *copes,* an incel term meaning any coping mechanism, from venting to their incel buddies online, to sex tourism in Southeast Asia. When the copes stop working, the final option is to *rope,* or die by suicide, the topic of an alarming number of posts.

The extremes aren't hard to find. There's a fair smattering of horrifying posts—violent racism and antisemitism, vivid rape fantasies, calls for random killings, and all flavors of misogyny, including a totally emotionless, painstakingly argued, thousand-word deep dive into whether advocating for the legalized torture of women violates the First Amendment.

Many of the posts read like term papers, cogently written, meticulously reasoned, and yet full of fallacies and false premises that are at the same time both dumb and chilling. Others are oddly pitiful ("why do foids hate me?"). The unifying theme seems to be a kind of outrage that women might be actual humans, with their own desires or agency.

But along with the hate speech, there are also a fair number of posts about the pain of loneliness that are surprisingly vulnerable and emotional.

"Lemme paint a picture," writes one young guy with the username @hopeisajoke. (This is pretty typical of online incel handles, which seem to tend toward either hate-speech or despair.)

> Imagine a guy like me, an incel, and I mean incel. I-N-C-E-L.
>
> I've known of how ugly I am for a long time now thanks to people making it abundantly clear. It wasn't just bullies at school or anything like that. I've been pointed at and laughed at by

women in public and at the gym, so I understand I'm not easy on the eyes.

Could you imagine how it must feel after years of sadness because of being not lusted after, could you imagine what it would feel like then for a woman to come up and want to have sex with me?

What so many people get wrong is that I or people like me want sex and sex alone. No! I know that my first time is going to be awkward and I'm most likely going to have some performance problems, hell, we might not even have sex at all, but that's not the point! I don't want sex! I want what comes with it!

Being in that position is so vulnerable, and she chooses to be vulnerable with me! Of all people she chose me.

My confidence would skyrocket and for the first time in my life I'd be able to go:

"Hey. I'm not as ugly as all those people who laughed at me said I was. I just had sex, so surely I can't be that detestable, right?"

Once I'm able to be lusted after, I'd like to build a future with a woman with a love that we cultivated together.

I hope I do.

His guileless rawness punches me in the gut. I message @hopeisajoke asking if he would be willing to talk to me, and I'm surprised when I hear back from him the next day, even though he is unsure.

"I get a lot of people who message me wanting to 'understand' me and study me as if I were some zoo animal for them to gawk at," he explains. "They don't really see me as a human being. More like a new species they need to understand out of fear."

I try to reassure him that that is the whole point—that I do want to listen to him as human. He seems momentarily reassured, but the next day he is nervous again. Now he is concerned that I might be from the FBI.

"It wouldn't be the first time something like that happened," he tells me.

"Has the FBI ever been in touch with you?" I ask.

"No, but incels have this paranoia that the FBI are after them. I mean, the world thinks incels are these alt-right white men who plan to kill everyone."

"Is that a fair characterization of incels in general?" I message back.

"Not at all," he replies immediately. "I mean, incels are so much more diverse. Like Black men for example who always had to deal with being hypermasculine. Who felt like they had to be gangsters and athletic and had to have some hustle going on. So many Indian men and Asian men and Black men hate themselves on the boards. They hate their own skin so fucking much, they wished they could peel it off. That's why I always laugh whenever people say incels are these alt-right white guys. Like no sir—we probably got more diversity than Apple and Google who always shout about inclusivity."

For some reason I am compelled to fact-check him on this point. It's hard to get reliable data on incel demographics, but the one survey that does exist, a 2020 poll that one of the main incel sites carried out of its members, suggests that he is right. Around 55 percent of incels in the survey identified as white and the remaining 45 percent were pretty equally divided among Black, Latino, Asian American, and American Indian. (A comparable proportion of Google's employees are white and the vast majority of the rest are Asian American, with a tiny number of Black programmers.)

Without ever really agreeing to a formal interview, @hopeisajoke—or James, as I now call him—and I start to talk regularly over Google Chat. I start keeping the chat window open on my computer most of the day, and we message each other back and forth while I'm scrolling through Instagram or feeling predinner despair or procrastinating about writing this book. I'm surprised to find that I enjoy his company.

James is a twenty-year-old who is studying finance at a Midwestern community college, living with his parents in a small city, and working part time as a supermarket cashier. He tells me that he grew up "decently poor," not middle class, but with enough food on the table. In his own words, he is "short and ugly" (he will never turn his camera on, so I can't form any opinion on this), and he was horribly bullied all the way through school.

"All twelve years of it," he tells me. "School wasn't just a prison like so many people describe, it was worse. It was a jungle. Every time I'd get off the bus and my feet planted themselves in front of the school's main gate, I would think, 'Where can I hide so they can't hurt me? Where can I hide so they can't laugh at me?' "

When I ask James if he is willing to share any specifics, I am surprised at the story he chooses—not one of violence or beatings (although he says he suffered those frequently), but about a more subtle humiliation. He tells me about a time that he went with his mom to pick up his sister after school. His mom left him in the car, and he started to doze off. Hearing a noise, he opened his eyes a crack and saw three girls in the backseat of the car in front, pointing and laughing at him.

"That moment in my life really cemented to me how women see me," he tells me. "I am ugly to them. I am a laughingstock to them. I will never be lusted after by them. I will never be loved by them."

It's a common theme on incel forums that even though they were bullied by both boys and girls, and often more harshly by boys, the incels tend to single out girls for blame in particular. I ask James why he thinks this is.

"Being hurt by other people hurts a lot," he replies. "But being hurt by the people that you're trying to attract? That you're trying to be liked by? That's worse than a knife to the jugular."

James had just one close friend during his school years, and they were inseparable throughout elementary school. But the pair lost touch when James's family moved away the summer before sixth grade.

"After I moved and lost my friend, I would try to make friends. I would literally force myself to be in people's presence, but nobody wanted me. I'd act like I was interested in the same things they were interested in, just to be in their company, but nobody wanted me."

He can't remember exactly when he first stumbled on the incel forums, but he knows it was when he was somewhere between the ages of fifteen and eighteen, a desperately lonely and depressed high schooler.

"I think it was a slow sinking into the movement," he remembers. "I was orbiting the pickup artist world and Men Going Their Own Way [a hard-line men's separatist group], just looking at it from time to time, and then I stumbled upon the IncelTears subreddit. That's when I first got to know what inceldom was."

IncelTears is a forum on the chat site Reddit, not for incels themselves, but devoted to ridiculing them—a place where feminists and others post content ranging from political pushback against incel ideology, to outright mocking of their perceived loserdom. But ironically, instead of acting as a deterrent, it became James's gateway into the movement. Identifying strongly with the image of a lonely, sex-starved young man, he sought out the incel forums themselves and immediately felt at home.

"I found my comfort," he tells me. "I found people who went through the same thing, and it felt so wonderful. It was a combination of knowing that there were others like me and also how they treated me. If I went to the 'normal' men in society with my issues of not being able to be lusted after and being generally hated by women, then they'd just laugh at me and boast about how many women they fucked and call me a virgin loser. A man's masculinity is dependent upon how many women desire him and how many women he's slept with. It's wrong and I hate that idea and I personally don't believe in it, but it is what it is."

To his surprise, James found that among incels, he was able to be emotionally open and vulnerable in a way he had always found impossible to be with most other men.

"It has always been very difficult for me to talk about my emotions," he says. "The only place I've been able to is incel forums and spaces online. The idea of bearing my burdens and never crying has been a constant thing as I was growing up. It's something you just know as a guy. You just know. You feel it. Most men don't confide in each other like that unless they're BEST friends, like they have known each other for years. Even then it's a bit unlikely."

"Incels are more emotionally open with each other than most men?" I ask him, surprised.

"Yeah," he replies. "We don't really put up a mask to each other. We have nothing to be proud of or macho about. All of us are incels. We are all sad. Nothing to brag about—no muscles, no nothin'. We talk like that all the time to each other—expressing our deepest fears, what we wanted."

I think of all the other boys I have interviewed. Of Oliver, who described his close friends as a "very unsupportive support system" and told me that he had kept his emotions hidden for so long he had become "emotionally constipated." Or Jordan, his roommate, who had never felt able to have an emotionally honest conversation with a male friend until he was in college.

I think of Cameron and Jayden, two young men of vastly different racial and economic backgrounds who had both used the exact same phrase in describing what it was like to be a boy around other boys: "You can never let your guard down." They had virtually nothing in common. But they both constantly felt the need to put up a facade of invulnerability—one through hilarious banter, the other through naked aggression. Even in both of the boys' therapy groups, which I visited, the guys had a hard time opening up in the presence of their male peers.

In some twisted sense, the way James was describing the incels made them sound like the most emotionally open all-male group I had encountered so far. The irony of this hit me hard. I had spent all this time searching for a space in which boys and young men felt they could disregard masculine norms, take off the mask, and be vulnerable with each other. I thought I might find it in some kind of feminist affinity circle, or a therapy group run by a soft-spoken vegan. But instead, I had found it right here at the heart of the manosphere, in Toxic Masculinity Central.

. . .

Dr. Sarah Daly is an assistant professor of criminology at Saint Vincent College, in Latrobe, Pennsylvania. Her work focuses on incels. After interviewing several of them herself, she now believes that paradoxically, their inability to participate in systems of masculinity can give incels a degree of emotional freedom that other boys and young men don't have access to.

"It's something I was not expecting," she tells me. "They just talk about their feelings a lot. So, in a way, all of the things that ostracized them because they're not masculine enough are seen as badges of honor in the incel community. That they've been victimized, that they've been looked down on and bullied. So those things make them 'true incels' in their circles."

Incels have a tense and conflicted relationship with traditional masculinity. In many ways, their conception of manhood as a hierarchy—with Chad, the square-jawed alpha on top; the lesser beta males scrabbling for Chad's table scraps below; and the tragic incels at the bottom—is a less sophisticated version of many classic feminist theories of masculinity.

The Australian sociologist Dr. R. W. Connell was the first to argue that masculinity is inherently hierarchical, and that in order for a dominant form of masculinity to exist, "lower value" men must be subordinated. Now most gender theorists agree that masculinity is a hierarchy in which the men with the most social and cultural power are at the top, with less powerful, often more effeminate men below. In this hierarchy, all of these masculine subtypes sit above women, who are, by definition, at the bottom of the pile.

In this paradigm, sexism isn't just an incidental by-product of masculinity, it's foundational to the whole idea. The subordination of women is built into the system, necessary for masculinity's very existence. Misogyny is sexism's more emotionally volatile cousin, a rotten blend of sexist power structures and human rage.

The manosphere as a whole is strangely obsessed with masculine hierarchies—alpha males, in particular—and how to game the system and rise to the top. Some incels dabble in "looksmaxxing," but at heart, where they differ from the rest of the manosphere cohort, is that while they buy into the basic terms of hierarchical masculinity, most incels have abandoned any hope of ever climbing the ladder themselves. The Blackpill, incel's banner ideology, is built on a rigid foundation of hopelessness.

Incels may be at the bottom of the pile of men, but of course, there is one group that they do sit above in the masculinity hierarchy, by definition—women. In this context, their misogyny makes sense. Demeaning women may not actually help them rise any closer to Chad on the manhood scale, but it does give them the unfamiliar experience of having someone, *anyone* to subordinate, all wrapped up in a prepackaged, semipolitical identity.

• • •

A couple of months have gone by, and I am still chatting with James online most days. He tells me that he loves Russian novels, but his favorite book is *Pride and Prejudice*.

None of his family or acquaintances know about his incel identity. "They would think I was a weird, demented loser." He talks about his plans to one day get a job in a bank, to make something of his life, but describes his mental health as taking a "long walk in the fires of hell." But during all these many hours of conversation, I never see what James looks like.

"I am biologically a man," he tells me one morning. "But I don't look like a man. I'm not tall, I have trouble growing facial hair. I don't have big, veiny hands. I don't fit into that image of male sexiness that women and men love so much. I just don't. And the thing is—these attributes—being tall, having a deep voice, having a big dick—are all treated with so much desire and positivity everywhere. In movies, in social media, in TV shows."

Incels in general are deeply preoccupied with their appearance, in a way that reminds me of the ambient self-loathing of female existence—the calorie counting and bikini body countdowns and antiaging creams and botox. I run this idea past James.

"It's interesting hearing all this," I tell him, "because growing up as a girl, then a woman, it always seemed like the impossible beauty standards were for us, and men could get away with looking like anything. Like you often see old, ugly guys with beautiful young women, for example, but rarely the other way round."

"Women have a *large* part in upholding these toxic ideals," he counters. "Women participate in body shaming men online a lot."

I'm interested in this new direction. "What have you heard in particular?" I ask.

"That short men aren't real men, that if you have a small dick, you aren't a real man.

"I remember two trends on TikTok: One was a song that went, 'Sorry. I don't like short guys.' And it would be all these girls and women who would flaunt their tall boyfriends as if they were trophies. Women who body-shame men, you would not believe the shit they say. They tell short men to kill themselves."

I quickly Google this, and I am shocked to discover he is right. I scroll through post after post of women telling short men to do exactly this, just a small subsection of a whole genre of short male–shaming posts, before clicking away.

"You're right," I admit to James. "And no one really remarks on it. It's true that in similar circles, if it was a man, say, fat-shaming a woman, there would be an outcry."

"Thing is," he replies, "the bounce-back for women seems so strong, *from everyone*. But if a dude gets body-shamed, I *rarely* see a woman standing up for us. Men are just free game to get made fun of."

I think about this. There is some truth in it for sure. My friends and I might well describe an insecure guy with something to prove as having a "short man complex," for example, without ever giving it a second thought, whereas none of us would dream of describing a woman as having a "fat girl complex." At one level this is clearly a false equivalence, a piece of lazy thinking that fails to acknowledge the wider power differential at play between men and women. After all, it's one thing to punch up with a joke, and quite another to punch down. As a general rule, it is acceptable, often healthy, to rib a group on the upside of power, but shaming directed downward is bullying.

But I wonder if we might be starting to overcorrect. Is body-shaming James—a vulnerable twenty-year-old with serious mental health issues, who has been repeatedly bullied throughout his life—really punching up? Clearly, the body-shaming of men is no justification for the kind of misogyny that abounds on incel forums, much less for murder. But it seems as though we are all caught in ever-decreasing circles of dehumanization. After all, we don't experience our lives or emotions as part of a political class, but as individuals. James is young enough to have no real first-hand experience of the centuries of objectification and impossible female beauty standards, of women being relentlessly judged for their looks, and shamed when they are found wanting. For him, the history is no consolation.

Throughout my research for this book, I have been surprised to see just how much of an issue body image had become for boys and young men. I had always thought that the male gender had mostly been given a pass on objectification and body shame.

But this has changed. Although men are still given way more aesthetic leeway than women, male bodies are suddenly up for appraisal and scrutiny. Young guys are self-objectifying on social media in an unprecedented way. I think of Ryan, the boy who had broken his back lifting weights, just to try to gain the ripped physique he had seen plastered over social media and in the superhero epics he loved to watch. Ryan was no incel—in fact he was repulsed by the manosphere—but he still felt so much pressure to achieve a kind of hypermuscled body type that he had shattered a vertebra. I think of the research that shows that boys are also starting to hate their own bodies in the same way that girls have always been subtly encouraged to. This might be inching us closer to equality, but it doesn't feel like progress.

• • •

At some point, I send James the philosopher Amia Srinivasan's famous essay, "The Right to Sex," about incels, particularly the incel killer Elliot Rodger, who opened fire on the sorority house in Santa Barbara; and the politics of sexual desire. The essay argues, among other things, that who is and isn't seen as desirable in a given society is at least in part culturally determined. James seems interested in the essay, and we discuss it back and forth over a few days. He seems particularly curious about this paragraph:

> Feminism, far from being Rodger's enemy, may well be the primary force resisting the very system that made him feel—as a short, clumsy, effeminate, interracial boy—inadequate.[1]

"What exactly could feminism have done to help Elliot?" James asks me.

I tell him that I think that Srinivisan is saying that feminism is really the only movement pushing back against the harmful effects of rigid gender expectations for both men and women. That the system of patriarchy that tells women they should be submissive and pretty and lacking in agency is the same system that tells men they should be tough and masculine and have a big dick and not cry. That we are all caught in it together, all on the same side. And, really, feminists are the only group actually standing up against that system.

He says he will consider this, but he sounds skeptical.

It's not hard to see why. The idea that feminism would feel like a helpful framework for someone like James to make sense of his own life, let alone Elliot Rodger, does seem, if not disingenuous, then at least a little unrealistic.

Much seminal feminist thinking acknowledges that patriarchy hurts men as well as women. In her book *The Will to Change: Men, Masculinity, and Love* (2004), for example, the author and social theorist bell hooks outlined in great detail the many harms that patriarchal norms bring to boys and men while cutting them off from their emotions and forcing them into a kind of rigid gender prison. Masculinity studies is a small but robust subfield of gender studies.

But it would be easy for someone in James's situation to miss this subtlety, given that quite rightly, men's issues have hardly been a priority for the feminist movement as a whole. Generally, the louder voices in the popular discourse have focused less on how patriarchy harms men and more on how it benefits men at women's expense. And although more nuanced gender theory sees both men and women as victims of patriarchy, for many high-profile, superonline feminists, a refusal to engage with men's feelings has become almost a point of principle.

The phrase "male tears" popped up on Tumblr around 2012 and has become the go-to sneer among millennial and Gen Z feminists when men express any kind of "we are the real victims" politicking. It served its purpose, helping to clarify the basic structures of oppression in people's minds, but the sentiment has become more widely adopted as a way of ridiculing or shutting down any expression of male pain.

Men have systemic power, without a doubt, but that framework is perhaps of limited use when trying to understand, say, the issues of a traumatized young man barely out of adolescence with no financial or social capital and serious mental health issues. For someone such as James, it can start to feel as though male emotions get dismissed from both sides. For every right-wing tough guy urging his crying son to man up, there is a voice from the left telling him that to voice his problems is to take emotional airtime away from a woman, whose suffering is more valid. These are not morally equivalent, of course, but in practice the impact can be similar. It's not hard to see why incel forums and manosphere spaces can start to feel like the only place that a troubled young man might find a sympathetic ear, or a sense of belonging or empathy.

Paradoxically, the same people who urge men to be more emotionally expressive are often also the ones who take a principled stand against hearing how men actually feel. This has certainly been true for James. He tells me that he wants to seek help, to find a therapist, and look for understanding and validation outside of the incel forums, but he is nervous that a female therapist would not be willing to listen to him.

"This idea that women are these eternal victims and men are these demons who oppress has been spread so far and wide," James tells me. "And it is true. For the longest time in human history, women never had rights, or anything at all. But this idea has been pushed beyond a certain line to the point where if a man voices any concern, they get deflected with all of their so-called privileges. Women just wouldn't care, and if they listened, they wouldn't sympathize or understand. They'd be like 'Whatever. You deserve it. Women have suffered more than you, so you have no right to complain.' "

I reassure James that a good therapist would listen to him and not judge, but it's not hard to see why he is concerned. The general lack of empathy and blanket condemnation, particularly online, can make it very difficult for young men to seek help when they need it the most. This, in turn, makes it more likely that they will give in to destructive impulses.

• • •

I am deeply torn. I am starting to worry that I am getting caught in the weeds with James, empathizing too much and losing my moral center. Talking to him, it is easy to start to see incels as these sweet little cuddlebugs and lose sight of the misogyny and violence of the movement.

"I need a grosser incel," I say to my husband that night. "A real scumbag misogynist."

"You need some new hobbies," he tells me.

Ian seems to fit the bill. His Twitter feed is deeply unlikable, the standard incel triumvirate: aggrieved, entitled, misogynistic.

His bio says simply, "Fuck all of you, honestly." His pinned tweet reads, "There's literally no point in having female friends. If they're not fucking you, it's worthless even talking to them. They just want you as an orbiter. Women make awful friends. They use and abuse but never help."

His feed is a mix of incoherent cartoons, stripped down misogyny ("Women have no fucking personality—they're so generic and predictable"), calls for incels to create their own home nation, one-liners that don't quite land even within their own morally desolate frame of reference, and tragedy. "In high school, I often spent the break in a restroom stall. Used to be the only place where I was safe, not being bullied by my classmates."

I message Ian and ask if he is willing to talk. Later that evening he replies, asking me to message him at an email address along the lines of "justkillmenow@hotmail.com," which, as he makes sure to clarify, is "not a business address."

Like James, Ian won't turn his camera on, and the conversation starts off awkwardly. I ask him what he does for a living. He tells me that he sells kitchens.

"That sounds fun!" I gasp, lamely overeager, groping to build some sort of rapport. "I *love* kitchens!"

"It's not. It's just all dealing with rich entitled women."

Honestly, he probably means me. The word *entitled* is used often to describe both my demographic, the Gen X Karen, a privileged white woman, poised to call the manager; and also his, the aggrieved online misogynist. *Entitled* is the feminist go-to descriptor for the incel mindset. I wonder briefly what any of us are entitled to in this life. Sex? Love? A nice kitchen?

Ian first came across the incel forums in 2016, while searching for martial arts content online. He had recently dropped out of college after several years of serious depression, mainly due to loneliness and repeated rejections from girls he wanted to date.

"Every night there was a party, and I was almost never invited," he remembers. "And if I'd go it was just depressing standing there, because everybody's taller than you. You start up a conversation and you notice immediately the girls are just not into it. You just think, 'What's wrong with me?' You just feel like a complete failure in every aspect."

Like James, Ian's first introduction to the incel movement was through a meme on Reddit, mocking incels as self-pitying losers. Identifying strongly, he decided to seek out the community and see for himself.

"I was taken aback a bit, at first, because there was some extremism there. The first thing I was thinking, was 'Holy shit, this is fucked up.' Like, I thought, 'These people are insane.' But there were also posts that just made a lot of sense."

"Like what?" I ask.

"People would just vent about their lives. And everybody was just basically in the same scenario as me. And one of the best things about it was that no one was sugarcoating the language. See, everybody lies online. Everybody pretends they have a good life, pretends like they're doing great. One of the best things about the incel community is that they're so honest. They don't give a fuck what people think. They'll not pretend to be anything. They'll just tell you how much of a loser they are."

Ian is happy to describe himself as a misogynist, fully owning the identity. But he tells me that he hasn't always hated women. He describes his realization that women were terrible as a sudden epiphany that sprang from a thread he saw on one of the incel forums.

The thread was a discussion about an experiment that has now become part of incel folklore, wheeled out regularly on the forums as evidence of women's shallow, heartless natures. In the experiment, a group of incels who had experienced multiple rejections on the dating app Tinder downloaded a picture of a Chad-like male supermodel, photoshopped a large swastika tattoo onto his arm, and made him a fake Tinder profile, complete with Nazi-sympathizing bio. According to Ian, the sexy fake Nazi got hundreds of matches and messages from women who were so desperate to have sex with him that they were prepared to overlook his politics, while the good-hearted incels of Tinder faced only repeated rejection.

As scientific proof of the moral depravity of the female sex, this experiment seems a little lacking. The irony of a man denouncing women for condoning problematic politics, when he himself identifies as part of a group that has repeatedly committed ideological mass murder, seems to be lost on Ian. But for him the evidence was incontrovertible. He wasn't worthless. Women were.

"That drove me insane," he tells me. "It just made me so depressed. I started to realize that women had no heart and no soul. They were incredibly shallow. Just interested in looks and money."

Ian insists that he is not concerned with looks himself. He doesn't need a Stacy and would be happy with almost any woman. But I'm still stuck on the Tinder experiment. "Has anyone ever tried it the other way around?" I ask him. "Where someone puts a picture of a very beautiful Nazi woman on Tinder and we see how many matches she gets from men?"

"I wouldn't date a Nazi girl," he replies, his voice thick with moral outrage.

"I mean, I wouldn't date a Nazi guy either . . ." I say, somewhat overdefensively.

"I don't believe you."

"You think I would date a Nazi guy?"

"Like if he was a supermodel, I don't think you would care if he's a Nazi."

My thoughts flit to my balding Jewish husband. Nazi supermodels are not my weakness.

"That's the proof I've seen," Ian continues. "Trust me, girls will not reject you if you're a Nazi. But I don't think any guy would date a Nazi girl. That's my actual genuine belief."

"You should try the experiment the other way around," I tell him, now stupidly overinvested. "Why don't you try it with a woman and see what happens?"

"I'm not interested in seeing what happens."

And then I realize this is exactly the point. Ian doesn't want his belief disproved. He relies on it. Misogyny is a defense for him, a thinly veiled cover story allowing him not to hate himself, to reclaim a shred of lost masculinity. The more terrible and shallow and incapable of love he proves women to be, the better he feels about himself. And the more pseudoscientific evidence he can amass to support this point, the more self-worth he is able to muster. Ian is doing what we all do to some extent. We come up with plausible stories to explain away our own inner mess and shame, a grand theory that externalizes our pain, locating it firmly outside of our own failures.

The psychologist Matt Englar-Carlson agrees that when it comes to incels, we need to look deeper. "In the stuff that's really shocking and misogynistic and violent, if you were to kind of decode that in some ways, it's probably about lack of connection and feeling hurt and feeling unseen and erased and like you don't matter. All these very human emotions," he says.

But by getting sucked into a debate with Ian about whether women are indeed Nazi-sympathizing monsters, no matter how strongly I am arguing the opposing case, I am allowing him to set the terms, to keep the discussion exactly where he wants it to be. At some level it feels like a microcosm of a wider problem, with Ian and me playing the parts of men's rights activist and feminist in an endless trolling contest.

• • •

Like James, Ian was badly bullied in high school.

"That was probably like the most humiliating part of my life," he tells me. "I just hate talking about it 'cause I hate the person I was back then."

"Why were you bullied?" I ask him.

"I'm very, very short."

"How short?"

"I'm five two, okay?" His voice catches. "Yeah, that basically made my life hell in high school because I couldn't defend myself and people just loved to pick on me. They loved to humiliate me. I was just so suicidal and depressed, and I just never wanted to go to school. I hated it. I think the stuff that happened to me in school is kinda my first step into nihilism, into believing in the Blackpill beliefs."

"Could you talk to your family about it?"

"I would be way too embarrassed to admit something like that, that I was weak or being bullied," he tells me. "You don't wanna tell your dad, 'Hey, Dad, kids are messing with me.' I would just feel so weak in front of him."

"Was it important to your parents that you weren't weak?"

"Yes. My dad is like one of the strongest human beings alive. Not just physically, I mean, but also his character. He's just, he has such a strong character and back then I was not strong in character whatsoever. And I think that was my biggest problem. I'm much stronger now. I've learned to be more aggressive."

"What about your mom?" I ask.

"I don't like talking to her. I never liked her," he says. I'm surprised at the baldness of this statement.

"Why didn't you like her?"

"Because I basically got most of my personality traits from her. In high school I was basically just like my mom. She was also very, very passive, very scared of everything. I was a gentle person, same as she was. And every time I told her something about myself, she'd say, 'Just like me.' And I hated it. Because they were terrible traits to have as a man."

• • •

Ian remembers the Elliot Rodger shooting well. It was a good two years before he started frequenting the incel forums, before he had even heard the word *incel,* but as soon as Ian saw Rodger's face on the news, he felt an affinity.

"He felt so relatable to me. I was watching the videos of him over and over," he tells me. "But in a fucked-up way. I thought he was insane. But he was bullied in the same way I was. And he had a lot of the same traits, a lot of the same life experience, down to dropping out, down to his roommates getting girlfriends and him complaining about it. Basically, it was my life.

"You know, the guy was absolutely mental," he tells me. "He saw the whole thing like it was a superhero movie and he was a supervillain. And he embraced that role. Even the way he dressed, the way he talked. Like his 'My Day of Retribution' video. I basically know that video word for word."

Ian adopts Rodger's chilling supervillain inflection and starts quoting. "Todaaaaay is the day of my retribution, the day in which you'll all pay." It is deeply unsettling.

"I watched that video tons of times. It was just pretty inspiring to see that he actually said something and did it—it wasn't just talking online."

"Have you ever thought about doing something similar?" I ask nervously.

"Of course. I have that fantasy every day," he replies, but then quickly clarifies. "I would never do it. Don't get me wrong—in case the FBI is listening—I would never do it. But of course, I have that fantasy all the time."

I pause, momentarily considering reporting Ian to someone. But then I realize that I have nothing to report, and no one to report it to.

"I mean that's basically my main daydream. You ask any incel, that's their main daydream."

"What is the daydream?" I ask. "Talk me through it."

"To grab a fucking gun, write a fucking note. One that gets famous, telling everyone to fuck off and then going and killing a bunch of people—specifically, Chad and Stacy."

• • •

There have been many attempts to profile and understand the motivations of mass shooters—their psychology and the cultural factors that drive them. At various times, researchers have pointed the finger at violent video games, bad parenting, loneliness, and mental illness. But if these things were the primary cause, then in theory, both males and females would commit mass shootings. In reality, the only thing that virtually all school-shooters, and almost all mass shooters in general, have in common is that they are male. There are extremely few exceptions. This is a gendered crime, an almost exclusively male response to loneliness and pain.

Adolescent girls are also isolated, bullied, and objectified. Young women get rejected, mocked, shamed, and excluded. But they almost never shoot people. The impulse to commit this type of violence comes not just from the experience of being lonely and depressed, but of being a lonely and depressed man. Our story of masculinity tells us not just that boys should be tough and aggressive, stoic and virile, but specifically that they should be heroes—special, notorious, superhuman. Masculinity comes with built-in inadequacy. By now I have seen in so many different ways how, operating under these impossible expectations, boys are almost doomed to failure.

A wide body of research shows that it is not masculinity itself that makes men violent, but the sense of shame that they are not masculine *enough*. A range of research shows that men who score high on measures for what researchers call masculine discrepancy stress—meaning, stress derived from a belief that they fall short of society's standards for manhood—are significantly more likely to be violent in a variety of ways, including intimate partner violence, sexual violence, and gun violence.[2]

One study from the Centers for Disease Control and Prevention's (CDC's) Division of Violence Prevention suggested that men who felt stressed about their self-perceived masculinity reported committing assault using a weapon at a rate that is a shocking 348 percent higher than in other men.[3]

A mass shooting, a one-off splashy act of terror and vengeance, is a quick way to reclaim masculine status, an easy shortcut to rebrand feelings of loserdom and rejection into a glorious avenging-hero narrative. The media frenzy that tends to follow every shooting, bestowing a twisted celebrity on the shooter, only feeds the beast.

"[You] have all rejected me . . . as an inferior man," said Elliot Rodger in his "Day of Retribution" video, shared across America by virtually every major news outlet. "You will finally see that I am, in truth, the superior one, the true alpha male." Like many mass shooters, he shot himself before anyone could take this coveted status away from him.

It is no coincidence that Elliot Rodger drew inspiration for his manner and methods directly from comic book supervillainy. This is the flipside of Andrew Tate, styling himself as Batman, the rich and powerful hero inside his Batcave. This was a vision of masculinity that was imprinted early, a grotesque way for him to claim a starring role in the hero-villain stories that were fed to him since childhood. And in a country where any disturbed boy can stroll past his local strip mall and walk away with an assault rifle, it was a vision that was shockingly easy to access.

• • •

"How likely do you think it is that you would actually do something violent?" I ask Ian, nervously.

"Well, let me just say I don't have a gun."

"If you did have a gun, then what?"

"I'd probably shoot myself."

His voice softens, saddens. "I don't think I have the actual capacity to kill someone else. You know, despite the way I talk, what I just said now, I definitely don't have that capacity to kill someone."

He sounds dejected, almost disappointed in himself.

"Why not?" I ask.

"'Cause I wouldn't be able to do it. I don't know why not. I just wouldn't, you know? I've always had trouble hurting other people. I've always cringed anytime I see someone hurt. I've had trouble hurting myself. I'd never be able to kill someone else, I think."

A note of self-hatred has crept into his voice. The image of himself as a mass murderer is less shameful to Ian than the image of himself as gentle or soft-hearted.

I ask him if he wishes things could be different—that there could be more ways for boys and men to show up in the world, and that a gentle, emotionally vulnerable boy could be valued and admired for who he is. To my surprise, he says no.

"I don't wish there were more acceptable ways for me to be," he tells me sadly. "I just wish I was different. I just wish women wouldn't raise boys to be pussies. You have to be tough as a man. I don't think you should allow boys to be gentle and soft."

Ian is so trapped within these punishing gender norms, he can't see an alternative, or even hope for one. The system isn't wrong, women are. But also, deep down, so is he.

"I've kind of accepted the idea that I could never actually be happy in life," he says. "Just miserable. I just keep sinking in more, more into my hatred." I try to reassure Ian, wheeling out all the "I Will Survive" type platitudes that my friends and I used to turn to when one of us got dumped or rejected. We are okay on our own; we don't need a partner to be happy. We need to love ourselves before we can love someone else. But to Ian they ring hollow.

"The difference is that those women—they're able to get a relationship again, they're able to get love again," Ian says, his voice flat. "Like what are you telling me? You're telling me I can be happy without ever being loved?"

It's hard to argue with this. We hear a lot about incels feeling entitled to sex. But what Ian wants, what most incels seemed to want deep down, isn't so much sex, but love. And surely some basic sense of feeling entitled to love is the very foundation of a healthy psyche. What makes Ian sick, what makes him misogynistic, is not overentitlement, but the very opposite—that at some level he doesn't believe he is entitled to love at all.

• • •

When James's name doesn't pop up on my Google Chat for a couple of days, I start to worry. He has told me several times that his mental health has been "down in the gutter for a long time now."

We associate incels heavily with mass violence, but these incidents are the exceptions. The exponentially bigger risk for these young men is suicide. A 2019 incels.co survey indicated that nearly 70 percent of incels suffered from serious, long-lasting depression and that over 67 percent had considered suicide. This echoes wider trends. Adolescent boys in general are one of the highest risk groups for suicide in most countries. In the United States, the suicide rate for young men is more than three and a half times that for their female peers.

For boys the stigma against seeking help is real. Adolescent boys are significantly less likely than girls to receive mental health care. In school settings, where large numbers of school counselors have been replaced with educational psychologists, who are focused more on academic testing than mental well-being, many are slipping through the net.

• • •

I'm relieved when James turns up again. He has been studying for his midterms. He has been trying to get out of the incel forums, to build a more hopeful life.

"Ever since this interview I've been noticing what people in the outside world are saying about incels," he messages me. "Like we're some cult trying to recruit as many followers into our fold as possible. But nobody in the outside world gets this unless you've been a part of the boards. You wanna know what happens when a fifteen-year-old boy comes onto the forums and posts, 'Hey, guys. Nobody at school likes me. No girl wants to date me'? People on the outside think we'd welcome that boy with open arms."

I think about this for a minute and realize he is right. It's true that I am fearful of a predatory manosphere, lying in wait to recruit any lonely, vulnerable young boy who happens to stroll past in cyberspace.

"But the fact of the matter is, we cuss him out," he tells me. "We tell him to leave. We tell him to try still."

"Why?" I ask.

"Because we don't want anyone to be like us. This fate of inceldom. Not because it's some special book club only the pompous and proud are allowed to enter, but because this fate is so fucking sad and depressing. Yeah, it's kinda hitting me a little now. But where else were we meant to go?"

James confides that sometimes, in his darker moments, he will go onto the incel forums and read the suicide notes that the guys sometimes leave. There is no real way of knowing how many of these young men follow through with their plan, but there are many of these notes.

"Now, you would think that these incels, based on the media, would say things like 'Oh, damn those women! If it wasn't for them, I'd so and so,'" he tells me. "But the fact of the matter is, all of them say the same thing. 'I want to be held. I want to be loved, I want to be touched. I want a future.' Those were their last words. Not woman hating."

I think back to Ian's misogyny, the repulsive sexism and violence and racism in incel spaces. I don't want to get too sucked into James's worldview.

"I kinda have a grim idea for you, if you want," he tells me. "If you wanna go a little deeper, there's a Reddit account that has pictures of plenty of the incels' suicide notes if you wanna read them?"

I'm not sure at all that I want to do this, but he sends me the link, and somehow before I know it, I am already scrolling through. In note after note, a young man, barely out of boyhood, describes his pain, his inability to go on when the "copes" stop working. He thanks his incel "brothers" and wishes them well on their own journeys.

The desperation is palpable, but so is the anguished sense of belonging and connection. In a deeply twisted way, the incels have found that sense of friendship and brotherhood that so many of the boys I had spoken to had been craving and were never quite able to access.

It makes me realize that the incel phenomenon is not an aberration, but perhaps the most extreme, but still logical, conclusion of many cultural, social, political, and parenting threads in boy culture, the strange blend of indulgence and neglect at the heart of male socialization.

These trends come together in their most terrifying expression in these groups, but their roots are deeper: a lack of nurturing for young boys, starting in early childhood; an unwillingness to listen to boys' feelings or teach them relational and social-emotional skills; a bombardment of glory seeking and hypermasculine hero narratives, which set up impossible expectations; a superonline culture, where boys can easily retreat into a screen-based world; an invisible epidemic of untreated mental health problems in young males; plus a deeply misogynistic society. Mix in some personal trauma and childhood bullying and the results can be both horrifying and tragic.

If we don't want boys to find their sense of belonging and intimacy in the manosphere, we urgently need to help them find it elsewhere.

• • •

My conversations with James and Ian stick with me for a long time, coagulating into a kind of sticky dread in the back of my mind. But at home, things are finally, slowly starting to get easier. A year since they were diagnosed, things are looking very different for our boys.

We had started Solly and Zephy on medication soon after the ADHD diagnoses. It took a few months of fiddling around to find the right drug and the right dosage, but when we finally do, it is transformative, both for them and for our family as a whole.

Almost overnight, Zephy goes from being hyperactive and emotionally dysregulated to being relaxed and focused and, often, mature. When he gets upset, he takes a few minutes in his room and calms himself down, instead of escalating into a three-hour rage. His new Ritalin-sponsored attention span has helped him throw himself into hobbies: speed cubing, piano lessons, playing the drums in a band called "The Bazonkers."

When school opens up after the pandemic, Zephy finds himself a new group of friends. They play soccer and basketball at recess, make endless penis jokes, talk about video games. The friendships are different from mine as a child, sure, but he is right in the thick of the third-grade social scene. He can still be wildly obstreperous, occasionally hyperactive, and it can take him an hour and a half to put his shoes on, but none of it feels pathological. With the ADHD treated, the signs of autism that we had seen seem to mostly melt away.

Solly is happier, too. He had always been prone to anxiety, to dark thoughts and spirals, but now these have loosened their grip on him. His moods even out and he becomes lighter in himself. He gets funny—not in a little kid way, but with a real, conscious wit, casually throwing in wry one-liners (although still with his fair share of "Poop! Heh, heh, heh" humor, too). He starts middle school and finds some equally idiosyncratic friends, who play chess every day in the library at lunchtime and share a million incomprehensible in-jokes. He has teenage mood swings, leaves his bedroom covered in old yogurt containers and wet towels, and yells that he hates us then apologizes wholeheartedly a few minutes later. He is usually great company—thoughtful, engaged, funny. Some days he still seems prone to neurodivergent hypersensitivity and becomes overwhelmed in a way that feels a little different from other kids of his age. Other days he just seems like any other quirky, tenderhearted preteen finding his way.

With Abe, it's really too early to tell whether his autism diagnosis will stick. He is sociable at preschool, playing happily with other children but equally happily by himself. Despite spending his entire life in the United States, he speaks with a full-blown English accent, seemingly drawn from a 1940s British wartime newsreel. He is obsessed with keys, driving us all to distraction with his once-every-five-minutes "What does this key open?" questions. On a special one-on-one day out with me, when I let him choose the activity, he chose a trip to an out-of-town lock store to buy a new padlock, followed by a manicure. He is way calmer than his brothers ever were and can sit patiently, without complaint, through an entire meal in a restaurant, and even a five-hour delay on a runway. He is painfully sweet, often empathetic, a tiny oddball, deeply normal. Is he autistic? Never. Rarely. Sometimes.

CHAPTER 7

"RAPE-CON"

My Uber driver and I are making small talk about the dehydration risks of the Colorado mountain air as we pull out of the airport.

"Last time I was out this way, I was pregnant," I tell him. "I'd gulp down a bottle of water and instantly be thirsty."

"What did you have? Boy or girl?" he asks.

"Boy."

"Oh, dear. That's a shame. Girls are much better," he tells me. "I have three boys and two girls. I much prefer the girls." I feel a familiar stab. I've heard so many variations of this basic sentiment, but people aren't usually quite so up-front.

"My boys are lovely," I counter, somewhat lamely.

"Oh, you only think that because you don't have girls. Boys can be sweet, but you should try girls, then you'll see. It's a whole different level."

We pull up outside the hotel and I wheel my suitcase to the reception desk, smarting with that ugly mix of defensiveness, disappointment, and shame that seeps through whenever someone lobs a #boymom pity bomb at me. I still give him five stars on the app though, because now he knows where I'm staying, and these are the minor self-protective measures that form the background noise of womanhood.

I'm out here for a conference and I'm already feeling conflicted and brittle. This is the annual weekend-long gathering for FACE, an organization that advocates for boys who have been accused of campus sexual assault. FACE stands, somewhat confusingly, for Families Advocating for Campus Equality. It is probably indicative of the political battle lines around this issue that I keep forgetting this, and instead my brain keeps defaulting to "Families *Against* Campus Equality." When I told my friends last night that I was headed to this conference, one of them started referring to the event as "Rape-Con." As a feminist of the #BelieveWomen school of thought, I feel like a traitor even being here.

Sexual assault is one of the defining political issues of our time, and as such, maybe one of the darkest parts of being a mother of boys. #MeToo had exposed sexual violence and harassment as deep, systemic fixtures of daily life. I was glad to see "Protect your daughters" evolve into "Educate your sons." It probably needed some tweaking around the edges, but it finally seemed as though we were starting to tell the right story about rape, to point the finger in the right direction.

Before this, the prevailing narrative had pitched women—sometimes with vicious misogyny, sometimes with a kind of disingenuous gallantry—as unreliable, untrustworthy, always somehow to blame. Now, after a couple of decades of activism, we had a new story, and we were just starting to breathe its air. We were finally holding men accountable, giving women not just credibility but full humanity. It was an exhilarating corrective, and I didn't want it threatened by anyone.

I had first heard about FACE via an article in *The New York Times* a few months before. The piece was factual and dry, in that old-school journalism way, which can sometimes feel as though in its precision impartiality, it leaves a major injustice unchallenged. The reporter had quoted a woman named Judith, the mom of a boy who had sex with a female student who was too drunk to consent. Even the phrase "had sex with" felt like a microaggression. Is it possible to "have sex" with a woman who is too drunk to consent? I wondered. Isn't that, by definition, rape?

"In my generation, what these girls are going through was

never considered assault," Judith told the journalist. "It was considered, 'I was stupid and I got embarrassed.' "

In my generation, too. I was a decade younger than Judith, but the misogynistic logic of my college years, back in the nineties, had been similar. The way we had thought—or rather hadn't thought much at all—about rape. I remembered all too well the atmospheric sexism, the assumed victim blaming, the constant pull toward self-doubt embedded in those words. "I was stupid and I got embarrassed."

My friend Rachel had been raped at a college party, though we didn't call it that at the time. She was drunk and had fallen asleep in the bedroom upstairs, waking up in the middle of the night to find the penis of the verbose boy from her Social Mores in Victorian England class inside her vagina. We had called this sex, too, back then. Still years away from #BelieveWomen, we didn't even have the consciousness, the vocabulary, the social permission to believe ourselves.

• • •

The FACE attendees are starting to gather in the bar in the lobby: a small handful of college-aged boys shuffling around in baseball caps and sweatshirts, and a much larger crowd of their mothers, petite, put-together white women in their fifties and sixties with coiffed blond bobs and jaunty scarves. A surprisingly large proportion of them have the same hairstyle as Betsy DeVos, Trump's former education secretary, who had become notorious for revoking Obama-era protections for survivors of sexual assault on college campuses.

It is a precondition of my being allowed to report on the conference that I am sworn to secrecy about its location. Cynthia Garrett, FACE's co-president, had told me earlier that several of the boys' families had been verbally abused and even threatened by feminist groups in the past, so they were being extra careful. I had bristled at this claim. The idea of rogue bands of feminists threatening middle-aged moms sounded so unlikely to me that I could feel myself getting defensive, wondering if this was a politically motivated exaggeration, a not-so-subtle dig at feminism itself.

Now I look around the lobby at these mothers and their sons. Each of them is intimately, inextricably connected with a young woman somewhere. A woman who woke up and cried and went to the Title IX office at her college and reported an assault. Who put herself through a drawn-out process of pain and bureaucratic invasiveness. Why are these mothers defending their sons, I wonder? Surely this kind of unquestioning support is part of the problem. No wonder some studies show that as many as 1 in 4 women are sexually assaulted during their college years, with this kind of enabling and indulgence going on in the background of their male peers' upbringings.

#BelieveWomen has been a heartfelt, if slightly un-nuanced response to centuries of women being disbelieved, ignored, and gaslighted. If it doesn't feel like an entirely neutral starting point for due process, then this overcorrection seems so trivial in comparison to the actual problem, which is sexual assault and the culture that encouraged it.

I had spent the previous night down an internet rabbit hole looking at examples of rape and rape culture on college campuses. They weren't hard to find: stories of major colleges turning a blind eye to sexual assault, in particular when the accusations involved high-value male students, like college athletes; frat-boy rituals that treated sexual violence as a hilarious punch line. I had read a leaked series of minutes from the weekly meetings of one fraternity—a snapshot of a group of entitled, oblivious male students and what they talked about when no girls or adults were around.

Disgusted, I had read through page after page of jokes about "rape attics," "rape tunnels," and even worse. The minutes shuttled between sex and objectification and assault and back to sex again, all part of the same horrifying misogynistic soup. I had listened to a recording of a group of drunk fraternity brothers guffawing and singing a truly chilling song about raping a woman until she dies and then exhuming her body to rape her again. "We buried her in a long pine box, she died from sucking too many cocks. . . . We dig her up every now and again, we fucked her once and we'll fuck her again, yo ho, yo ho, yo ho."[1]

In this climate, "false accusations" feels like a badge of bad faith—the All Lives Matter of gender relations, yet another bait and switch cooked up to discredit women. Sure, men are occasionally falsely accused of sexual assault. Even activist groups admit that there is a false reporting rate of somewhere between 2 and 10 percent.[2] But in a way, so what? Women's grip on equality still feels way too fragile to allow that story to take hold as any kind of major, widespread concern.

Besides, this is political. If any debate over the last few years has come to sum up the divide between right and left, rape versus false accusation is it. As president, Donald Trump—a man with multiple credible accusations of sexual assault against him, who had bragged about "grabbing women by the pussy"—positioned men as the real victims of #MeToo and himself as their defender.

"It's a very scary time for young men in America," he said. "You could be somebody that was perfect your entire life . . . and somebody could accuse you of something and you are automatically guilty." His son, Donald Trump Jr., chimed in, claiming that he feared more that his own sons might be falsely accused of rape than that his daughters might actually *be* raped.

Individual cases were litigated in the public imagination along political lines. Supreme Court nominee Brett Kavanaugh was accused of raping his classmate Christine Blasey Ford at a party in high school. It was almost unthinkable that a liberal could believe Kavanaugh, or a conservative, Blasey Ford, and the same ideological split lurked in the background of every case of sexual assault.

This was tribal and we had picked sides: on one side, the entire feminist movement; on the other, Donald Trump and a bunch of frat boys guffawing about their rape attic. Left versus right. Or rather—at least in my own demoralized, #MeToo battered brain—left versus wrong.

It is in this fighting frame of mind that I pick up my name

badge and enter the throng of Betsy DeVoses sipping wine in the lobby. I don't yet know that this conference will end up seriously shaking my worldview, challenging what I thought I knew about left and right, rape and consent, truth and perspective. And how we come to believe what we believe.

• • •

Someone hands me a glass of white wine, and I sit down at a table with a small group of moms, next to a woman who introduces herself as Diane. She smiles at me warmly, her face kind and tired. I tell her that I am writing about the conference and like a tightly coiled spring, she launches straight into her story.

Her younger son, Rob, had been away at college for barely a week during his freshman year, when he called her while she was in the grocery store, picking out laundry detergent. "He said, 'Mom, something's happened and I think it's really bad. This girl has accused me of raping her.' "

Rob told Diane that he was walking into class when two police officers stopped him outside the door and told him that they needed to bring him into the city police station for questioning.

"He's like, 'Are you sure you have the right kid?' He thought they might have meant his brother; his older brother was at the same college and was always in trouble. But they said, 'Oh yes, we have the right kid.' He told them, 'I can't miss this class,' and they just said, 'Too bad, you're coming with us.' "

According to Rob's version of events, a few days earlier, during rush week—the annual ritual at the beginning of the new school year, when fraternities and sororities recruit new freshman members—he had been out at a bar at an informal event organized by the fraternity he was hoping to pledge. After a few drinks, he and a few other students had gone back to his older brother's off-campus apartment to sober up before returning to their dorms, hoping to avoid the strict penalties for students found drunk on college property.

After a while, everyone had peeled off from the group and

headed home, except for Rob and a freshman girl who had been at another event at the same bar, where a handful of sororities had also been recruiting. In Rob's telling, the girl started flirting with him and kissing him, and eventually she whispered in his ear, "I want to fuck you."

Excited, he went upstairs to get a condom, and they had brief, awkward sex. Rob ejaculated quickly, and the girl laughed, saying, "Well, that's embarrassing." Rob offered to walk her back to her dorm, but she said no. So they went their separate ways, and he walked the two blocks back to campus alone. A few days later, she went to the police and reported the incident as a rape.

As Diane is talking, I find myself struggling to make sense of my own reaction. I can feel myself pushing back internally. My entire mental framework for assessing who is telling the truth in a story such as this is heavily weighted toward believing the woman, barely allowing for the possibility that Rob could be innocent. There had to be more to it.

"Why would she have done that?" I ask.

"We found out much later from our attorney that she had gone to the ladies' room, and the condom had fallen out of her," says Diane. "I didn't know that was even a thing. We think she got worried she might have been pregnant. She was from a very, very religious family. She needed a way to explain why she had had sex.

"Also, we think the other part of it is, remember the kids are rushing the fraternities and the sororities. And there is an unspoken rule in the sorority part of Greek life that girls don't just pull down their panties during rush because they might be proven to be fast, or a slut, and that would not be a proper girl for the sorority."

I think about the many layers of sexism in what Diane is telling me. The misogyny in the assumption that a woman might lie about being raped is trumped only by the misogyny that makes that woman's consensual sexuality so unacceptable that she would need to lie about being raped.

The police did not arrest or charge Rob, and he was free to go back to school and attend classes. But right before Christmas, he got a letter telling him that he must appear before a grand jury to determine whether there was probable cause that he had committed an offense.

The grand jury did not indict Rob and no charges or arrests were made. The family were hugely relieved and thought that was the end of it. But then, after spring break, more than eight months after the incident, he received a letter from the dean's office at the college saying he had been accused of sexual assault and that he would be investigated under the school's Title IX policy.

On most college campuses, sexual assault falls under Title IX, the 1972 law that prohibits any educational institution that receives federal funds from discriminating on the basis of gender. Under the law, colleges and universities are responsible for investigating all reports of sexual violence and making any necessary accommodations for student survivors to be able to access their education without fear. The school would appoint an investigator, who would gather evidence from all sides and then make a verdict on whether or not the assault happened.

"It was like having the sword of Damocles hanging over his head," says Diane. "It was horrible."

After sixty days, Rob received a letter stating that he had been found "not responsible" for the sexual assault, the Title IX equivalent of a not-guilty verdict.

The fallout from all this had dominated his freshman year, but Rob was insistent he would return to school for his sophomore year. "I've done nothing wrong and they know it," he told his mom. "Why wouldn't I go back?" But just a few days after school got out for the summer, he received another letter. Despite having already found him officially not responsible, the school was going to do another investigation, this time under a different system: their student code of conduct.

"We had a whole new investigation, as if the first one never happened," says Diane. "They couldn't get him under the Title IX policy. So they decided to go after him again. They told him he had to attend a meeting with the dean and that if he did not acknowledge his actions or take ownership, there would be another hearing on it."

This felt like a double bind to Rob. Either own up to a crime that he believed he did not commit or face another grueling investigation. Rob was unwilling to say he was guilty. And so the school decided to proceed with a second hearing, and a date was set for the middle of summer break.

"We only got three or four days' notice," says Diane. "And it was a holiday weekend, so you are paying higher fares and it's horribly expensive. But we got our ducks in a row, we got on a plane, and we got down there. Only when we got there, the dean says, 'Sorry, we have to reschedule. The girl can't make it.' "

A second hearing date was scheduled, and the family flew down again—more expensive plane tickets. And then more roadblocks followed. In accordance with their policy, the school had given Rob an adviser for the process, who was supposed to give him a packet of information, outlining the allegations against him and the evidence for them. But when he arrived at the hearing, the adviser told him he had none of that available. Rob was not given access to any of the evidence against him. He couldn't see the girl's report to the school and, because he had never been charged with a crime, he was also not allowed to read her original police report.

Despite all the setbacks and misinformation, after a second hearing, Rob was again found not responsible for what was effectively the third time. But the process had taken its toll.

"And those processes and the way he was handled," Diane tells me. "It was horrible. He was so traumatized he could barely get off the sofa. He was diagnosed with PTSD and anxiety, just anticipating what's going to happen to him by people who are in control of him and dumping him."

Rob sank into a deep depression. Although his friends at school stood by him, he found himself unable to socialize. "He was not well, emotionally and psychologically," Diane tells me. "His friends believed him, but he ended up losing them all anyway because he was so unfun—he was just so emotionally ill. I think, really, the bottom line is to have people accuse you of something that you just didn't do. In his mind it was worse than murder."

My thoughts flit to my own boys. The night before I came here, Abe had had a nightmare and had called out for me from his bed, still half asleep. "Do you know what a nightmare is, Mommy?" he asked me, a sleepy preschool philosopher. "It's when a train gets stuck in a tunnel and it can't get out." I climbed into bed with him, still able to make things right, just by my presence. He threw a hot little arm around my neck and fell straight back to sleep.

What would I believe, what I would do, if in fifteen years, he were to call me in tears from a dorm room somewhere to tell me he was being investigated for sexual assault? Would I have the strength to disbelieve him? As a feminist, would I be obliged to? I look around at the group of women gathered at our small table, listening to Diane tell her story, nodding along in recognition. They are all mothers of beloved sons, like me. Politically, these are not my people, but suddenly, I feel an affinity with them.

"You see a lot of this is about crazy girls," says Diane, and they lose me again.

• • •

In 2011, bolstered by a spate of surveys and media reports and high-profile cases that suggested there was an epidemic of sexual assault on college campuses, and that universities were consistently failing to tackle it or to listen to survivors, the Obama administration took action. It issued a new set of guidelines for how colleges should handle accusations, promising tougher penalties for those that did not comply. The administration sent out a letter to every college in the country that would fall under the new rules. This letter became known to both activist supporters and critics as the "Dear Colleague" letter.

"The statistics on sexual violence are both deeply troubling and a call to action for the nation," the letter read. "A report prepared for the National Institute of Justice found that about 1 in 5 women are victims of completed or attempted sexual assault while in college. . . . The sexual harassment of students, including sexual violence, interferes with students' right to receive an education free from discrimination."

As well as streamlining investigation and reporting procedures, the new guidelines mandated that colleges must start using a new, lower standard for determining guilt. Whereas previously there needed to be "clear and convincing evidence" that sexual harassment or violence had taken place for an accused student to be found responsible, now the standard would be changed to "the preponderance of the evidence." This meant that colleges were now required to find a student responsible for sexual assault if there was a 50.1 percent or more likelihood that it happened, a standard now known colloquially as "50 percent and a feather."

All this sent a clear signal that the administration was listening to women. It was taking the problem of sexual assault seriously and communicating to colleges that they were no longer allowed to turn a blind eye or let these acts of violence slide.

The letter was no showpiece; the Obama administration enforced the guidelines vigorously. Colleges hired Title IX coordinators to oversee investigations and spent millions of dollars establishing assault prevention programs and overhauling reporting and investigation procedures.

The cause became highly political. President Trump revoked these new protections for accusers, and feminist groups and survivors' organizations, as well as left-leaning politicians, pushed back strongly. Biden's administration then restored most of the Obama rules, and the battle continued, each side fighting for control not just of the procedures, but of the narrative itself.

• • •

"What do you think of Trump?" asks a heavyset Midwestern dad the next morning at breakfast, gripping an absurdly tiny coffee cup in his meaty hand.

"I like him," says Cynthia, FACE's director. The other parents at our table nod approvingly.

I dodge the question. "Do you see families from across the political spectrum?" I ask instead.

Another mom, who has introduced herself as Linda, steps in to answer. She had already told me the night before that her son was expelled in his freshman year of college, when a girl accused him of sexually assaulting her after what Linda said he had believed to be consensual drunk sex.

"Have you ever heard of cognitive dissonance?" Linda asks me now.

I nod. I had researched cognitive dissonance, the phenomenon whereby our brains try to debunk or avoid information that contradicts our own deeply held beliefs, at various times for my work.

"When we get liberal families coming to us there is terrible cognitive dissonance," says Linda. "They can't believe their own party has done this to them, and they drift away from us. So most of our families are conservative."

• • •

Cognitive dissonance is a reasonable description of my own state of mind as I talk to Frank, one of the few dads attending the conference alone. He is blustery and formal, bristling with dates and facts and policy specifics. His son, Frank Jr., a Latino boy with a dual diagnosis of ADHD and a language disability, was accused of raping an unconscious girl after they had both been drinking heavily at a fraternity event at a bar. Frank Sr., an alumnus of both the college and the same fraternity, had received a call from the fraternity's president telling him that his son had been accused of sexual assault and warning him there was going to be a Title IX investigation.

"My initial response was 'Send him to the dogs,'" Frank tells me. "If he did this, he deserves it." But when he got hold of his son on the phone, Frank Jr. had a different perspective on what happened. He told his dad that the only time he and the girl had

had any form of sexual contact, it had been she who initiated it and he who had been semiconscious. He said they had been in the backseat of his car together after a night of drinking. She had removed his pants and tried to perform oral sex on him as he flitted in and out of consciousness. But a combination of alcohol and the Adderall that he was taking for his ADHD prevented him from maintaining an erection, and she had given up.

Frank Jr. and the girl agreed that this is how the first part of the night happened; she did not dispute his version of events up to this point. It was their accounts of what happened next that diverged. In Frank Jr.'s version, the pair had gone back to his fraternity house, he had passed out drunk on his bed, and she had left. But in her version of events, when they got to Frank Jr.'s dorm room, she was the one who passed out, unconscious—on a beanbag on the floor—and he had raped her.

Later witness testimony appeared to corroborate his version, with other fraternity members saying that she had visited their rooms after leaving, both apparently unharmed, and within a timescale that didn't allow for an assault to have taken place.

After talking to his son, Frank called the dean of students at the college and made the counterclaim that it was actually his son who was the victim of sexual assault. He referred to the earlier part of the night, in the backseat of the car, when the girl had performed oral sex on Frank Jr. when he was semiconscious and too drunk to consent. Frank argued that because Title IX rules apply to both men and women, a separate investigation should be launched into the assault of his son. The dean refused on the spot, telling Frank that he believed this was a retaliatory move, and if his son were to pursue it, there would be repercussions for him.

I'm momentarily stumped by Frank's move and don't know what to make of it. Technically he is right. Title IX does apply to both men and women, and of course, boys can be sexually assaulted too (boys account for about 1 in 6 victims of sexual assault). But still. As Frank is telling me the story, I can feel myself mentally pushing back, sympathizing with the dean's view.

"So do you feel as though your son actually was sexually assaulted in this situation?" I ask Frank. "Or was this more a tactic to get him out of trouble?"

"Clearly he was," says Frank. "He was passed out, he couldn't consent."

I push. "But would he ever have framed it that way if he wasn't being accused himself? Would he have ever gone to the office and reported it as an assault?"

"I don't know," says Frank. "We'll never know that. But it's really irrelevant. Once the university learned that he was sexually assaulted, they had a legal obligation to investigate."

I can't help feeling as though launching a full investigation into that incident as a sexual assault somehow trivializes the problem of gendered violence. I don't envy the dean's position, when, after a young woman came in to tell him that she had been raped, her accused rapist had claimed that it was actually he who was the victim. I can see how Frank's counterclaim of assault seemed retaliatory, invoking a technicality and willfully ignoring the structural (and physical) power imbalances in a situation, the wider injustices at play.

The "Who's raping whom?" conundrum sounds like an ad absurdum example from a college philosophy class, but it turns out that Frank's son's case was not an outlier. It has become an increasingly popular tactic among Title IX lawyers defending male students accused of assaulting a young woman after a drunken or murky sexual encounter, to make a counterclaim that the boy was himself assaulted. As one lawyer attending the FACE conference whispers to me later off the record, "It can become about who runs to the Title IX office first the morning after."

Frank's attempt to launch a counterinvestigation never got off the ground, but the investigation into the girl's accusation against his son gained momentum. Frank believes that there was a series of due process violations in both the investigation and the hearing. He gives me a long list of these, including that his son was forbidden from presenting the testimony of his key witnesses; that evidence was suppressed; that his son did not get equal speaking time during the hearing; and that no accommodations were made for his language disability.

There was no DNA evidence or a hospital report in the case. The girl had gone to the hospital and the nurse there had asked her to save her underwear in a bag. But the girl had left the hospital before they could examine her or administer a rape kit. The university claimed it did not have the capacity to test the girl's underwear, and she did not go to the police or press criminal charges. Without hard evidence either way, the school's investigation found Frank Jr. responsible for sexual assault, and he was expelled.

"The investigator and the hearing officer both said there's no evidence that a sexual assault occurred on her," Frank tells me. "They had to make credibility determinations. So the investigator determined that she is more credible than he is. Well, she's this white girl who's articulate and cute. My son is Hispanic, a little overweight, with a full beard. He has language-based learning disabilities and stumbles over his words. How do you think he is going to present?"

"So you think there was a racial element to this?" I ask.

"I do, I think it's bias," he replies. "Everyone in the process was white. And we're not ones to play the race card. We have never done that. But when you look back, there probably was a bias there. There was no evidence, but the hearing officer said, 'Clearly he touched her somewhere.' Well, no, it's not clear. It's not clear at all."

• • •

Frank is not the only one raising concern about the potential for racial bias in these types of campus sexual assault cases. When hard evidence is lacking, alcohol is involved, and recollections are fuzzy, colleges and universities have to decide whose story, whose perspective, and whose "facts" are valid. At some basic level, they are adjudicating not just which individual human, but also which social category of human, is to be trusted. Historically, women have not fared well in these battles of credibility, and as a feminist, I have always fought hard against this form of subtle, legally sanctioned gaslighting. But race is also an important component, and narratives involving race and gender play out in complex ways in these kinds of cases. The racist trope of a predatory Black man preying on an innocent white woman is an old American story, and one that throughout history—*To Kill a Mockingbird*–style—has led to some egregious false accusations and violent consequences.

It's almost impossible to get any hard data on how race plays into these Title IX investigations. The Office for Civil Rights oversees how colleges and universities respond to sexual assault allegations, but it does not require them to collect any data on the race of either the accused or the accuser. So it's not surprising that experts in the field, and those involved in adjudicating these kinds of cases, are increasingly voicing concerns about the subtle racist narratives that are playing out in the adjudication process.

In an article for the *Harvard Law Review,* Janet Halley, a feminist and professor at Harvard Law School, writes, "American racial history is laced with vendetta-like scandals in which Black men are accused of sexually assaulting white women that become reverse scandals when it is revealed that the accused men were not wrongdoers at all. . . . The general social disadvantage that Black men continue to carry in our culture can make it easier for everyone in the adjudicative process to put the blame on them. . . . Case after Harvard case that has come to my attention, including several in which I have played some advocacy or adjudication role, has involved Black male respondents."[3]

Another Harvard Law professor, Jeannie Suk Gersen, who has written extensively about due process issues in campus rape cases, echoed Halley's concerns in an article for the *New Yorker*. She had spoken to various administrators and faculty members who work on sexual misconduct cases, and they had told her that "most of the complaints they see are against minorities."

This is not true of the FACE crowd, however, which, Frank's

son aside, is almost entirely made up of upper middle class white boys and their conservative families. And I am still trying to figure out how to assess the stories they are telling me.

Listening to them, I find myself scrambling to construct some kind of mental framework that squares what they are saying with my own basic worldview. Are their sons lying, or at least distorting the truth, to serve their own ends? Tweak a tiny factoid here, a perspective or motivation there, and suddenly a situation can look very different. Would I hear something very different if I talked to the girls in these stories? Or are the boys' accounts accurate, but their cases just bizarre outliers, unfortunate for sure, but not indicative of anything much more systemic than bad luck?

After breakfast, we wander into the large hotel conference room, laid out wedding style, with several round tables and a podium at the front. I find a seat next to Cynthia, FACE's director. She tells me that we are about to begin a family sharing session, in which people will stand up and tell their personal stories to the group.

One by one, around twenty parents of college-aged boys—mainly mothers, but a handful of fathers—take the microphone and recount their sons' experiences, their voices cracking as they talk.

The stories themselves are remarkably similar, and by now I am familiar with the format. With minimal variation, a typical account goes something like this: Seemingly out of the blue, the boy gets a letter from the school's Title IX office, or the equivalent, telling him he has been accused of sexual assault. This communication often provides no further details about which incident it refers to. Usually the boy can guess. Sometimes he is baffled. He traces it back to some drunk sex, which he believed at the time to be consensual. Sometimes he has text messages from the girl or other evidence to back up this belief, but often he has little to go on.

He is then launched into a protracted Title IX investigation, which can drag on for several months, or with appeals, even years. While the investigation is in progress, the boy is sometimes suspended from school. If he is not, he is often subject to verbal and occasionally physical attacks on campus. His friends disown him, fellow students shout "rapist!" at him in the hallways.

The investigation process itself is confounding and punitive. He doesn't get the chance to see the evidence against him until the hearing itself, or to fully prepare his case. There is a single investigator who both gathers the evidence and makes the determination, with no other voices in the mix. Often this person is a sexual assault advocate or activist, working from a starting point of #BelieveWomen, which, at least in his view, biases the investigation against him from the outset.

If his parents can afford it, he engages a lawyer, but the lawyer is often not allowed to speak at the hearing itself. The hearing is typically short, and he doesn't get the chance to ask the questions he wants to ask, to put his case in a manner he sees as fair. He is not allowed to cross-examine the girl or challenge her account. Over and over, the families claim their sons did not receive due process and were assumed to be guilty from the start. The verdicts themselves are wildly inconsistent.

Sometimes there are also parallel criminal proceedings. In almost all of these cases, the boy is found not guilty in criminal court, or the case is thrown out. There is rarely enough evidence to convict him of any crime by the higher standards of the criminal justice system, which must find him guilty "beyond reasonable doubt." This leads to the bizarre circumstance in which he is found responsible by his university for a crime second only to murder in severity, but never convicted or even tried for the same offense in criminal court. Whether he is found responsible or not responsible in the university proceedings, his reputation and his self-esteem are often shattered. In each of the stories I hear today, without exception, he becomes severely depressed.

"Pretty much every one of our kids has said they have considered suicide," Cynthia whispers in my ear.

One after another the moms stand up, starting their stories with the words "My son was accused." At first, I saw this passive-voice grammatical construct as a refusal to take responsibility, a kind of corporate-style "Mistakes were made" type of obfuscation. Now I am wondering if it is actually a way of capturing a lived experience that had its own momentum, its own runaway-train logic, beyond anyone's active control.

The stories make for scary listening. But still, I can't shake the feeling that there has to be more to all this. These parents have such incentive to see their sons in the best possible light. It just doesn't seem possible that all these boys were so squeaky clean, that the system is so stacked against them, and that these allegations really just came out of thin air.

"Do you ever get cases where the boy is guilty?" I ask Cynthia.

"You know, sometimes someone will call us with a story, and I will think that the boy is creepy or that he crossed a line," she tells me. "But we believe in due process, guilty or innocent."

Due process. I am feeling disorientated now. How did we get to the point where that was a right-wing cause? However tempting it is to correct the narrative en masse for the horrifying history of violence and gaslighting women have endured, since when did it become a progressive position to argue that anyone—no matter how white or male or privileged—should not receive due process, a fair hearing?

• • •

There are only a handful of boys at the conference, probably less than five: one nervous, slightly sweaty teenager in a baseball cap at the breakfast buffet with his mom, levering up slices of processed cheese from a platter in the chiller cabinet; a gangly, almost painfully polite young man with a copy of the French philosopher Simone Weil's book *Gravity and Grace* under his arm; and a couple of good-looking jocks, whom I'd seen knocking back beers at the hotel bar the night before, firing out alpha male pheromones. I might have known any of them in college myself when I was their age. Universities just seem to have a set number of vacancies for the same basic student archetypes, which they keep refilling over and over across the years, with only the faces changing.

Back in the conference room, the two young jocks I'd seen at the bar last night sidle in through the back door. They have changed clothes and are now wearing matching sweatshirts with the words WHITE MALE emblazoned on the front and bright red MAGA hats. They hover in the back of the room, suddenly menacing.

Cynthia looks over at me and whispers in my ear, "This issue drove a lot of people to Trump."

Then one of the WHITE MALE sweatshirt boys steps up to the podium and taps on the microphone. The room goes quiet.

"I'd like to introduce our next speaker, Professor Aya Gruber. She is a law professor at Colorado University, winner of multiple awards, and an intersectional feminist."

The words "intersectional feminist" sound profoundly incongruous coming out this boy's mouth, like a preschooler discussing his crypto portfolio, or your grandmother talking about her OnlyFans account. But for me they have a strange effect. I realize that throughout the weekend, until now, when someone was speaking, no matter how traumatizing their experience or convincing their words, I have been listening with a kind of tight skepticism, my brain on hyperalert, mining for flaws and inconsistencies in what they were saying. A suspicious little metronome tapped in the back of my mind with an insistent "Can you really be trusted?" and "Surely there must be more to it," and "You must have done *something*." Perhaps this is a similar phenomenon to whatever happens in the brain of a conservative when a woman says that she has been raped. "How can I be sure you aren't lying?" and "It can't have been *that* bad," and "What did you do to provoke this?"

Then this one phrase, "intersectional feminist," so unmistakably the language of the left, in all its invoking of the invisible power imbalances hovering in the background of every human encounter, tweaks some kind of tribal instinct in me. The phrase feels like a secret handshake, a signal telling me that this is someone I can trust to tell me the truth. It gives me permission to relax and listen with an open mind. I'm surprised at the strength of this effect as Gruber walks up to the microphone, tiny and chic in a red blazer and exquisitely cut black pants.

• • •

Aya Gruber is one of a small but growing band of feminist scholars from the left who are pushing back against the campus antirape activist movement, and what they see as a mass failure of due process which it has provoked. In a 2016 essay for the *Colorado Law Review,* she wrote:

> Antirape activism is a cultural juggernaut that has heralded a new era of discipline . . . on campus. This essay is critical of many facets of the phenomenon, and I write it with a sense of trepidation, in a climate where being a good feminist—or anything other than a raging misogynist—necessitates supporting expansive rape definitions, eschewing due process, and favoring swift punitive action.

Gruber's work focuses on a phenomenon called *carceral feminism,* which is the idea that in an attempt to tackle gendered violence, feminists are agitating for an ever more illiberal justice system. When it comes to sexual assault, progressives who would normally be critical of authoritarian punishment, police overreach, and mass incarceration, are "switching sides" in order to be better feminists.

"They're going to take that megaphone and shout about it and call these guys rapists and say, 'They should do life in prison.' And they think that this is a progressive stance," Gruber tells me when I talk to her later. "That's the difference between me and a lot of feminists. They don't think it's complicated. They think it's simple."

Gruber sees this trend as being particularly acute and problematic on college campuses, driven by a widespread belief that there is a mass epidemic of sexual assault in universities. This idea was bolstered by the statistics and surveys that suggested that 1 in 5 or 1 in 4 female students will be raped or assaulted during their college years.

"That was the narrative a lot of the activism was based on," Gruber tells me. "That we need a make-up punishment system for these guys to keep us safe."

But, she points out, dig a little deeper and these statistics are somewhat misleading.

The 1 in 4 figure, for example, can be traced back to a 2014 survey by the Association of American Universities, which includes in its definition of sexual assault any form of unwanted sexual contact, including touching over clothes and sudden kissing, even when the "victim" of the action did not herself define what happened as an assault.

Gruber points out that these studies stand in stark contrast to another survey, by the Department of Justice, which is almost never mentioned by activist groups, that used a narrower definition of sexual assault: the not wholly unreasonable sounding "forced or coerced to engage in unwanted sexual activity." Using this definition, the study put the rape and sexual assault rate for college students at a significantly less horrifying sounding 6 in 1,000.

But when it comes to adjudicating sexual assault accusations, Title IX offices are usually working with much broader, and often inconsistent, definitions of sexual assault. In a bid to tackle the more subtle forms of coercion, the term has expanded to the point where it can now potentially encompass almost any form of drunken, icky, or unfulfilling sex.

For instance, the idea that drunk students cannot consent to sex is now written into many college Title IX codes and policies. The charge of "rape by intoxication" exists in criminal law too, but in practice the bar for a conviction is very high. But in Title IX proceedings it has come to potentially encompass any sex that students have while drunk or otherwise intoxicated. These policies were presumably meant to catch the Brock Turner–type cases—the Stanford athlete who raped an unconscious girl behind a dumpster. But taken to the letter, this definition would make me, and probably the majority of people who ever had sex in college, into rapists. It can often leave college administrators trying to parse out the blurry intricacies and complicated feelings of a night of bad sex, in which both parties were drunk.

This is just one way in which the definition of what can be considered a sexual assault has incrementally expanded. In most universities now as well as in several U.S. legal jurisdictions, the standard is now something called *affirmative consent,* meaning that consent in any sexual encounter should be explicitly stated and not just implied, and that consent should be freely given and enthusiastic, rather than grudging or coerced.

Enthusiastic consent is clearly a cultural norm that we should be teaching in sex education for kids of all genders. Many legal experts also argue that affirmative consent can work well in the criminal justice system where there are stronger due process protections in place for the accused. But in the college setting, the ambiguities can be a particular minefield.

As Gruber tells me, the problem with affirmative consent is that there is no official or legal definition of what it actually means in practice, or of how anyone can know for sure if they have obtained it. There is no agreement as to what form of words or set of actions might count as consenting, and the parameters are constantly shifting.

The vast majority of the time, this isn't a problem. Most sex is, of course, uncontested and few people want a college bureaucracy or government agency mandating a set script for them to use in the bedroom. The absence of set rules for what exactly constitutes affirmative consent only matters when there is a dispute—when wires get crossed, signals get missed, emotions are messy, and especially, when alcohol or drugs are involved.

By some definitions of affirmative consent, only a verbal "yes" is good enough; nonverbal signals, no matter how enthusiastic or explicit, don't qualify. But as Gruber points out, this requirement that both parties need to explicitly say the word "yes" in order for sex to be legal, would make a lot of consensual sex that people have every day into a crime.

Even an enthusiastic "yes" (or yes! yes! *yes!*) isn't necessarily enough to qualify as consent, because, quite rightly, under these codes, consent needs to be ongoing and can be withdrawn at any time. And while by many definitions, the consent itself must be expressed verbally, withdrawing consent, in theory, doesn't have to be. If consent is withdrawn nonverbally, it might well be unclear, especially to an inexperienced teenager, when someone has changed their mind.

Asking for consent repeatedly throughout sex seems like the obvious answer, but boys are still operating under significant social pressure to come off as confident and masculine and not hesitant or weak, and often fear that the "Is this okay? Is this okay?" guy invites ridicule. It's also, I am shocked to hear, not a foolproof strategy. According to Gruber, in some cases, asking too many times to escalate the sex can even be seen as a form of coercion in itself.

"Affirmative consent is extremely fraught terrain," says Gruber. "There are so many contradictory messages. This idea that you are either a rapist or you're not—it doesn't cover the complexity of the modern sexual landscape. It's not that women lie or they don't lie. Human beings behave in messy, complex ways."

Across the board, Gruber argues that the changing culture around sexual assault and consent draws on old sexist tropes and paradoxically can end up reinforcing regressive gender norms.

"In one sense millennial feminists are trying to upend this culture, where women and men have totally different relationships to sex and sexuality," she tells me. "Where men are pursuers who always want sex and women are gatekeepers who are ruined by sex. But their very program relies on maintaining these norms."

Gruber also echoes others' concerns about racial and social bias. She reiterates the idea that when a legal system starts to overreach, it is usually the poorest and most marginalized, and in this case, particularly boys of color, who are the most affected.

"When you use that broad of a brush, it makes a lot of things criminal," she tells me. "And the people who end up getting ensnared in the system are not always the right people. It's either totally random and idiosyncratic or it's marginalized people."

It's clear from talking to Gruber that this topic is confusing even for top legal scholars to navigate. It occurs to me how impossible it must feel for teenage boys, who, since birth, have generally received miserably inadequate training in the subtleties of human social and emotional dynamics. They are told on the one hand, that they need to be masculine and domineering and confident, and on the other, that if they overstep by the tiniest smidge, they will ruin someone's life.

"In general, it's such a bad model of creating a healthy relationship with sexuality for teens and young adults," Gruber says. "Sex is now a totally dangerous and fraught proposition for both men and women. For women it's caught up in all these old tropes of ruination, and traumatized women and women's adversity to sex. And for men it's bringing the hammer down, and punishments, and sexual shamings. It just feels so freaking unhealthy to me, and ultimately, it is so tribal and just lacking in empathy for everybody else.

"We have this crisis of masculinity that's ruining our country, and you think it helps things to have this top-down authoritarian system? What's it doing? Remember these are *boys*. Their political identities are being formed. And, you know, I really wonder how we're forming these identities."

• • •

The MAGA hat boys in the WHITE MALE sweatshirts seem like they might be a good example of Gruber's point about how this issue is shaping boys' political identities. As the conference is drawing to a close, I pull one of them aside. On closer inspection his "MAGA" hat actually says, MADE YOU LOOK AGAIN.

Mark is surprisingly thoughtful when we sit down to talk. He tells me that the experience of being accused of sexual assault in college radically changed his politics. In his freshman year, before the accusation, he had actually been a liberal activist. "I volunteered on Bernie Sanders's campaign," he tells me. "I probably would have said 'Believe all women' before this."

His story by now feels familiar. A girl accused him of raping her on a residential trip for an academic club they both belonged to. There were several witnesses who backed him up, and a school investigation found him not responsible. But, as in many other stories I had now heard, the school insisted on a full second investigation and hearing, in which they reversed their decision and found him responsible.

In the second investigation, Mark felt as though the school was out to prove he was guilty from the start. They didn't listen to key witness testimony, and he was forbidden from presenting certain pieces of evidence, including the fact that his accuser was taking an antidepressant that in rare cases can cause hallucinations.

Mark was suspended from school for three years while the process was ongoing. And although he was eventually allowed to graduate (something he believes to be a bizarrely unjustifiable decision, given that he was eventually found responsible for rape), he had become deeply depressed and traumatized by the process.

Mark brought a lawsuit against the university, one of several hundred suits brought by male students accused of sexual assault against their universities since the new Title IX rules were introduced.[4] He won. In the state court decision in his lawsuit, a lengthy document outlining dozens of violations of due process, the judge wrote, "Here, a university held a hearing to determine whether a student violated its student code of conduct. Noticeably absent was even a semblance of due process."

Mark was awarded a six-figure settlement, but the money barely covered his legal costs. He was diagnosed with PTSD and depression. The whole experience radicalized him, dramatically moving his politics and belief system to the right.

"It was a kind of political transformation," he tells me. "But it was actually so much more than that. It was a kind of spiritual, epistemological transformation of just realizing that so many things I had taken for granted were not actually true."

I look down at Mark's WHITE MALE sweatshirt. "What do you think about feminism and feminists now?" I ask him.

"I think that their policies are misguided and contribute to a lot of real-world suffering," he says, his voice tight. "I find their ideas to be evil."

My head is spinning as I head back to my room to collect my things, ready for my flight home. Is there something, however twisted, in the victimhood narrative of men on the right? Are we radicalizing boys into ideologies of hate? I never thought I would ask the question, but has the culture of #MeToo gone too far?

I press the button to call the elevator, and the door opens to reveal two men. They are in their forties, wearing suits, business travelers, already a little tipsy from the bar. "Going up?" one of them asks me. "Going down," I say.

The man grabs his crotch. "Oh yeah?" he asks lewdly, cueing up what is clearly a favorite line. "Go down on me."

• • •

I leave the FACE conference feeling deeply uneasy. How can we tackle the problem of sexual assault and take women seriously while still giving men and boys a fair hearing?

I keep thinking about my conversation with Aya Gruber: "It just feels so freaking unhealthy." How did we get to a point in which the dominant narrative around sex has become one of abuse, of old sexist tropes, ruination, and shaming rather than joy, pleasure, and connection?

As a society we are finally getting a handle on trauma, and the sneaky ways it can show up in relationships, but we are less comfortable with pleasure—with eroticism and togetherness and play. It doesn't seem like a good environment for developing a healthy sexuality, let alone a generous and connected approach to relationships and intimacy.

This scares me. Solly is twelve now, just starting middle school, and Zephy is not far behind. This is the climate in which they will learn about sex and relationships, form their early sexual identities, have their first sexual experiences.

Like any terrified feminist mom, I have already crowbarred the word *consent* into approximately one million conversations about wrestling and kissing, and whether it's okay to say "no" to hugging grandma. I have talked to the boys endlessly about respect and bodily autonomy, all with a slight undertone of panic. These conversations are crucial. Sexual assault and harassment are still frighteningly common, including for teenagers.

But I also want my sons to have a story around sex that is centered in more than just harm, to have the freedom to develop a joyful sexuality that is all about mutual pleasure and exploration and human connection, the same things that I would want for a daughter. But in this high stakes, heavily politicized atmosphere, with such a backlog of abuses for men to atone for, I am starting to wonder whether this is even possible.

CHAPTER 8

SEX AND SEXISM

Maybe it's just that I don't really want to think about my sons having sex at all.

In itself, this feels like a pretty reasonable aversion for any parent. When I was a teenager, my dad once told me, only half jokingly, that "kids know that their parents have sex, and parents know that their kids have sex, and let's never speak of it again." This approach was absolutely fine by me. To this day, I try to block out the chilling possibility that my parents once had sex and that my children might one day do the same.

I'm British and my natural tendencies skew a little prudish, which means that at some level, I find conversations about sex excruciating, anyway. But I probably would have felt on firmer ground if I had had girls, instead of boys. Obviously, it's much easier to romanticize the perfect parenting performance I would have delivered with a hypothetical daughter, than face up to my fumbling incompetence with my actual sons. But with a girl, at least, I would have been clearer on how I would want to frame the conversations about sex and relationships, the messages I would want to pass on.

Of course, I would have talked to a daughter about safety—about birth control, and STIs, and the possibility of assault. But I like to think that I would have also centered the sex discussions around pleasure. I would have talked to her about the orgasm gap and the fact that women have historically been so busy pleasing men that they didn't even know what they wanted themselves, let alone felt able to ask for it. About all the many ways in which we frame sex around male desire, and how we might be able to change the story.

I probably would have used these conversations as a way to exorcize my own demons from the relationship self-help canon of advice books that formed the backdrop to my own dating years in the nineties and early two thousands. These seemed mostly to be about encouraging women not to trouble men with their pesky feelings and needs.

"Don't call him." "Never chase him." "Have no expectations of him." "Follow *The Rules.*" *He's Just Not That into You.* These were the guiding principles offered to women when I was single. (Even though it might have prevented a few #MeToos, there was no *She's Just Not That Into You.*) The logic underpinning this value system was a strange combination of evolutionary psychology ("Men are biologically programmed to be the pursuers") and market economics ("Increase demand by reducing supply"). Any unguarded admission of actual human feeling was, of course, evidence of repulsive neediness. As my friends and I used to say at the peak of our dating nihilism, "The one who cares the least, wins."

The irony is that now, masculinity influencers and "pickup artists" are recycling a version of the same tedious evo-psych in reverse, encouraging men to pretend to be emotionally uninvested as a way to manipulate women into sleeping with them, apparently unaware that women have been doing the same to them for generations. Perhaps, like many sexist ideas that are pitched as evolution, this belief system is brought to us not by biology, but by patriarchy.

I would have done my best to stop my fantasy daughter from disappearing down a black hole of man-pleasing invisibility, and instead would have encouraged her to figure out her own desires and claim her own pleasure, to be assertive with her partners about what she wanted and what she didn't want. Especially if boys were her thing, I would have encouraged her to focus on her own needs and reassured her that her partner would be juuuust fine.

In other words, pretty much the exact narrative about sex that would be disastrous to communicate to my boys.

The story that I would have passed on to a daughter feels rooted in hope and pleasure and self-actualization. But as a mother of sons thinking about how to talk to them about sex, I am struggling to find a way to frame the discussions in anything other than panic. In the post-#MeToo era, at some level the only message about sex that seems reasonable to give to boys is one of harm reduction. The wider cultural narrative around male desire is so steeped in a history of wrongdoing that it can easily end up casting boys as little more than predators-in-waiting. In this story, the best we can hope for from boys' emerging sexuality is to minimize the damage it is likely to cause. Of course we need to educate boys about consent, but I wonder what this is doing to boys psychologically, to have their own sexuality and desires framed from the outset as inherently harmful.

In this heavily freighted moment in history, the job description for a mother of sons seems to be narrowing further and further, her expectations, goals, and hopes shrinking to a single pinprick measure of success—to raise a boy who won't rape anyone.

• • •

For someone who cringes a little at the prospect of talking about sex, I am doing a fair amount of it, spending many of my working hours interviewing boys about their sex lives (or lack of them). Since the FACE conference, I had been hoping to get beyond the topic of assault, to hear about boys' experiences of sex outside of the long shadow of #MeToo. Because as glad as I am that we are finally talking about consent and becoming aware of all the murky, underhanded ways that violation can show up, a part of me is also casting around for something a little more hopeful to hold on to.

I want some indication that #MeToo has achieved more than just fear, that the discussions and fundamental rethinking sparked by the movement have actually helped young people have more consensual, communicative, and mutually pleasurable sex. I am now keen to hear tales of healthy relationships and fun exploration and experimentation, some narrative about sex that isn't essentially one about assault.

But the more teenagers I talk to, the more I am starting to realize just how much the fallout from #MeToo dominates their experience of sex and sexuality. In one sense, this is progress. Boys are finally being held accountable not just for straightforward cases of rape or assault but also for the more complex, invisible power dynamics—the subconsensual persuasion and pressure that can easily tip the experience of a sexual encounter into something coercive, unpleasant, or frightening. Although it's impossible to know how much this affects their actual sex lives, in my conversations with boys, I am surprised at just how sophisticated their understanding and vocabulary around these issues now seems to be. Perhaps they just know the right words to say to impress a middle-aged feminist, but in both conservative and liberal communities, the boys I talk to are keenly aware of the issues surrounding consent and assault. In many cases, they are several steps ahead of the limited sex ed they receive at school.

"Have you seen the 'tea video'?" nineteen-year-old Oliver asks me.

I have. "Tea and Consent" was a viral and highly praised animated video originally commissioned by a branch of the UK police force, which is often used to teach the concept of consent in schools and elsewhere.

"Consent—it's simple as tea," the title page reads.

"If you are still confused about consent, just imagine instead of initiating sex, you're making them a cup of tea," chirps a no-nonsense British man in the voice-over. "If you say, 'Hey, would you like a cup of tea?' And they're like, 'Uh, I'm not really sure,' then you can make them a cup of tea . . . but be aware that they might not drink it. And if they don't drink it . . . don't make them drink it." (Cue animation of one stick figure waterboarding another stick figure with a cup of tea with road-sign-type red line through it.)

"If they are unconscious," the voice-over continues, over a picture of a passed-out stick figure, "don't make them tea. Unconscious people don't want tea." He wraps up his analysis of the issue that is currently confounding legal scholars, Title IX coordinators, and juries across the country with the jaunty conclusion, "If you can understand how completely ludicrous it is to force people to have tea when they don't want tea . . . then how hard is it to understand when it comes to sex?"

Clearly, as recently as 2015, when the Stanford swimmer Brock Turner raped a passed-out Chanel Miller behind a dumpster, the idea that an unconscious woman was not able to consent was either not obvious to boys, or if it was, they felt entitled to ignore it, so these basics in consent education were important. But Oliver thinks this message doesn't go nearly far enough.

"You're throwing boys out there saying, 'Don't give unconscious people tea.' But what about everything else?" he says. "I find that really problematic because then it boils this down to this really small, simple thing, where like sexual assault and rape is so complicated."

In general, the boys I speak to have a pretty nuanced understanding of the issues surrounding consent, but somehow this does not seem to be translating into a healthier culture around sex. For the most part, the boys don't seem to be using their newfound insights to help them have better, more mutually rewarding sex. Instead, they seem to have settled into a place of dread and avoidance.

Over and over again, the boys I interview refer to "cancel culture" at their high schools and college campuses. At first, I am confused. The phrase itself is a pretty tired trope of the online culture wars, used to refer to the mass social boycotting of public figures who are perceived to have transgressed. These takedowns are generally characterized as either an important way to hold the powerful accountable, or as a grave threat to freedom of speech, depending on the politics of the person talking (I have some sympathy with both of these positions). But in both conceptions, the targets are generally people with social power: celebrities, high-profile academics, or creepy, overindulged auteurs.

But the boys are talking about something different. Cancel culture in high school is not so much a democratizing force, punching up to the rich and powerful, but a relatively new, unofficial system of retribution and justice that teenagers mete out to each other. And for the most part (though not exclusively), this is a punishment targeted at boys.

High school cancellation is a kind of dramatic and elaborately coordinated form of social shunning. The boy's picture shows up on social media, often with a caption calling him a rapist or an abuser. No one talks to him in the hallways or invites him to hang out or sits with him in class or at lunch. His friends stop talking to him, and any who do risk being canceled themselves. This treatment often goes on for months or even years.

From what the boys are telling me, in some parts of the country, particularly in coastal, liberal communities, cancellation is now a pretty mainstream part of the high school experience. I am surprised at how many of the boys I speak to have either been canceled themselves or have witnessed a friend or classmate going through it.

In some ways, cancel culture is working as an effective deterrent. Many boys have changed their behavior when it comes to sex (though often motivated as much by terror as by genuine compassion or understanding).

"My greatest fear is getting canceled," twenty-year-old Henry, a college sophomore in Chicago, tells me. "I've only hooked up with one girl since being at college, and I just kept being like 'Is this okay? Is that okay? Is this okay?' Like any time we would do anything, I'd be like, 'Is this okay?' "

The process of cancellation often starts online, with students creating "cancel pages" on Instagram or another social media platform, where they display pictures of the faces of the boys they are accusing. Survivors can also contact these pages, asking for their own abusers to be featured.

"There is an entire page deck on Instagram of local abusers in our community," Wilbur, a gay nineteen-year-old in California tells me. "I was DM'd to follow this page to 'stay aware.' "

As a survivor of sexual assault himself by an older man, Wilbur has long seen himself as an activist in this area. He even did his senior art project about sexual assault and advocating for survivors.

"I saw it as using my privilege to help the girls at my school in confronting these people," he tells me. At first Wilbur was glad to see the cancel pages emerge. "I felt like it's keeping your community safe and creating awareness around people who are genuinely dangerous, especially within girl communities."

It was his brother who first saw Wilbur's own face on one of the cancel pages. The post described a sexual encounter that Wilbur had had in his junior year of high school with a sophomore boy. He had asked the younger boy to go with him to a party. Everyone had been drunk and taking drugs, and they had ended up having sex upstairs in a bedroom. Wilbur had had uncomfortable feelings about the encounter himself, turning it over and over in his mind afterward.

"I was still a minor, so there was nothing illegal about it," he tells me. "But I've learned a lot about consent and power dynamics and how although it's not a huge age gap, how much difference in experience there can be between a sophomore and a junior."

Even so, seeing his image on the cancel page was a huge shock.

"It was very, very, very invasive and so public," he tells me. "And the thing that bothered me the most is it's like I was grappling with what had happened. I was grappling with the fact that I did something wrong, and that I hurt someone's feelings, but it never crossed my mind that I was these huge trigger words, like 'rapist' or 'abuser.' "

When the allegations went public, Wilbur's friends started falling away.

"I totally just sat back and watched all these close friends and acquaintances just disappear from my life. It's all over social media. You just watch your follower count drop, and drop, and drop, and drop. I had a panic attack, and I just crawled into bed and just shut it out. I was horribly, horribly depressed and stripped of my identity."

Wilbur's story is long and complicated, and in a way, impossible for me to adjudicate. As in many of the stories I had heard at the FACE conference, and from other teens I spoke to, there were a million subtle modifiers as to how each of the people involved might have perceived what had taken place—a multitude of complicated missteps and shifting communications. But the cancellation was swift and absolute, with no room to hear differing points of view or make amends. Wilbur was no longer a complex human, a survivor of sexual assault himself, figuring out his own sexuality and place in the world.

If the Title IX systems that I had heard about at FACE had often seemed arbitrary and draconian, the unofficial systems of justice and punishment that teenagers have cooked up on their own are even more lacking in nuance or forgiveness.

"It equates all these people, no matter what the situation is," Wilbur tells me. "No matter if it's a serial rapist or if it's someone who DMs someone inappropriately or just someone who contacts the page to have their story featured. Then it creates no conversation, you know, no gray area. There's no place for people to process, or to move forward. You're put in a box and you can't move out of it."

Across the country in a smallish liberal town on the East Coast, fourteen-year-old Evan had a similar experience at his public middle school. In the winter of his eighth-grade year, he was invited to a party at a friend's house following a school basketball game. He went with Christina, his best friend since elementary school. A group of them were hanging out in one of the bedrooms upstairs, chatting and ribbing each other, but later in the evening the rest of the group dispersed, and Evan and Christina found themselves alone. They were chatting and flirting and at one point, Christina took Evan's hand and placed it on her knee. Excited, he moved his hand upward, to her thigh. The mood changed, Christina told him that she didn't like what he had done, and he removed his hand immediately. After a moment of awkwardness, they both went downstairs and rejoined the party.

The next day Evan and Christina texted each other. Christina told him that what he did was not cool. Evan—who had had many conversations with his parents about consent and assault—took full responsibility and apologized. She accepted his apology and it all seemed to have blown over, with the pair returning to their usual friendly texting, riffing on a long running in-joke they shared about a family of pandas.

But a few days later, Christina messaged Evan again and this time her tone was different. "What you did was a sexual violation," she wrote. "You assaulted me." For the remainder of the school year no one talked to Evan. He sat alone at lunch. When his class picked partners for pickleball in PE, he was left with no one. Whenever he approached a group of kids at recess, they fell silent, and turned their backs. His friends formed new group chats that didn't include him. What hurt the most was that even his best friend Zach didn't stand up for him. Previously sociable and popular, Evan became withdrawn and socially anxious, not wanting to leave his bedroom.

Evan and Christina's story leaves me torn. For so long, girls and women have been disbelieved and ignored to the point where they often can't even trust their own feelings about a sexual encounter. Boys pressure them into acts that feel uncomfortable or violating, and they often can't even really pinpoint why. The culture encourages boys to feel entitled to girls' bodies, and girls—who are socialized to be people-pleasers—are often under subtle cultural pressure to give them what they want. This is a tricky and insidious problem that is hard to capture with the vocabulary of assault.

But the vocabulary of assault was what was available to Christina. She presumably felt powerless and angry and used the limited tools on offer to her to express that anger. It is understandable that any woman might take a few days to make sense of her own experience, even to herself, and especially a young teenager. A girl in Christina's situation even five to ten years ago would have been expected to just suck up the violation, not to say anything or rock the boat. Girls in general are depressingly used to operating in a constant climate of low-level sexual harassment—of sexual comments, smirks, and demands for "nudes." It is, in one sense, progress that a teenage girl now feels able to articulate when she feels violated, and her experience deserves to be heard and validated.

But is it helpful for anyone in this situation to frame what happened as a sexual assault, with hefty social consequences, rather than a case of an inexperienced teenager missing the mark and hurting a friend? Does Evan deserve to be treated as a sexual predator with all that goes along with that? I'm not at all sure. A key defense of cancel culture is that it punches up. That it is a direct and democratic way for the less powerful to hold the more powerful accountable. But when we are talking about teenagers, the power structures don't seem quite so simple or immutable. In order for teen cancel culture in its current form to be justifiable, we should be seeing a clear structural imbalance of power, tipped heavily in boys' favor. Perhaps this was once true, but now the reality seems way more complex. Is there still a substantial power differential between an adolescent boy and an adolescent girl? And if so, what does that really mean in practice? Is it really helpful for Christina, or any teenage girl in a similar situation, to see herself as a victim of a sexual assault, rather than as a participant in a sexual encounter between two peers with equal negotiating power?

Listening to boys talk about this new punitive landscape, it occurs to me that this is in part a continuation of the same problem that adults have with baby boys, the same inability to see boys as fully vulnerable, and to treat them as children in need of protection. High school boys, like high school girls, are still figuring stuff out, working out how to have sex, how to be people. In many ways, casting teen boys as fully formed sex offenders doesn't so much challenge stereotypes as help reinforce them.

Perhaps we should rather be seeing both boys and girls as children, navigating the complex task of forming their identities and sexuality, and use these kinds of situations as a way to start conversations rather than shut them down, and find a way to approach these painful and complicated parts of growing up with empathy for all involved.

• • •

With the looming threat of cancel culture on the one hand, and the lingering pressure to be dominant and masculine on the other, boys are now caught between two contradictory sets of expectations, which at times can seem impossible to reconcile.

Because while #MeToo tried to set new standards for boys and men, the old expectations of masculinity are still very much in circulation. Boys are expected to conform to relatively unexamined and unreconstructed masculinity norms—the same basic rules that have been fed to them in numerous ways since childhood.

In this set of rules, boys are told to be strong, commanding, and even domineering. When it comes to sex and relationships, they are still expected to take the lead—to make the first move and to come off as confident and assertive. And they are still heavily policed for any behavior that might come off as overly feminine. The threat of emasculation—of being branded a faggot or a pussy, even by implication—still looms large in the teenage male imagination.

According to one wide-scale survey of teenage boys, 1 in 3 reported that they still felt pressure to "dominate or be in charge of others."[1] A similar number said they felt pressure to join in when other boys talked about girls in a sexual way, and 1 in 4 said they felt pressure to hook up with a girl. According to the boys surveyed, these pressures come from all over, including from family members (especially fathers), friends, and classmates, as well as images of masculinity drawn from popular culture and porn.

And while sexuality as a whole is becoming more of a fluid concept for those who identify as female or nonbinary, with sexual identities such as bisexuality or pansexuality becoming increasingly normalized, the same progress has not been made for cisgender boys. According to a wide range of data, young women's sexual identities are shifting rapidly, with reported rates of same-sex attraction and behavior skyrocketing. But the same datasets show that young men's sexual identities and practices have mostly remained static, with the vast majority of them identifying as exclusively heterosexual, and a small minority as gay, likely because rigid masculinity norms still preclude much exploration.

Boys are working within two conflicting systems: one that demands they be sensitive, cautious, and emotionally nuanced, while the other encourages them to be domineering, emotionally stunted, and borderline aggressive. And the consequences of failure can be severe in both systems. Stray too far in one direction, and you are a pussy. Stray too far in the other, and you might be canceled. As twenty-year-old Zach put it, "It feels like we are set up to fail."

Dr. Jessie Ford is a sociologist at Columbia University whose research centers around gender and sex, particularly on college campuses. One of her major research projects looked at gender roles and expectations for young people through the lens of "unwanted sex." By this she means the flavor of icky sex that isn't quite assault—no one is forcing or coercing anyone—but more the kind that people don't actively want, but end up going through with because of perceived social pressures, or because they don't quite know how to say no.

This is a phenomenon that writer Melissa Febos calls *empty consent,* in which we consent to touch that we don't want or feel ambivalent about, a common experience for women in a culture in which they are socialized to please men and center male needs.

Since #MeToo we have heard a fair amount about these kinds of sexual encounters from a female perspective. But people of all genders have unwanted sex, including boys and young men. Ford found that, depending on how the questions are phrased, somewhere between 7 and 27 percent of straight men reported at least one unwanted sexual incident during their college years. Their descriptions of these events, and their reasons for going along with them, provide a unique insight into the expectations around masculinity that are still bearing down heavily on boys.

After interviewing dozens of college students of all genders and sexual orientations about their sex lives, and in particular their experiences with unwanted sex, Ford was struck by the extent to which straight boys are still locked into rigid gender roles, and still feel under heavy pressure to adhere to some pretty old-school masculine norms.

"The things the boys were saying—it felt like a guy in the 1950s would be saying this," Ford tells me. "Those hegemonic toxic norms around masculinity are still very much intact. They are so pervasive and so invisible."

The boys Ford interviewed often ended up having sexual encounters that they really didn't want or desire because they believed that to say no would invite shame or ridicule, since a "real man" would never pass up an opportunity for sex with an attractive woman.

Tyler, one of her eighteen-year-old interviewees, described these thought processes when a woman climbed on top of him in his dorm room after a party, and started having sex with him. "I didn't want to be in that position because sex still was something that was kind of an emotional thing for me," he told Ford. "But in the back of my mind I'm thinking about this girl telling weird stories about me to her friends. . . . Guys are supposed to enjoy sexual intercourse under any circumstances . . . I was still playing the role of someone who wanted to be in that moment. I wanted to stick to the conventional script."

Some version of the same fears was echoed by many of the boys Ford interviewed.

"The socialized pressure around male performance and competence is really ingrained and the men can't really escape it," she tells me. "Men are just so afraid of being a wuss or a virgin or gay."

Ford had expected to hear from boys that these pressures came mostly from their male friends, as a fair amount of research suggests that masculinity is largely a performance by men for the benefit of other men. But she was surprised to hear how significant a part girls played in upholding these rigid gender expectations, and the extent to which girls are policing boys' masculinity. What showed up repeatedly in her research is that although women might want the "Is this okay? Is this okay?" guy in theory, in reality, that is often not what they actually find sexually desirable.

"Women are very much a part of creating these double standards for men," Ford tells me. "On the one hand, he needs to be confident and know what he's doing and make the first move. But at the same time, he shouldn't take things too far or be pushy or be gross. But also, if he doesn't make a move, 'What's his problem?' There were times when I was listening to them and thinking, *This feels impossible.*"

• • •

Dr. Mark Ruffalo is a therapist and professor of psychiatry at the University of Central Florida. He sees adolescent boys (among other populations) in his private therapy practice and is becoming increasingly concerned about the feelings of stress and paralysis they are expressing about sex and relationships.

I first come across Ruffalo on Twitter, when he tweets out a call to other mental health professionals, asking if any of his colleagues in the field have noticed a similar phenomenon to something he is coming across more and more often among his straight adolescent male patients: that they are deeply reluctant to date girls or get into relationships with them. This is not because they are living in any kind of hedonistic, casual sex hookup culture, but rather because they claim they would rather be at home alone, watching porn and masturbating (or "practicing self-gratification," as Ruffalo quaintly calls it). The responses came flooding in from therapists who were seeing similar trends.

Ruffalo's tweet catches my attention in part because, although patients in therapy are a self-selecting group, and probably at the more extreme end, I know from my own research that his clients are not complete aberrations but part of a wider trend. Mirroring the downturn in all other forms of in-person social contact, this generation of adolescents is actually having less sex than any teenagers since the 1970s.

The proportion of adolescent boys reporting no partnered sexual activity at all almost doubled in the last decade, now hovering at around 45 percent. For high school girls that figure is now close to 75 percent.[2] (Although as a rule, people seem to feel way more comfortable with the idea of teenage girls remaining celibate than teenage boys, so there have been fewer anguished think pieces about sexless women and their potential threat to society.)

Of course, the fraught climate around assault and cancellation is only a part of what is driving this downward trend. According to researchers, various potential causes show up in the data for the decline in young adults' sex lives.[3] For young women, the primary reason that emerges is that they are drinking less alcohol; for their male counterparts, it's the fact that they are more likely to still live with their parents than previous generations, and in addition, they are apparently too busy playing video games to have sex. (Perhaps parents who are keen to lure their teenage boys away from screens should point them toward the research that shows that men who play video games every day cut their odds of having sex in half in comparison to men who never game.)

But this type of data-based research isn't quite able to get at the psychological truths behind this decline and what is really going on for young people emotionally behind the scenes. So I message Ruffalo directly and ask if he would be willing to talk to me about his experiences with his patients. He is reluctant at first, not seeing it as his role to overinterpret or to make any great cultural claims. I reassure him that he can just tell me what the boys are saying to him, and I will happily overinterpret on his behalf, and eventually he agrees.

Ruffalo tells me that he has now seen the phenomenon a handful of times. A boy, always heterosexual and usually between the ages of sixteen and eighteen, will claim in therapy that he just isn't interested in dating or finding a girlfriend.

"Boys are saying to me, 'It's much more gratifying for me to watch porn and please myself than to have sex,'" says Ruffalo. "It's not even that they don't want relationships because they are chasing some kind of bachelor lifestyle. It's just isolation and self-gratification."

"Is this just boys?" I ask him. "Or are girls doing the same?"

"It's definitely specific to boys," he confirms. "There is still a great desire among the girls I see to find a boyfriend."

Ruffalo is in his thirties and sees this as a huge shift since he was a teenager. "When I was young, we lived for socializing and dating," he remembers. "It's all we talked about."

When I press Ruffalo to try to dig deeper into the reasons why these boys might be retreating from real-world sex into virtual substitutes, he sums up the issue with two words: "Fear and ease." In other words, real-world sex is scary—both psychologically and politically loaded, whereas porn is convenient and emotionally undemanding.

Ruffalo's fear-and-ease framing strikes a chord. While most social change is slow and subtle, this generation of teenagers has lived through two major cultural shifts in quick succession that have each radically changed the sexual landscape. The first of these was the advent of the smartphone and the explosion of online porn, allowing the modern teenager instant access to almost any virtual sex act that his vivid hormonal brain can conjure. The second major cultural shift was the #MeToo movement and its aftermath, including the swift ferocity of teen cancel culture. Taken together, these two social and cultural transformations have fundamentally altered the risk-reward calculation of sex.

I ask Ruffalo about the "fear" side of the equation. What are the boys he is seeing actually afraid of? He rattles off all the usual anxieties—the same angsty roadblocks that every human who has ever considered a romantic or sexual relationship has had to face down at some point. Rejection, exposure, performance issues, flat-out humiliation, not being enough. But in the era of cancel culture, there is now an added terror. "They're scared of getting accused of something," Ruffalo tells me.

And while the sexual climate has become unusually fraught and the potential downside of any sexual encounter chillingly apparent, it has never been easier to retreat from sex entirely. Representing the "ease" side of Ruffalo's conception, porn is providing boys with an alternative, a way to bypass the fears and horrors of real-world relationships completely.

"Tech has played a huge role," Ruffalo tells me. "You can jump on the internet and find whatever you want to see. Things that could never be re-created in actuality. There's so much variety, so much novelty. Boys are asking themselves, 'Is it worth it to have relationships?' "

• • •

This push-pull of fear and ease is something that twenty-two-year-old Ryan (not one of Ruffalo's patients) has long grappled with. We first met Ryan back in chapter 3, the boy who had shattered a vertebra in college while weight training, trying to bulk up to achieve the hypermuscled look of the online fitness influencers.

Now Ryan has a girlfriend, Hannah. She is in the next room as we talk over Zoom, and during our conversation he occasionally breaks off to call something out to her affectionately. Ryan and Hannah met at a music festival last year, putting an end to a long period of depression and self-imposed celibacy for Ryan.

He had lost his virginity early, in eighth grade—a brief fumble with a girl in the restroom at a swim meet. Ryan was already familiar with porn at this point. He had seen his first porn video three years earlier, in fifth grade, on the phone of a boy who was passing it around class. "It was exploratory kind of stuff—boobs and vagina, basically," he tells me. He started masturbating in fifth grade, too, as puberty hit. But it was when he got his own smartphone in middle school that his porn use quickly escalated.

Ryan dated a few girls casually through high school, but never had sex with them. And as time went on, he started to spend less and less time pursuing real-world relationships, and more and more time watching porn on his own. By the time he got to college, he was starting to worry that his porn habit was becoming obsessive.

"It would get to the point where I was doing it several times a day, instead of going out and pursuing people or interactions," he tells me. "It became like, as soon as I get the urge, I got to take care of it. Now looking back, I just did it way too much."

"Why do you think you were using porn instead of trying to meet girls in real life?" I ask.

"I think it was an ease thing," he says. *Ease*. The exact word that Dr. Ruffalo had used. "It was easier for me to just stay inside and do this in between doing my lectures."

"You mean it was easier literally in terms of convenience?" I ask. "Or do you mean emotionally and socially easier?"

"All of the above," he replies. "I kind of got to the point where I convinced myself that it was almost preferable to just do that. I convinced myself I didn't need a woman because I could just do this myself."

Since childhood, Ryan has long suffered from anxiety and self-esteem issues, always carrying around the nagging sense that he had something to prove, that he wasn't quite worthy of friendship or love. These feelings had nothing to do with porn, but porn became an easy way for him to avoid them.

"It's not like the porn or masturbation was the pivotal thing," he tells me. "But it was definitely a factor when it came to why I would avoid relationships, or why I was able to avoid them for as long as I did."

Through porn, Ryan was exposed to all kinds of sex that he would likely never have encountered in real life. "It used to be incredibly diverse," he tells me. "It would be every sort of situation—BDSM stuff, public stuff. For somebody who had absolutely no concept of what sex was and what real relationships are and how those intertwine, it was just very damaging. It distorts what sex is."

"What was damaging about it for you?" I ask.

"Everything, from the size of the dudes' dicks to the fake plastic surgery that half of the chicks have—it's like everything involved in it is fake. And especially as a young kid, I didn't know that. I didn't have enough experience with sex to acknowledge that."

"Did you find that you were comparing real girls' bodies to porn stars' bodies?" I ask him. It's a theory I have heard a fair amount—that boys and men who watch a lot of porn become overly judgmental and critical of women's bodies in real life, comparing them to an unrealistic standard. But for Ryan, it wasn't other people that he scrutinized. It was himself.

"It was more me comparing myself to that," he replies. "Unless you're endowed with one of those . . . *things* . . . it's hard not to be like, well, *damn*." Ryan blushes slightly and turns his head away from the camera. "And then suddenly I'm expecting myself to be like that."

"Did it make you feel bad about your body?" I ask.

"Oh, yeah, for, for a long while. If I didn't have the experience that I do, I think it would still impact the way that I view myself. It's like, you don't have any of that experience and you can't discern between what porn is and what life is. And so suddenly you're thinking that you are inadequate and that you won't ever be enough for somebody."

• • •

It would be easy to use Ryan as a kind of case study to illustrate the dangerous effects of pornography. He carries a lot of shame about his relationship with porn, but there is also something about the way that he is talking, the way he understands his own experience, that feels a little rote. It's as though he has absorbed the cultural discourse, the checklist of talking points about the harms of porn, and is now reciting them back to me, as though he assumes this is what I want to hear. The arguments are familiar: Porn gives teenagers body image issues and distorted views about sex. It warps their minds, so they are unable to distinguish between fantasy and reality. It is addictive.

I have similar experiences talking to other boys, too. They are all extremely porn literate. Every boy I speak with watches porn regularly, and most of them were exposed to it young, generally around fifth grade. One boy told me he had seen his first porn video in kindergarten at a birthday party, when a group of five-year-olds snuck into the kid's dad's study and watched two women perform oral sex on a pair of penises whose owners were out of shot. He had concluded that they were both licking popsicles and had noted the coincidence that they had both chosen the same flavor.

The boys are all intimately familiar not just with the various categories and types of porn but also, to my surprise, with the wider critique around porn's negative effects. One by one, they tell me that they are worried that porn is addictive and distorting; that it would stop them from enjoying real-world sex; that it demeans women; that it might cause erectile dysfunction; that it is seedy and disgusting. It is almost as if they feel they have to recite this list to me as some kind of social penance.

Perhaps this isn't surprising. Porn shoulders a lot of blame in our current cultural moment for where we are going wrong with sex, in a way that deeply implicates teen boys and young men. It's one of the few issues on which both left and right are often broadly aligned. The religious right and the feminist left may arrive at their conclusions via a different rationale and sensibility, but they share a deep moral squeamishness about porn, and in making their cases, they often point to similar harms. (Liberal sex ed in America often feels nearly as rooted in fear as the Jesus-and-abstinence variety.)

Both left and right argue not just that porn makes boys avoid sex altogether, as Dr. Mark Ruffalo suggests, but also that it turns them into rabid, uncontrolled sex monsters. Both sides argue that porn is addictive, and boys watch way too much of it. It distorts what sex is in the real world and normalizes more "pornified," demeaning, and sometimes violent or dangerous sexual practices. They argue that the bodies on display are so fake and surgically enhanced that they trigger body image issues, and that as a whole it exposes boys to sexist imagery and ideas that carry over to real life.

In fact, when it comes to porn, the religious right often co-opts the language of the feminist left. "Porn use is correlated with . . . a greater objectification of women and a greater acceptance of 'rape myths,'" claims one antiporn website run by conservative Christians, a population that generally seems happily unperturbed by rape myths and objectification when it comes to, say, slut shaming or abortion rights.

Perhaps the writers lifted the claim from a *New York Times* op-ed that approached the issue of porn from a liberal feminist perspective. "Among college men, pornography use has been associated with seeing women as disposable, and for both sexes, a stronger belief in rape myths," it says, linking to a study from researchers at Rutgers University and the University of Michigan as evidence.[4]

When I click through, I see that the study, entitled "Less Than Human? Media Use, Objectification of Women, and Men's Acceptance of Sexual Violence," doesn't look just at porn but also at various types of media and their correlation with young men's objectifying and potentially violent beliefs about women.

The study does, indeed, find a correlation between boys watching a lot of porn and the likelihood that they see women essentially as objects who exist mainly in service of men's desires, rather than subjects in their own right. These beliefs are then in turn correlated with greater acceptance of rape myths such as "she was asking for it" and "she was wearing the wrong clothes," as well as more frequent acts of sexual deception (as measured by a scientific instrument called, slightly comically, the Blatant Lying subscale).

What neither the religious nor the feminist antiporn crusaders mention when they quote this study is that in its findings it wasn't just porn that encouraged boys to objectify women and buy into rape myths. Various types of mainstream TV were doing the same job. The boys in the study who watched reality shows such as *The Bachelor* held similarly sexist beliefs about women as those who watched a lot of porn. (Perhaps this is unsurprising; another analysis of primetime dating programs found that in these shows women are referred to as sexual objects around once every ten minutes.)[5]

And even more likely to be correlated with objectifying beliefs and the acceptance of rape myths than watching reality TV among young men, was watching a lot of televised sports. This link between sexism and sports-watching is actually confirmed by a number of other studies. It is obviously not that the sports themselves directly feature rape myths or objectification but rather that watching a lot of TV sports is likely a proxy for greater buy-in to wider value-systems of masculinity.

When I tell my husband that watching sports is similarly correlated with objectification and rape myths for boys as watching porn, he snorts and says, "Oh, America's gonna love that." His skepticism is understandable. In a country that has a deep historical attachment to both TV sports and sexual shaming, we are far more comfortable scapegoating porn than digging deeper into the wider stories about masculinity that permeate the culture.

Porn sells boys a myth about manhood—that men are hypermuscled, dominant, aggressive, and obsessed with sex. Ryan compared himself with this image and found himself wanting. But these expectations are nothing new. Porn is just a more sexualized version of the same masculinity narrative that has been fed to boys, including Ryan, in different variations since birth. In this story, men are strong and dominant heroes. Male pleasure and agency are the main event, and women are peripheral characters who exist mainly for their pleasure and gratification. Ryan's ideas about masculinity had been seeded long before he ever saw porn, something he had actually told me himself.

"Every time you flip on a superhero movie, you're seeing this crazy physique, and then suddenly I'm expecting myself to be like that?" he had said. "Trying to shape your mentality of what it means to be a man, there is a feeling of just never being enough."

Without a doubt, porn plays a significant role in shaping teenagers' views around sex and sexuality, especially in the era of the smartphone. But when we blame porn for these things without digging into the wider culture, we are missing a huge piece of the puzzle, and can easily end up giving larger systems of masculinity a free pass.

• • •

The evidence for the adverse effects of porn on the adolescent psyche is actually relatively limited. In a widescale review of the available research about porn's negative impact, some studies show links between exposure to pornography and violent attitudes or behavior in boys, but several more show that for the vast majority of males, "frequent exposure to sexually explicit material cannot be linked to increased levels of sexual aggression" and any links apply to only a small percentage of males, who are already predisposed to sexual violence.[6]

There is no objective definition of "porn addiction" and it is not a recognized diagnosis. Generally, experts start to become concerned about a person's porn usage only when that person themself perceives that they have a problem or that their porn habit is dysregulated or out of control and is having a negative impact on their life. Research suggests that one of the key reasons people start to feel this way is not so much the actual amount of porn that they consume, or any objective evidence that their usage is out of control, but rather a belief that porn itself is somehow shameful or immoral. In other words, the porn itself is not the problem, but the shame surrounding it is. This is a phenomenon known as *moral incongruence*—meaning that when people continue to engage in behaviors that don't align with their own value systems, they start to feel ashamed and guilty and angry with themselves, and as a result believe they must have an addiction.

One meta-analysis concluded that how frequently a person watched porn only slightly predicted feelings of addiction, but that shame and moral incongruence heavily predicted those feelings, even if the users don't objectively watch that much porn.[7] This research focused on religious shame, specifically, and it is likely that that is the variety that cuts the deepest, but the feminist left can also seem oddly committed to the project of porn shaming.

As for the critique surrounding porn's impact on body image, the picture is also more complicated than the media discourse suggests. Again, a lot gets blamed on porn that might actually originate elsewhere. One of the main critiques of porn is that both the women's and men's bodies featured are unrealistic, lacking in diversity, and often surgically enhanced, causing young people to compare their own and their partner's bodies and find them wanting.

There is real truth in this picture. While a fair amount of queer, feminist, and other alternative porn genres exist, for the most part, mainstream pornography features relatively similar body types. But punishing standards for female beauty and a lack of diversity in acceptable body shapes is hardly a problem that is confined to porn. There is likely a wider range of women's bodies on display even in mainstream porn than in almost any Hollywood movie or episode of *Love Island*. Several of the boys I spoke to picked up on this, confiding, often unprompted, that they preferred more realistic body types in the porn they chose to watch. "I like the more amateur stuff," twenty-year-old Henry told me. "Like not the super heavily produced stuff. I like it to be more realistic, I guess."

It's not easy for an adolescent boy to be completely frank about his porn preferences in an interview with a middle-aged mom of three. But the idea that straight men might actually be drawn to more diverse body types when watching porn is backed up by research from Pornhub, the go-to destination for adult content for most of the boys I spoke to. Each year Pornhub publishes statistics about what their users search for by age and gender (although for legal reasons this research applies only to viewers at least eighteen years of age). These statistics provide a unique insight into what people actually watch and desire, as opposed to what they feel they should say they watch and desire.

Last year, the third most common term searched on Pornhub by young men was "mature," a category that generally refers to videos starring women in their forties and fifties.[8] As a woman firmly in this demographic myself, it's hard to know whether to take this information as creepy and oedipal or, in a culture in which older women's sexuality is generally portrayed as either grotesque or invisible by mainstream media, oddly flattering.

Similarly, porn is often blamed for the rise of the so-called "porn vulva." This is the idea that porn stars' genitals are generally neat and hairless with small, contained inner labia, and that as a result, young women are increasingly feeling ashamed of their own vulvas, believing that boys will find them disgusting in comparison to the porn version. Some are even seeking out labiaplasties, a form of cosmetic surgery that reduces and shapes the labia.

In 2017, the American College of Obstetricians and Gynecologists raised concerns that the rates of young women seeking labiaplasty had risen sharply over the last few years, and suggested that pornography was driving the trend. But as a group of porn stars point out in a piece for Refinery29, perhaps porn is unfairly blamed for this. Even mainstream porn shows a wide diversity of vulva types, they argued, and way more than, say, WebMD.[9] It's a fair point. Solly will likely get a better education in the diversity of women's bodies from porn than from the book on puberty for boys that we ordered for him from Amazon, which features hand-drawn illustrations of eight differently shaped penises and only one, very neat, vulva.

Surprisingly (at least to me), when it comes to body image, porn seems to have more of a negative impact on boys than on girls. In one longitudinal study of nearly two thousand Dutch teenagers, for example, researchers found that exposure to pornography was associated with body dissatisfaction for boys, who were particularly concerned about their stomach and abs, but had no negative body image effects for girls. It isn't clear why this is the case. Perhaps because boys watch more porn in general, or more likely, because girls are marinating in body objectification across the board, so porn is but a drop in the ocean of female body shame.[10]

• • •

The feminist anti-porn argument is rooted in a wider critique of so-called "sex positive" feminism, and the idea that it sold girls and women a lie.

The theory, argued by Ariel Levy and others is that while on the face of it, women were "empowered" by a hyper-sexualized culture that encouraged them to wear revealing clothes, shave their pubic hair and have casual sex without being "slut shamed," what actually ended up happening was that female sexuality became commodified in service of male pleasure. Raunch culture was really more a display for the benefit of men rather than a true expression of authentic female desire. In this argument, sex-positive feminism did not, in fact, liberate women sexually, but instead incentivized them to perform their sexuality for men. Now girls and young women are under huge pressure to please their male partners and to be the "perfect slut" rather than pursuing their own actual sexual pleasure or agency. According to this critique, porn played a major part in this process.

In both the religious and the feminist worldviews, porn is generally framed as something that boys and men enjoy and that girls and women are either exploited by, or at best, tolerate. In both conceptions, boys and men benefit from porn, and girls and women are harmed by it. Porn is an expression of men's sexuality, the ultimate manifestation of the male gaze, and women are presented only as accessories to this, objects of men's desires rather than subjects with their own sexual agency. Porn's ubiquity in teenagers' lives allows boys to set the terms for sex.

When I spoke to teens, some of their responses fit neatly into this picture. Amira, a nineteen-year-old girl who recently graduated from her Northern California high school, described an intense hookup culture among her peer group, in which sex was increasingly "pornified" and both boys and girls tended to center boys' desires.

"It's like they are looking at you with porn eyes," she tells me. "It's easier to objectify you. Never in high school did a man ask what I wanted during sex. It wasn't intentional. They were just so focused on what they wanted, and I wasn't comfortable telling them what I wanted."

Amira's experience makes sense in a culture in which girls are heavily socialized to put aside their own desires in order to please, and children of all genders are subtly encouraged to believe that boys and men are the main characters in any story. But although those power dynamics are real and important to acknowledge and unpack, they are not the whole story.

For other young people that I spoke to—both boys and girls—the picture that emerged was perhaps more complex than the feminist critique would allow. It did not seem to be a simple equation that porn aligned perfectly with boys' interests and desires, while girls had no authentic interest in it of their own. Boys are also objectified by porn in ways that can lead to pressure around body image, masculinity, and sexual performance. And, notably, girls are real sexual agents, who also use and enjoy porn for their own sexual pleasure.

Although more boys than girls consume porn regularly, various data shows that young women watch a fair amount of it, too. Porn consumption statistics for viewers eighteen years old and up show that slightly more than a third of pornography is consumed by women and that this figure is rising every year. Considering the stigma that still exists around women watching and enjoying porn, this is likely to be an undercount. The trend is driven by younger women, a fact that suggests that for teenagers younger than 18, the numbers are likely to be even higher. When I talked to teens themselves, they generally confirmed this.

Amira told me that her female college roommate used to watch porn on her phone while she was in the room, and many of the boys I interviewed told me that their female peers talked openly about enjoying it, too. It's possible, of course, that these girls are only watching porn as a way to research strategies to please the boys in their lives and have no sexual interest in it themselves. But this idea smacks of an (almost certainly apocryphal) story about Queen Victoria, that when nineteenth-century lawmakers were drafting the British legal code outlawing homosexuality, they did not include lesbianism, because the queen could not believe that women would ever have sex at all if it wasn't a wifely duty they carried out at the behest of men.

But a fair amount of research shows that women and girls not only consume and enjoy porn but also enjoy more sexual satisfaction as a result. According to research by the psychologist Dr. Sean McNabney, of Indiana University, women who watch porn during masturbation report higher satisfaction.[11] Other research shows that when couples watch porn together as part of their sex lives, the woman is more likely to have an orgasm.[12]

When we keep rehashing the idea that porn exists exclusively for the pleasure of men, we paradoxically make women's desires even more invisible. Perhaps if we were to remove the stigma about women watching porn for their own gratification, girls would be better able to explore, own, and communicate their own sexual needs and preferences. This in turn would send a strong message to boys, that girls' pleasure is as important as their own, and that boys should be taking some responsibility for ensuring that it happens.

• • •

Unpacking the gendered complexities of porn's influence feels like a particularly urgent task, given how quickly the norms are changing for young people when it comes to violent sex. Whether you choose to see this cultural shift as "youngsters experimenting with kink" or as an "alarming normalization of dangerous and potentially abusive sexual practices" will depend on your sensibilities and values. But either way, more violent practices, ranging from spanking and face slapping to choking and strangulation, have now become a relatively mainstream part of sex for many college-aged kids.

I was shocked to learn just how mainstream. According to one study of the sexual behaviors of nearly five thousand American college students,[13] among those who had had any kind of partnered sexual experience, 43 percent had choked a partner, 47 percent had been choked themselves, nearly 60 percent had been lightly spanked, and 12 percent had been slapped across the face during sex.

It's something that is familiar to Amira. "It's a common thing in high school hookup culture," she tells me. "People assume that everything is on the table. They slap you in the face. It's less violent with people who don't watch a lot of porn."

But this shift can't all be attributed to pornography. When the students were asked what specific influences led them to want to try out these practices, only around 20 percent of men and 5 percent of women said they had learned about these practices by watching porn. The rest (both men and women) mainly said they thought it sounded exciting or fun or that they had heard about it from peers or partners. In another study by the same authors that focused specifically on college women's experiences with choking as part of sex, when the participants were asked about what influenced them, they mentioned the movie *Fifty Shades of Gray,* as well as fan fiction, as often as they mentioned porn.[14]

The media discourse around choking echoes the wider discussion around porn and sex more generally, in its hefty use of gender stereotypes. Choking is often talked about as something that boys desire, and that girls, at best, endure to please their male partners, or feel under pressure to consent to. (At worst, it's something horrifyingly dangerous, which boys inflict on girls without their consent, as an act of sexual violence.)

But as with porn, the research paints a much more complex and nuanced picture about the gender dynamics involved. Dr. Debby Herbenick is the director of the Center for Sexual Health Promotion at the University of Indiana. She is also the principal investigator for the National Survey of Sexual Health and Behavior and the author of much of the cutting-edge research into the normalization of choking and other forms of violent sex among young people.

A complex and slightly different picture emerges from her in-depth qualitative interviews with male and female college students about their experiences with choking and strangulation (technically what they are describing is strangulation, but the terms are often used interchangeably) as well as from larger scale quantitative data. Some of the young women Herbenick interviewed did, indeed, talk about this kind of rough sex as unwanted or indicated they felt pressure to go along with it for their partners' pleasure.

"I fake moaned a lot when he was choking me 'cause I felt like, I'm also a people pleaser. I like to make people happy," said one female participant. "But also at the same time I'm just like, 'I don't necessarily fully like this. I wish it was different.' "

But this woman was one of the exceptions. Although they were rarely the ones to initiate it, the majority of the women Herbenick interviewed about their experiences with choking told her that they actively enjoy and desire this kind of sex, often describing it with adjectives such as "exciting" and "exhilarating." And one of the reasons they gave most often as to why they enjoyed it was precisely because it reinforced traditional gender roles and made boys seem more manly and dominant.

"Gentle sex . . . it's like, I feel like he's not as masculine. . . . I don't feel as excited," said one female participant when asked about her experiences with both more tender, loving sex and more violent practices. "It's just like, 'Oh, okay, very normal,' but it's not, I don't feel any type of strong emotion. . . . It's not as exciting to me. That feels like they're less masculine."

When it came to choking and other forms of kink, girls played a major role in policing boys' masculinity. On the flip side, while many of the boys that Herbenick and her team interviewed did authentically enjoy these more violent practices, others felt under pressure to engage in them so as not to come off as unmasculine. The researchers underscored this idea in their analysis of the interviews.

"Rough sex—with its assertion and dominance—was equated with a stereotypical expected and desired masculine behavior," they wrote. "Men who did not engage in this or were wary of it were criticized for their lack of maleness."

Herbenick and her team's research on choking suggests that the whole framing of rough sex as something that men desire and women tolerate is inadequate to really understand the complexities and contradictions of desire. These nuances were perhaps even more unexpected and difficult to untangle when it came to the issue of consent. Across the board in her research, engaging in rough sex acts such as slapping and choking without prior discussion or consent was worryingly common. But to my surprise, actually significantly more men than women reported that they had been slapped or choked without their explicit consent.

Of the students who had engaged in choking behaviors, more than 1 in 4 of the men said that their partner had "never asked me for consent . . . they just choked me anyway" while less than 1 in 5 women reported having this experience. Similarly with slapping, nearly half of the men who had been slapped reported that it had happened without their explicit consent, while for young women that figure was "only" a third.[15] This data was so surprising to me that I had to go back and check it several times.

It is crucial to note that these things are not equivalent. There is a real, substantive difference between a man choking a woman without consent and a woman doing the same thing to a man. When it comes to violent sex, the power differential between men and women is not just some theoretical abstraction in the feminist literature, but very real in terms of actual size and strength. Women are seriously vulnerable in this situation—a man choking a woman poses a genuine threat to her physical safety, something that is far less likely to be true the other way round. Even if a woman is not in immediate physical danger, the experience of being choked by a bigger, stronger person without consent is frightening and potentially traumatic.

These kinds of practices also need to be set in the context of a long and horrifying history of male violence against women. While intimate partner violence can happen within any sexual or romantic relationship, it is for the most part a gendered crime, with men abusing women in the vast majority of cases. The boundaries between so-called rough sex and domestic violence can easily become blurred in both symbolic and very material ways. As evidence, women's advocates point to an almost 90 percent rise in the use of the so-called rough sex defense in court, in which a man who has murdered his partner during sex is able to claim that it was just consensual, rough sex that "went wrong."

Although there are ways it can be done more safely, any form of asphyxiation is extremely dangerous, and it is alarming that young people are doing this without careful discussions around consent and safety. Anyone engaging in any form of kink needs to have open and honest communication at every stage.

But as cultural norms around sexuality evolve, formal sex education is getting further and further from the way sex actually looks in real life. Parents and educators urgently need to have open conversations with adolescents that reflect the real ways in which young people actually have sex, in a nonshaming way, including discussing both kink and porn openly and honestly. We need to talk about crucial issues of consent and safety in a real-world context, and acknowledge the complex, conflicted emotions that young people of all genders experience around sex and desire.

And while well-intentioned as a way to protect women from male pressures and violence, the gendered understanding of both porn and kink as things that boys and men unequivocally enjoy and benefit from and that women and girls endure or tolerate, can actually make it harder for young people to own and discuss any experiences or emotions that deviate from this narrative. This, in turn, can end up shutting down crucial conversations. We need to make space in any discussions to talk both about girls' desires, excitement, and pleasure from this kind of sex, and also for boys' fears, vulnerabilities, and reluctance. Only when we realize that sex is complicated for everyone—exciting, scary, conflicted, messy, painful—can we start to develop more healthy, consensual, equal relationships.

• • •

It's not just sex. The same tired gendered scripts that tend to dominate the discussions of porn and kink are also still very much in circulation when it comes to boys and relationships more generally.

Just as there has been a notable lack of acknowledgment of girls' own authentic desire and sexuality—that girls want sex, with or without intimacy—there has also been a corresponding lack of discussion about boys' need for connection and love.

When they are toddlers, people throw around the phrase "Boys are like dogs," casting them as animals at the mercy of basic biological urges, rather than emotionally complex humans. We carry a version of that story forward into male teenagers with sex.

At some level, the discourse that has been handed down about teenage boys has barely shifted in forever. And now, in the post–#MeToo era, it has been reinvigorated, gaining a new exploitative cast. In this narrative, boys are only interested in sex and have no real investment in relationships. Relationships are essentially a concession that boys make to girls, who, in turn, are only interested in love, with no genuine sexual interest or desires of their own. It is a story that, though it has gone through various different iterations, is surprisingly unchanged in its fundamentals since my grandmother's generation and before.

As a mother of boys, this story has never made intuitive sense to me. When I think about my own sons, their constant drive to connect with me, their hunger for intimacy and love and for my approval and attention, the whole narrative seems off. How do boys go from affection-seeking cuddlebugs to emotionally bankrupt sex monsters in just a few years? Can it really be just a question of hormones? Add 500 ng/dl of testosterone to the veins, and all need for warmth and attachment disappears? It doesn't seem right.

Our dehumanizing characterization of boys as emotional voids on sexual hyperdrive can easily become self-reinforcing. The story itself puts pressure on boys to conform to these gendered expectations, unwittingly shaming them for their feelings and denying them the full range of emotional expression.

Of course, teenage boys want sex. They crave it, deeply and urgently. But as a recent body of research (as well as common sense) confirms, they also crave intimacy and relationships in roughly equal measure to girls. Wide-scale surveys into boys' desires and motivations around sex and relationships show that, contrary to the tired story that they are "only interested in one thing," boys are as emotionally invested in relationships as girls are, and in many cases more emotionally affected by the ups and downs of romantic entanglements.[16] When researchers at the State University of New York, Oswego, surveyed a racially and economically diverse group of tenth-grade boys about their motivations for dating and having sex, the top reason for boys pursuing a sexual relationship with a girl, as noted by 80 percent of the boys asked was, "I really liked the person."[17]

This seems to fly in the face of what the therapist Dr. Mark Ruffalo had told me—that his adolescent male patients were claiming that relationships weren't worth the hassle, when they could just pull out their smartphone and watch a choking video. But somehow, this seems less like a reasoned choice than a rationalization of their own avoidance.

All the boys I interviewed, pretty much without exception, from macho players to lonely incels, actually craved connection and love. When I asked them questions about sex and porn, they answered them. But what they really wanted to talk about were the specific girls and boys they loved—their secret crushes and broken hearts, the relationships they were in, and the ones they wished they were in.

Marshall told me about his painful, year-long sixth-grade infatuation with his best friend, Lincoln, the thrilling, searing, will-it-won't-it tension of that year and the overwhelming pain of seeing Lincoln turn up to the pool the summer before seventh grade with a girlfriend. Gary told me all about "the beautiful, beautiful girl" whom he loved all through college. "We broke up in May and that was the worst heartbreak I have ever experienced," he said. I spoke to boys who were in relationships, boys who were desperate for them, and boys who were terrified and avoided them. I didn't speak to a single boy who only wanted sex, with no deeper connection.

These boys' emotional lives were rich and complex, and agonizing in the way that only adolescent romance can be. While their friendships often sounded alien to me, their romantic crushes and rejections sounded painfully familiar. In many ways, lacking the kind of emotional intimacy and connection that many girls experience in their platonic connections, boys seemed even more emotionally reliant on their romantic ones. Hearing them talk like this actually soothed the soul of my own former teenage self, who always feared that the boys my friends and I spent our days obsessing over never gave us a second thought, beyond the prospect of sex.

But despite these preoccupations, in the sex ed these boys received at school, there was almost no mention of relationships or romance.

"It was just completely about safe sex," Oliver tells me. "In fifth grade, what we got was basically a list of every STD and what sex act you need to do to get it. And then you get older and the closest they get to talking about healthy relationships is just how not to rape people."

Oliver isn't the only one to have this experience of American sex education. Any meaningful discussion of relationships is mostly absent from the curriculum, which tends to focus more on disease and danger rather than joy and connection.

It doesn't have to be this way. It's a cliché at this point to pick a Northern European country and then compare a random aspect of American life unfavorably against it, but the U.S. system does stand in stark contrast to the Netherlands, where sex education is fully centered in relational learning. In her book *Not Under My Roof: Parents, Teens, and the Culture of Sex* (2011), the sociology professor Dr. Amy Schalet takes a deep dive into Dutch sex ed and the attitudes of Dutch teenagers and their parents more generally toward sex and contrasts it to the American system. She points to a Dutch sex ed syllabus called Long Live Love that talks about sexual development. It covers both risk and pleasure, but roots all of it in the idea that teenagers are relationally driven and wired to fall in love.

The Dutch curriculum is careful to address gender stereotypes around sex, placing emphasis on encouraging girls and young women to assert their needs and desires, as well as encouraging boys to open up about their feelings. As Schalet writes: "[The Dutch] leave room for boys to think of themselves as romantic, of having feelings. And it's not that American boys aren't romantic, it's that everything in their culture tells them that they shouldn't be."

While the Dutch parents Schalet interviewed generally saw their sons as fully emotional beings who fell in love hard and often and engaged with them about the ups and downs of their relationships, American parents across the political spectrum tended to caricature their sons as walking bags of hormones, having internalized the tropes of masculinity so effectively that they didn't question them, even for their own children. As one liberal American mother Schalet interviewed put it, "Most teenage boys would fuck anything that would sit still." But if we are not even able to see our own sons as relational and vulnerable, then how will they ever be able to incorporate that into their own sense of self?

The Dutch emphasize the similarities between boys and girls in love and sex, rather than the differences. It's an approach that might appeal to Oliver. When I ask him whether he thinks girls and boys really are that different when it comes to these things he replies:

"More and more I'm seeing the similarities as I get older. It's interesting because you start off by thinking, 'Oh, boys just want sex and girls won't have sex because girls only want to have love.' But more and more I'm seeing that all these different dynamics are not really to do with gender. I see a lot of boys that really want love."

• • •

Just a couple of weeks before the end of the school year, we get an email from Solly's middle school. Next week, the sixth graders will be starting sex education, as part of their science lessons. The topics covered will be Menstruation and Reproduction, Pregnancy and Contraception, and Healthy Communication.

I try to kick off some Healthy Communication of our own the following week, by asking Solly what he has learned in class. He tells me that I should stop asking embarrassing questions. But eventually, he volunteers that they had to draw a Venn diagram about what people with penises and people with vaginas have in common.

I don't know what Solly wrote on his Venn diagram—our Healthy Communication didn't extend to him sharing that information. I think about what I would write if I were to do this exercise, and especially what would I put on the outer edges, the parts that didn't overlap. Do the differences just come down to body parts and periods? Or are they really something deeper, something that comes from being socialized from birth into one of those categories—what the world decides about you, which subtle system of expectations and pressures it tracks you into?

But the focus of the assignment was not about differences, but about commonalities, and I am glad about that. It's not quite the Netherlands, but it's a start, and I think we can all learn from this emphasis. It makes me think about how easily and unwittingly I had bought into the stereotypes. I had decided without really questioning myself that conversations about sex would have been so much easier with a daughter than with boys, the script so different.

It's not that there is no truth to this. There are different cultural contexts and histories to discussing sex with boys and with girls. But honestly, all the "empowerment" talks I would be having with my fantasy daughter are based on a stereotype, too, and she likely would have found them shrill and grating. Because both of these heavily gendered hot takes are only a small part of the story. People with vaginas and people with penises do have more commonalities than differences. All of us are complex beings, who fall in and out of love, crave both mindless sex and deep romance, wield power and succumb to it, get hurt and hurt others, screw up and try again.

Maybe I should be focusing more on the middle part of the Venn diagram, the similarities, talking to my boys exactly in the way that I would naturally talk to a daughter. Treating them as fully rounded people in all their messy contradictions.

We aren't there yet. When I ask Solly about whether kids at middle school are starting to date, or have crushes, he says, "Oh yes, everyone is doing it." But he had given it some thought and wouldn't be getting involved himself because there is a "100 percent breakup rate."

But I will keep asking, keep trying to avoid the simple, reductive gender stories and be as honest as possible about the messy ways we all—with penises, with vaginas—experience desire and pleasure, power and powerlessness, vulnerability and tenderness.

Because, as it turns out, boys are like humans.

WHAT DO WE DO ABOUT IT?

In the fall, Abe, my youngest, heads off to kindergarten, almost toppling under the weight of his brand-new backpack. I'm full of end-of-an-era feels. With three children, widely spaced, we have been stuck in the joyful brutality of the preschool years for well over a decade now. I'm tired and ready for this next phase of life. But the heft of my last baby's giant backpack pulling against his small body is making me question this readiness.

Abe takes his place in the line of kindergartners, behind two similarly fearful looking little girls, and a male teacher welcomes each child as they file past. "Hi, sweetheart," he says tenderly to the first girl in line, then "Hi, sweetheart" again to the second girl. When it's Abe's turn, the teacher's tone changes, drops an octave, fills out to a manlier register. He lifts up his hand in a high five and booms out, "Hi, buddy!"

There's a lot of "buddy" when you have sons in America. It's how the world relates to them. Abe hasn't even made it through his first hour of kindergarten and he has already been tracked out of the "Hi, sweetheart" system and into the "Hi, buddy" system. But the "hi buddying" starts even earlier than that. The labor and delivery nurse called Zephy "buddy" as she cleaned the vernix off his body, not wanting to emasculate him with the word *sweetheart,* even on his first day on earth.

It's not hard to see where girls lose out in the sweetheart/buddy divide. "Sweetheart" is patronizing. It diminishes girls, subtly seeding their exclusion from the unofficial networks of power, the social back channels where buddies slap each other on the back and make decisions. But perhaps less obvious is just how much boys lose out in this divide, too.

Buddies and sweethearts carry different emotional and social burdens. A buddy is a peer, someone to grab a beer with. A sweetheart is a cherished darling in need of love and nurture. We take care of sweethearts, but not buddies. While "sweetheart" centers emotion and intimacy, "buddy" is an early initiation into the performance of masculinity in all its avoidant fist-bumping and defensive overcompensation.

As parents and educators, we do this to boys with the best of intentions. We call them buddy instead of sweetheart to help them survive in a system in which the costs of appearing weak or feminine are still very real. Masculinity lives right on the edge of humiliation, always just a tick away from transgression or failure or even violence. "Hi, buddy" is just one vowel sound away from "Hey, *buddy,*" which is basically the opener to a fight.

Most popular feminist writing has focused heavily on how boys and men benefit from patriarchy, but less on how they are harmed by it, what they lose in terms of care and nurturing, emotion and connection. Of course, in order to register this as an actual loss, we need to truly believe that these things are worth having in the first place. To value emotional intimacy not as a nice to have add-on, or "fine for girls," but as something weighty and significant enough to be seen as aspirational for boys and men. This would require attaching real importance to the behavior and cultural norms of women.

The logic easily starts to collapse in on itself. As a society we tend to assign a higher cultural value to male concerns and trivialize those associated with girls and women. This gendered hierarchy means, in turn, that we tend to overvalue power and undervalue intimacy and the expression of emotions. "Girl power" is an aspirational slogan. It's hard to imagine much demand for BOY NURTURE T-shirts.

Talking about how patriarchy also harms men is a different conversation from the "Men are the real victims" chest-beating of the right. Patriarchy is a complicated beast. For men and boys, privilege and disadvantage are intertwined, feeding off each other in a way that makes the injuries hard to pinpoint. But at some deep level, in this system, men get everything except the thing that's most worth having—human intimacy.

Because despite all the buddy-buddy backslapping, masculinity can often be the enemy of deep connection. Right from their first moments, boys are given less nurture and care, depriving them of tenderness and understanding. We learn to care for others by being cared for ourselves, so this early discrepancy starts off a lifelong pattern of loneliness and disconnection.

As they grow up, masculine norms harm boys in other ways, too, telling them to value competing over relating, winning over connecting, fighting over cooperating. Our ideals for masculinity teach boys that vulnerability is humiliating, that they need to be physically and emotionally untouchable. Shame is built into the foundations; the expectations are by definition impossible to meet, leaving men and boys living with the constant prospect of humiliation and failure.

Much of this happens below the radar, communicated in a million invisible social transactions. The buddy-sweetheart moment was so minor, so well-meaning and harmless on its face. But this invisibility makes masculinity a slippery target. We are starting to become aware of its worst excesses. Now we can pinpoint the truly toxic norms and behaviors—the assault and violence, the shootings and most overt instances of misogyny. But we fail to see the million more subtle, subtoxic ways that masculinity limits the humanity of boys and men.

Tweaks such as "healthy masculinity" or "aspirational masculinity" are not really challenging the basic idea that a boy needs to be masculine in order to be seen as worthy. Instead, they subtly reinforce the idea that masculinity itself is non-negotiable. I would rather see a world in which "aspirational masculinity" rings as sexist and regressive as "aspirational femininity."

We have tended to frame "Smash the patriarchy!" as a punitive measure, a loss for men and boys, rather than a gain. But really, they only stand to benefit from throwing off these debilitating norms and pressures. This is not about losing power but about gaining freedom and connection, an opportunity to become more fully human. This is a hopeful project for all genders, and we should sell it as such.

• • •

But how do we make these changes in practice?

For me, the first step was naming the problem. Thanks to my mom's involvement in the women's liberation movement, I grew up with great, finely tuned sensors for identifying sexism that affected girls. "That's sexist!" I would cry when I saw the pair of doctor and nurse costumes in the toy store, the doctor modeled by a boy, the nurse by a girl. Or when my elementary school teacher said, "We need four strong boys to help move the chairs," or when all the princesses in the movie were being rescued by princes, or when anyone used the phrase "man and wife." ("Woman and husband," ten-year-old me would snarl.) I was primed to recognize these slights and had the vocabulary to call them out. Because of the work my mom and her generation of feminists put into this project, now almost any fifth-grade girl could spot those affronts in a heartbeat and demand better.

I want boys to have the same level of awareness of where they are missing out, be able to identify and name the impossible pressures placed on them, and to ask for change.

With boy stereotypes, the sexism is often trickier to spot, and the insidious creep of masculine pressures harder to name. Often it is as much about what is missing as what is on display. Once I started to notice the absence of relational role models for boys, for example, and our failure to flag it or care about it, I saw it everywhere. There are shockingly few representations of boys in books or TV shows or toys that center relationships, friendships, and nurturing as the main narrative through line and not just a minor subplot, shoved in between bouts of dragon slaying and princess rescuing.

I am consciously trying to expose my boys to as many stories about friendships and relationships as possible. I would love to give them role models of boys and men, not just performing great feats of bravery or strength, or embarking on great adventures, but having great friendships and connections, taking on emotional labor, taking care of people and their feelings.

I try to encourage my sons to watch gender-neutral shows, marketed to both girls and boys, that feature boys taking on more relational roles, even if in limited ways. Sometimes this is just about social permission. When Zephy got into Japanese anime, I was surprised that he was naturally way more drawn to the *shojo anime,* or "anime for girls," which features more relational and emotional themes than the more monster-fighting, adventure-focused *shonen anime,* or "anime for boys." If he had understood what the Japanese terms meant, he almost certainly would have nixed *shojo anime* before even trying it, but the language barrier means that the gender segregation was invisible to him, thereby freeing him to just like whatever he likes. Unfortunately, American gendered norms and marketing are all too obvious to him.

Naming the glaring absence of relational role models for boys as sexism and calling it out is the first step. As soon as I became aware of this lack, I started doing this with my sons. I had long been the kind of dogmatist mother who never used the shorthand "he" for train engineer or firefighter or plumber, always taking great pains to spell out laboriously, "he or she or they."

Now I do the same work calling out the more invisible sexism or exclusion of boys from relational roles, the harmful expectations and assumptions around physical toughness, aggression, and emotional stoicism. I try to point out the absence of boys in friendship or social or caregiving roles, to make them aware of the lack. "Why are there no boys in this, do you think?" or "Why do the boys not get to be friends, too?" I'll ask them about the Baby-sitters Club, or Ivy and Bean, or Lego Friends, or Disney's *Frozen*, taking pains to pitch this as something desirable they are missing out on. "Don't you think it's sexist to assume that boys don't have friends, or feelings?" Usually, they either find this deeply irritating or they ignore me. But I think at some level they are taking it in, at least absorbing these questions into their understanding of how the world works. Wherever they end up taking it, I want to make the invisible visible, to give them some sense of what is missing and what might be possible for them, a language to understand their own experience and to challenge it.

And lo and behold, right before this book goes into production, I go to Target to buy a Lego set for Abe and am pleasantly surprised: After ten years of featuring almost exclusively girls and women, the Lego Friends franchise has been rebranded to be more inclusive of boys. The packaging is no longer hot pink and purple, but teal. And the new cast features three boy characters along with five girls. Abe loves his set, featuring two boys hanging out in "Leo's Room." It may be painfully slow, but progress is starting to happen. At last the culture is starting to recognize the invisible exclusion of boys from these roles and register it as an actual loss.

I call out the more insidious masculine stereotypes with my sons, too. "Why is the boy character always the one who hates school?" I ask. "Why do you think he needs to be so strong and tough—is that really an important quality for being a good person?" "Do you think fighting is the way to solve this conflict? What might be a better way?" "Do you think he might actually be scared in that situation and not feel brave at all?"

I do all this inconsistently and messily. The idea is not to get them to be perfectly scripted feminist citizens, tiny woke ambassadors faultlessly executing my agenda. I screw up constantly, and so do they. I'm lazy, imperfect, exhausted, strung out. They push back, and roll their eyes. But I'm trying and so are they, and I want to create space for us all both to try, and get it wrong, and try again.

I'm willing to be annoying in service of this project. I remember when it was considered humorless and deeply unattractive for feminists to point out that endless stories about beautiful princesses being rescued by handsome princes might be sending some problematic messages, or that Barbie's body shape transposed to a real woman would have her in the hospital with a feeding tube. Or that it might be a problem that the cat and bunny inhabitants of Richard Scarry's Busytown books assigned the city jobs to the boy cats and bunnies while the girl cats and bunnies stayed home to clean the kitchen.

Thanks to a generation of feminists that was willing to stand proud and be annoying, the Busytown jobs were redistributed along more egalitarian lines; you can now buy a SMASH THE PATRIARCHY coffee mug at Walmart, and the *Barbie* movie sounded like it could be quoting from a gender studies textbook. While of course the job is not finished, norms and expectations for women and girls have been transformed in a generation. Now I want to channel my own annoyingness in service of challenging stereotypes for boys, too.

I don't expect any grand revelations, but I want to create a climate of critical thinking around these issues and the subtle impact they have on boys. For so long, male socialization was the default normal. I want it to be open to question and debate, in the same way that we have been able to critique and analyze female socialization.

I'm incredibly lucky to be raising my sons with Neil for so many reasons, among them that he is a full participant in all this. He knows firsthand how hard it is for adult men to find deep connection. As we have gotten older, he sees the stark difference in our friendships—how intimate mine still are—how when I see my friends we still talk for hours about our lives and emotions and how we help each other out when times are tough—and feels a kind of envy. He never had a model for this kind of friendship himself growing up, and he wants better for our sons. So he puts in the hours at bedtime talking with them about their feelings, and organizes playdates and checks out the Ivy and Bean books from the library and plays dollhouse with Abe, even though it doesn't come naturally to him. He was the one who suggested the *shonen anime* for Zephy. He has always called our boys sweetheart, never buddy.

• • •

One evening we have some friends over, and the grownups are chatting in the living room. Nine-year-old Zephy is upset about something and comes in to snuggle with me on the couch. My friend tells me that she is surprised to see him do it. She doesn't have her own kids, but she thinks that her similarly aged nephews would be too embarrassed to cuddle with their mom in public. I ask her if her same aged nieces would feel the same way, and she says no.

The conversation makes me sad. My friend is from a country where masculinity norms are perhaps even more rigidly enforced. In the United States, public snuggling with their mother might still be acceptable for boys at age nine, but probably not at fifteen and definitely not in adulthood, whereas it would likely still be considered socially acceptable, even sweet, for girls. We have somehow just collectively accepted a kind of mass disconnection for boys, an idea that care and affection is emasculating, and that a close relationship with their mom is somehow an embarrassment. We need to call out these sexist narratives and normalize intimacy between a mother and her son, and for boys in general. We can do this by prioritizing connection for boys, starting from a young age, with the care and nurture we give them. To treat boys as our sweethearts, not just our buddies, and give them the same level of empathy and touch and tenderness as we give our girls.

A friend of mine told me about the work she had done after college as a counselor on a phone helpline. In the training session she received before starting, the head counselor told the trainees that as a rule, when women called the helpline, they described experiencing all kinds of complicated and subtle emotions. She used a color metaphor to illustrate this, describing these more detailed emotional descriptions as vermillion, ochre, and magenta. In contrast, the men who called tended to have a more limited emotional palette, more red, blue, and green. In order not to overwhelm or confuse them she advised the counselors to talk to men about their emotions only in very basic terms: happy, angry, or sad.

I want my boys to be able to understand and name the vermillion and ochre of emotions as well as the blue and red. I spend some time browsing various "feelings posters" online to hang on their bedroom walls, that include a wider emotional range—annoyed, disappointed, embarrassed—with accompanying aggrieved cartoon figures. At the very least this might give them a more effective vocabulary to describe their feelings about my newly politicized parenting. But in the end, I delete them from my Amazon cart. It's all a little too on the nose for my taste. I'd rather the boys got their grounding in emotions in more organic ways than memorizing them from a chart. Instead, I try to talk to them about emotions in real life—to name and understand their own, to work through them, and to make space for all of them, and make space for all of them.

In addition, we all need to encourage our boys to become more attuned to other people's needs and emotions in the same way that we have always expected from girls. We need to get boys to write the thank-you notes and remember the birthdays, to think about how their friends and family might be feeling in any given situation, to notice that Grandma is looking sad at Thanksgiving and go and sit with her.

As they grow up, we should prioritize connection for boys, to consciously correct for the built-in isolation in male culture. Even before we consider academics or sports or extracurriculars, we should carve out time for connecting with peers and with family. We need to do this intentionally, to schedule it if necessary, and to protect it fiercely.

Where have I landed with screen time? Honestly, the last thing any American parent likely needs in this moment is more guilt about screens. For most of us raising young children in a country with few social or cultural supports for parents, and where childcare is scarce and expensive, screen time is often a necessary sanity saver and childcare provider. As children grow up, screens—and everything they entail—are a key way in which they interact with the world. We are not going to be able to eliminate them.

The way I have made my peace with the screen-time issue is to identify the problem as *one of displacement* and recognize its gendered nature. Data shows clearly that boys are displacing social time with screen time significantly more than girls. Given that boys are already at a disadvantage when it comes to social and emotional learning, we need to fight this. But it seems as though we are more likely to make progress with this not through banning screens but by carving out and prioritizing face-to-face, screen-free social time with friends as regularly as we can.

For us, at least, this means pushing through some excruciating discomfort as our sons' hangouts and playdates with friends inevitably end up with various boys wandering around aimlessly, asking repeatedly when they can next play video games. I have come to the uneasy conclusion that it is worth holding the line, at least some of the time. It's so easy to let screens become a crutch for boys, but without them, eventually they build the social stamina to amuse themselves in other ways. I'm sure many kids play together easily and willingly screen free, but for us it has required some endurance and commitment. We have found that clarity is helpful. Saying "You can have one hour of screen time on this playdate at five o'clock" works better for us than "Maybe you can have some screen time later."

Firm boundaries (otherwise known as mild threats) also work well for us—"If you nag us for screens before that time, then the offer goes away." Perhaps this just reinforces the belief that screen time is the most exciting possible activity, but for our kids that conviction is already so embedded that it likely won't make much difference. At least this way we can leverage it to our own advantage. Similarly, we try to hold firm on enforcing some protected screen-free time connecting with family most days. And as my friend Elissa says, "lead with joy." We try our best to make this family time without devices feel like a fun gain instead of a punitive loss. Occasionally we even succeed.

What else? Just as we aim to do with girls, we should try to resist biological essentialism and limiting language about boys, such as "Boys will be boys"; "Boys can't sit still"; "Boys are reluctant readers"; and "Boys are like dogs." These stories don't just normalize bad behavior and perpetuate low expectations; they limit boys' horizons and sense of self. For too long we have seen the biological differences that do exist between young boys and girls as evidence that as parents there is nothing we can do. But instead, we should be seeing these differences as a reason to do more. We need to give boys a more expansive, less suffocating story about their own possibilities and place in the world.

Perhaps when we talk about boys' ability to become thoughtful, well-rounded, relational beings, we would do well to borrow from the inspirational "sky's the limit" tone we use to talk about girls' prospects, aspirations, and abilities. But first we need to question how our own internalized sexism colors what we actually consider to have true value. When we say "The sky's the limit" we are generally talking about power, about career aspirations and financial success. But the real "sky" in any well-lived life is not wealth or power or a seat in the boardroom, but meaningful relationships with other human beings.

All this work needs to come from a place of love. I want us to teach our boys to fight for gender equality by rooting our feminist critique in empathy, not opposition. To recognize that we are all trapped in an oppressive system together, rather than casting boys as either the enemy, a bunch of would-be predators, or fair game for mockery. For this we need to really listen to boys and not dismiss their pain or quash their concerns. It's tempting, especially as a feminist, or a mom operating from a place of panic, to dig in hard when a boy says anything in the neighborhood of "#MeToo has gone too far" or "Andrew Tate makes a lot of good points." But we should listen, with empathy and understanding, to try to hear what is going on underneath. Ask questions about our boys' experiences and show curiosity about them rather than dismissing them outright. Acknowledge that things are not black and white and that while male privilege is real, it is also a complex equation with privilege and harm entangled. Boys are more likely to listen if we acknowledge the complexities of, say, cancel culture or false accusations, or changing power dynamics between boys and girls, rather than dismissing these things outright.

Mostly, we need to demonstrate to our boys the importance of connection and intimacy by building the best relationships we can with them. The culture often dismisses teenage boys as grunting monosyllabic lumps who have no interest in connecting with their parents. But this is far from my experience. My boys crave connection, and connection is at the heart of loosening the grip of masculinity. We need to really engage with boys and listen to what they are telling us, to make them feel, in the words of Kade Janes, the founder of Iron Gate, "safe and heard." Discuss their feelings and other people's. Take an interest in their passions and concerns and share ours with them. Take them seriously as people and treat them, not as "boys" and certainly not "like dogs," but as full complex humans, finding their way.

• • •

In the spring we get an actual dog. She is calm, with a moderate amount of energy—nothing like a boy. In our house, at least, when it comes to reductive stereotypes, it seems as though gender trumps species. This is the push and pull of the whole experience for me. Gender doesn't matter. Gender matters deeply. And back again.

It dawns on me that after years of barely getting through each day, I am starting to enjoy motherhood, to cherish this time with my boys. Now that they are older, a little more regulated, and a little more medicated, and their wild savagery has settled a bit, I am happier. The culture of motherhood has changed since I started out, and now we have greater permission to speak up about the hard parts. I found the raw physicality of the early years overwhelming and unpleasant, and I'm happy to own that. White knuckling it through each day, breaking up wrestling matches is not my skill set, and I don't want it to be. Motherhood is much easier when I am less afraid that someone is going to end up in the emergency room.

The boys are stepping into themselves. In third grade, Zephy has a glorious gang of friends, who charge around and talk about video games nonstop and go to sleepovers at one another's houses every weekend. It's all very stereotypically boyish—physically relentless, good-natured, emotionally low stakes. Zephy is an action kid: his body still full of wild energy, but it's a little more channeled now. He loves learning and mastering new skills. Ritalin has been life changing; his brain is no longer a box of captive frogs, and this allows him to settle into a calmer, more honest version of himself.

His level of emotional insight is now impressive; he can parse his own emotions with nuance and self-awareness. He still doesn't really see it as his role to do this for his friends, but he is starting to step up to an almost painfully sweet big brotherly role with five-year-old Abe. Yesterday they were playing basketball together in the driveway. I could hear Zephy coaching Abe, encouraging him, cheering with genuine excitement when he made a shot. When Abe banged his foot on a fence post and cried, Zephy enveloped him in a hug and stroked his hair. Abe laid his head on Zephy's lap, and they stayed like that for several minutes.

• • •

The autism diagnoses that had once felt definitive and explanatory now feel odd. In some moments, they still make total sense, in others they seem almost absurd. Maybe these classifications aren't as immutable as the DSM would have us believe, and humans aren't as categorizable as we like to think. Of course, the ability to pinpoint and diagnose conditions such as autism is important—lifesaving, even—for many reasons, including explanation and identity and a way to access support. But the labels can also be reductive.

I try to wear the diagnoses lightly, and not overidentify with them. This is a privilege—my sons live at the margins of neurodiversity, and they get to make some choices around it. I think about the labels a lot. Do they help or obfuscate? Do they fence the boys in, or give them an identity that is freeing, a sense of belonging? Ultimately, that is for them to decide.

It's hard to talk about parenting neurodivergent children in a way that both acknowledges the hard parts and doesn't paint neurodivergence as a defect. It's a balance I still struggle with. I don't want our "happy ending" to be that the diagnoses were just an unfortunate mistake.

Because of the way the testing process works, unless we spend thousands of dollars to re-test them, my sons' diagnoses remain valid. If some future version of the boys finds the labels useful—if identifying as autistic or neurodivergent helps them make sense of any part of their experience, or allows them to access support or identity or community, they can use them and make sense of them in any way they choose. And if a future version of me needs them to cling to, to help explain my own parenting fears and failures, they are available to me too. But for the most part, at least for now, they barely feature.

We probably will never have a definitive answer on exactly what is going on with our sons: the unique ways that their neurons fire and connect, the ways in which they are different from other people and the ways they are the same. What's in store for their futures. But then, what parent does? The thrill and the terror of not knowing are the heady gamble of parenthood, the heart of deeply loving another human.

• • •

As he approaches his thirteenth birthday, Solly starts preparing for his bar mitzvah, the Jewish ritual that marks the official start of manhood. It occurs to me that in Biblical times, middle school boys could clearly sit still long enough to study ancient Hebrew texts for many hours each day. *Take that, biological essentialism!* I think to myself.

Solly must learn a portion of the Torah to chant in the synagogue on the day. Bar and bat mitzvah students often study their portion for months in advance, generally a Biblical story or obscure piece of Jewish law that they must scour for meaning. Solly's is about priestly robes. It goes into soporific detail about the design specifications—the exact detailing, the embroidery, the colors. "God seems very controlling," observes Solly.

I enjoy talking with him about his portion, seeing how his mind works. True to form, I remark on the fact that the priests in question are all men, that there are no women in the story, and that the role of priest is handed down from father to son, with no mothers or daughters in sight. We talk about how this centering of men was the reality for pretty much every society that has ever lived until just a few short decades ago. Men were the only people who truly mattered for most of human history. It's important to set any conversation about how patriarchy harms boys in this context.

Solly takes it well. We talk a bit more about the priestly robes, the exact significance of the purple and crimson yarns, the gemstone adornments. It's slow going trying to find the relevance for a modern preteen. But as we are slogging through, Solly breaks in with a query.

"How does meaning start?" he asks me. "Who gets to decide what things mean?"

I'm stumped. In many ways his question cuts right to the heart of who we are as people, and how we live alongside one another. Who *does* decide what things mean?

"We all do," I tell him eventually. It's incomplete, but it's true. Every person on Earth has to navigate their own path through this central question. To sift through the meanings that others impose on us and choose the ones we want to hold on to.

Categories—boy, girl, masculine, feminine, autistic, neurotypical—can help us make meaning, but they can also flatten it. Personhood lives in the particulars, in what Doris Lessing called "the unique flame" of the human personality—the parts that don't fit.

Masculinity has gone mostly unexamined for too long. We

have accepted it as some kind of biologically determined inevitability, rather than a set of decisions that humans have made about meaning. I don't want to make my sons' meaning for them, but I want to give them the tools to think and notice—to question and analyze, not to just accept the chokehold of masculine expectations as an inevitable part of maleness.

Their generation is already throwing out the old rules on gender, opting out of the old binaries and options altogether, making choices that are new and exciting. But somehow cisgender boys mostly got left behind in those discussions. I want the same freedom for my sons and for all boys—the same ability to question, to be fully human, to loosen masculinity's grip, to throw out the old rules and make their own meaning.

I'm excited to see what meaning they will make.

ACKNOWLEDGMENTS

First, thank you, always, to my agent, Steve Ross, the wisest mentor and most generous cheerleader, and to my editor, Michele Eniclerico, to Shannon Welch, and the rest of the team at Harmony for picking up the project so enthusiastically and for their steady and wise guidance. Also, thank you to Peter Catapano at *The New York Times*, for his ongoing support.

My deepest respect and thanks to all the boys who talked with me so openly and generously and shared their lives and dreams and fears. You give me hope for the future.

Thank you to Kent Toussaint and the staff of the Teen Therapy Center, Kade Janes and the staff and residents of Iron Gate, and Dr. Niobe Way and the staff and students of the Browning School for their openness and generosity in allowing me to report on their work.

Thank you to the two wonderful researchers who set up interviews and other research opportunities—Orla Katz-Webb and Carmen Warder. Also thank you to Lance Knobel for tapping into his network and to Salma Rached.

No words can be written without childcare—thank you to the wonderful Tatlin Johnson and Finnegan Graham.

Various people have read and commented on drafts of this manuscript, including Nick Mamatas, Kelly Webb-Lamb, Liz

Jackson, and Jo Ann Finkelstein. Thank you for all your wise insights, comments, suggestions, and Oxford commas.

Bonnie Alexander read every draft, thrashed out every structural snarl, and debated every point with me and made this book so much better. Thank you. Your brain is a wonder and I'm so lucky to have had access to it this past year.

With love and gratitude to Ayala Avitzour, who could be listed under almost any of these categories. You have helped me in so many ways that I can't even quantify.

I'm deeply grateful to my dear therapist, Dr. Nathan Greene, boy expert, who has guided me through this season of life with generosity and wisdom.

Writing this made me realize how lucky I am in my female friendships. Thank you to Ana Balabanovic, Jo Paterson, Georgia Moseley, Tiffany Thomas, Hanna Simmons, Hannah Michell, Tara Conklin, Helena Echlin, Lauren Schiller, Jill Egan, Leigh Carroll, Maria Yacoob, Tania Branigan, Annabelle Nabarro, and Hetty Whippman. Thank you and love also to my sister Sarah Vaughan, James Vaughan, and Katie Vaughan.

With all gratitude to the Peacocks—Elissa Strauss and Yael Goldstein-Love—for our ongoing brilliant daily discussions of motherhood, gender, psychoanalysis, life, death, and skincare. You sharpen my thinking and make my life so much richer.

With deepest love and admiration for my mother, Constance Whippman, the best, most inspiring role model, who set all this in motion in 1982, when she wouldn't let me have that Barbie, and for my very special dad, Michael Whippman, who did all this and more before anyone else did.

Neil Levine. You have so many domestic credits stacked up from the support you have given me for this book that you will never be able to spend them in this world. I love you so much and am so lucky to get to share this life and these boys with you.

Solly, Zephy, and Abe Levine. Wild things. Thanks for choosing me as your mom. You make my heart sing.

CHAPTER 1: BOYS WILL BE BOYS: OFF TO A BAD START

1. Rhoshel K. Lenroot, Nitin Gogtay, Deanna K. Greenstein, Elizabeth Molloy Wells, Gregory L. Wallace, Liv S. Clasen, Jonathan D. Blumenthal, Jason Lerch, Alex P. Zijdenbos, Alan C. Evans, Paul M. Thompson, Jay N. Giedd, "Sexual Dimorphism of Brain Developmental Trajectories During Childhood and Adolescence," *Neuroimage* 36, no. 4 (July 15, 2017): 1065–73, https://doi: 10.1016/j.neuroimage.2007.03.053.
2. Melissa Hines, "Prenatal Testosterone and Gender-Related Behaviour," *European Journal of Endocrinology* 155, supplement 1 (2006): S115–S121, https://doi.org/10.1530/eje.1.02236.
3. Greg L. Drevenstedt et al., "The Rise and Fall of Excess Male Infant Mortality," *PNAS* 105, no. 13 (2008): 5016–5021, https://doi.org/10.1073/pnas.0800221105.
4. Benjamin Zablotsky, Lindsey I. Black, and Stephen J. Blumberg, *Estimated Prevalence of Children with Diagnosed Developmental Disabilities in the United States, 2014–2016*, NCHS Data Brief No. 291 (Hyattsville, MD: National Center for Health Statistics, 2017), https://www.cdc.gov/nchs/data/databriefs/db291.pdf.
5. Allan N. Schore, "All Our Sons: The Developmental Neurobiology and Neuroendocrinology of Boys at Risk," *Infant Mental Health Journal* 38, no. 1 (2017): 15–52, https://doi.org/10.1002/imhj.21616.
6. Richard Reeves and Sarah Nzau, "Poverty Hurts Boys the Most: Inequality at the Intersection of Class and Gender," Brookings Institution Report, June 14, 2021, https://www.brookings.edu/articles/poverty-hurts-the-boys-the-most-inequality-at-the-intersection-of-class-and-gender/.
7. Sebastian Kraemer, "The Fragile Male," *BMJ* 321, no. 7276 (2000): 1609–12, https://doi.org/10.1136/bmj.321.7276.1609.
8. Schore, "All Our Sons."
9. Jan Kunzler, Katharina Braun, and Joerg Bock, "Early Life Stress and Sex-

Specific Sensitivity of the Catecholaminergic Systems in Prefrontal and Limbic Regions of Octodon Degus," *Brain Structure and Function* 220, no. 2 (2015): 861–68, https://doi.org/10.1007/s00429-013-0688-2.

10. Ian Weaver et al., "Epigenetic Programming by Maternal Behavior," *Nature Neuroscience* 7 (2004): 847–54, https://doi.org/10.1038/nn1276.

11. Kathryn Gudsnuk and Frances A. Champagne, "Epigenetic Influence of Stress and the Social Environment," *ILAR Journal* 53, nos. 3–4 (2012): 279–88, https://doi.org/10.1093/ilar.53.3-4.279.

12. Maayan Pratt et al., "Maternal Depression Across the First Years of Life Impacts the Neural Basis of Empathy in Preadolescence," *Journal of the American Academy of Child and Adolescent Psychiatry* 56, no. 1 (2017): 20, https://doi.org/10.1016/j.jaac.2016.10.012.

13. Ri-hua et al., "Fetal Gender and Postpartum Depression in a Cohort of Chinese Women," *Social Science and Medicine* 65, no. 4 (2007): 680–84, https://doi.org/10.1016/j.socscimed.2007.04.003.

14. Dana Sinclair and Lynne Murray, "Effects of Postnatal Depression on Children's Adjustment to School: Teacher's Reports," *British Journal of Psychiatry* 172 (January 1998): 58–63, https://doi.org/10.1192/bjp.172.1.58.

15. Robyn Fivush, "Exploring Sex Differences in the Emotional Content of Mother-Child Conversations about the Past," *Sex Roles* 20, nos. 11–12 (1989): 675–91, https://doi.org/10.1007/BF00288079.

16. Katharine Johnson et al., "Gender Differences in Adult-Infant Communication in the First Months of Life," *Pediatrics* 134, no. 6 (2014): e1603–e1610, https://doi.org/10.1542/peds.2013-4289.

17. Ana Aznar and Harriet R. Tenenbaum, "Parent-Child Positive Touch: Gender, Age, and Task Differences," *Journal of Nonverbal Behavior* 40, no. 4 (2016): 317–33, https://doi.org/10.1007/s10919-016-0236-x.

18. Ana Aznar and Harriet R. Tenenbaum, "Gender and Age Differences in Parent-Child Emotion Talk," *British Journal of Developmental Psychology* 33, no. 1 (2015): 148–55, https://doi.org/10.1111/bjdp.12069; Jennifer S. Mascaro et al., "Child Gender Influences Paternal Behavior, Language, and Brain Function," *Behavioral Neuroscience* 131, no. 3 (2017): 262–73, https://doi.org/10.1037/bne0000199.

19. Darcia Narvaez, "Why Worry About Undercared for Males? Messed Up Morals!" *Psychology Today*, January 15, 2017, https://www.psychologytoday.com/us/blog/moral-landscapes/201701/why-worry-about-undercared-males-messed-morals.

20. James W. Prescott, "Body Pleasure and the Origins of Violence," *Bulletin of the Atomic Scientists* 31, no. 9 (1975): 10–20.

21. Pratt et al., "Maternal Depression," 20; Anne-Claude Bernard-Bonnin, Canadian Paediatric Society, and Mental Health and Developmental Disabilities Committee, "Maternal Depression and Child Development," *Paediatrics and Child Health* 9, no. 8 (2004): 575–98, https://doi.org/10.1093/pch/9.8.575.

22. Chanda Rawat and Ritu Singh, "The Paradox of Gender Difference on Emotional Maturity of Adolescents," *Journal of Human Ecology* 58,

no. 3 (2017): 126–31, https://doi.org/10.1080/09709274.2017.1305610; Smritikana Ghosh, "Emotional Maturity Among Adolescents," *International Journal of Indian Psychology* 7, no. 4 (2019): 570–73, https://doi.org/10.25215/0704.065.

23. George E. Vaillant, Charles C. McArthur, and Arlie Bock, *Grant Study of Adult Development, 1938–2000,* dataset, version 4.6, 2022, Henry A. Murray Research Archive at Harvard University, https://doi.org/10.7910/DVN/48WRX9.

CHAPTER 2: "GIRL STORIES": WHAT WE ARE FAILING TO TEACH BOYS ABOUT BEING HUMAN

1. Plan International, *The State of Gender Equality for U.S. Adolescents* (2018), https://planusa-org-staging.s3.amazonaws.com/public/uploads/2021/08/state-of-gender-equality-summary-2018.pdf.
2. National Center for Education Statistics, *Student Reports of Bullying: Results from the 2017 School Crime Supplement to the National Crime Victimization Survey,* July 2019, https://nces.ed.gov/pubsearch/pubsinfo.asp?pubid=2019054.
3. Carolyn M. Barry et al., "Emerging Adults' Psychosocial Adjustment: Does a Best Friend's Gender Matter?" *Psi Chi Journal of Psychological Research* 18, no. 3 (2013): 94–102, doi: 10.24839/2164-8204.JN18.3.94; Melikşah Demir and Haley Orthel, "Friendship, Real-Ideal Discrepancies, and Well-Being: Gender Differences in College Students," *Journal of Psychology: Interdisciplinary and Applied* 145, no. 3 (2011): 173–93, https://doi.org/10.1080/00223980.2010.548413; B. J. Bank and Suzanne L. Hansford, "Gender and Friendship: Why Are Men's Best Same-Sex Friendships Less Intimate and Supportive?," *Personal Relationships* 7, no. 1 (2000): 63–78, doi: 10.1111/j.1475-6811.2000.tb00004.x. For a summary of the research on this, see Stéphanie Langheit and François Poulin, "Developmental Changes in Best Friendship Quality During Emerging Adulthood," *Journal of Social and Personal Relationships* 39, no. 11 (2022): 3373–93, https://doi.org/10.1177/02654075221097993.
4. Anita P. Barbee et al., "Effects of Gender Role Expectations on the Social Support Process," *Journal of Social Issues* 49, no. 3 (1993): 175–90, https://doi.org/10.1111/j.1540-4560.1993.tb01175.x.
5. François Poulin, Anne-Sophie Denault, and Sara Pedersen, "Longitudinal Associations Between Other-Sex Friendships and Substance Use in Adolescence," *Journal of Research on Adolescence* 21, no. 4 (2011): 776–88, https://doi.org/10.1111/j.1532-7795.2011.00736.x.
6. Judy Y. Chu, *When Boys Become Boys: Development, Relationships, and Masculinity* (New York: New York University Press, 2014).
7. Maite Garaigordobil, "A Comparative Analysis of Empathy in Childhood and Adolescence: Gender Differences and Associated Socio-Emotional Variables," *International Journal of Psychology and Psychological Therapy* 9, no. 2 (2009): 217–35; Jolien Van der Graaff et al., "Perspective Taking and Empathic Concern in Adolescence: Gender Differences in Developmental Changes," *Developmental Psychology* 50, no. 3 (2014): 881–88.

8. Daniel B. Hajovsky, Jacqueline M. Caemmerer, and Benjamin A. Mason, "Gender Differences in Children's Social Skills Growth Trajectories," *Applied Developmental Science* 26, no. 3 (2022): 488–503, https://doi.org/10.1080/10888691.2021.1890592.
9. Manuela Barreto et al., "Loneliness Around the World: Age, Gender, and Cultural Differences in Loneliness," *Personality and Individual Differences* 169 (February 1, 2021), https://doi.org/10.1016/j.paid.2020.110066.

CHAPTER 3: BOY STORIES: THE SCRIPTS OF MASCULINITY

1. Mark Aguiar, Mark Bils, Kerwin Kofi Charles, and Erik Hurst, "Leisure Luxuries and the Labor Supply of Young Men," *Journal of Political Economy* 129, no. 2 (2021): 337–82, reported in Quoctrung Bui, "Why Some Men Don't Work: Video Games Have Gotten Really Good," *The New York Times*, July 3, 2017, https://www.nytimes.com/2017/07/03/upshot/why-some-men-dont-work-video-games-have-gotten-really-good.html.
2. Centers for Disease Control and Prevention, *Youth Risk Behavior Survey: Data Summary and Trends Report 2011–2021*, 2023, https://www.cdc.gov/healthyyouth/data/yrbs/pdf/YRBS_Data-Summary-Trends_Report2023_508.pdf.
3. Peixia Shi et al., "A Hypothesis of Gender Differences in Self-Reporting Symptom of Depression: Implications to Solve Under-Diagnosis and Under-Treatment of Depression in Males," *Frontiers in Psychiatry* 12 (October 25, 2021), https://doi.org/10.3389/fpsyt.2021.589687.
4. Centers for Disease Control and Prevention, *Suicide Rates, by Sex, Race, Hispanic Origin, and Age: United States, Selected Years 1950–2019,* table, https://www.cdc.gov/nchs/data/hus/2020-2021/SuicMort.pdf.
5. Pew Research Center, survey of U.S. adults, conducted August 8–21 and September 14–28, 2017, summarized in Juliana Menasce Horowitz, "Americans' Views on Masculinity Differ by Party, Gender and Race," Pew Research Center January 23, 2019, https://www.pewresearch.org/short-reads/2019/01/23/americans-views-on-masculinity-differ-by-party-gender-and-race/.
6. Gregory Seaton, "Toward a Theoretical Understanding of Hypermasculine Coping Among Urban Black Adolescent Males," *Journal of Human Behavior in the Social Environment* 15, nos. 2–3 (2007): 367–90, https://doi.org/10.1300/J137v15n02_21.
7. Christopher Bartneck, et al., "Have LEGO Products Become More Violent?," *PLoS ONE* 11, no. 5 (2016), https://doi.org/10.1371/journal.pone.0155401.
8. Crystal Smith, "Word Cloud: How Toy Ad Vocabulary Reinforces Gender Stereotypes," Crystal Smith (blog), last updated September 20, 2017, http://crystalsmith.ca/word-cloud-toy-ad-vocabulary-reinforces-gender-stereotypes.
9. Plan International, *The State of Gender Equality for U.S. Adolescents,* 2018, https://planusa-org-staging.s3.amazonaws.com/public/uploads/2021/08/state-of-gender-equality-summary-2018.pdf.

10. Karen M. Skemp, Renae L. Elwood, and David M. Reineke, "Adolescent Boys Are at Risk for Body Image Dissatisfaction and Muscle Dysmorphia," *Californian Journal of Health Promotion* 17, no. 1 (2019): 61–70, https://doi.org/10.32398/cjhp.v17i1.2224.
11. "Andrew Tate," https://hopenothate.org.uk/andrew-tate/.
12. Keith J. Yoder et al., "EEG Distinguishes Heroic Narratives in ISIS Online Video Propaganda," *Science Reports* 10, no. 1 (2020), https://doi.org/10.1038/s41598-020-76711-0.

CHAPTER 4: "FEMINIZING THE CLASSROOM": BOYS AND SCHOOL

1. Sean F. Reardon et al., *Gender Achievement Gaps in U.S. School Districts*, CEPA Working Paper No. 18-13), Stanford Center for Education Policy Analysis, 2018, https://cepa.stanford.edu/content/gender-achievement-gaps-us-school-districts.
2. National Center for Education Statistics, table 233.20, "Percentage of Public School Students in Grades 6 through 12 Who Had Ever Been Suspended or Expelled, by Race/Ethnicity and Sex: Selected Years, 1993 through 2019," *Digest of Education Statistics: 2021*, https://nces.ed.gov/programs/digest/d21/tables/dt21_233.20.asp?current=yes.
3. National Center for Education Statistics, figure 1, "Actual and Projected Undergraduate Enrollment in Degree-Granting Postsecondary Institutions by Sex: Fall 2010 through Fall 2031," Fast Facts: Enrollment, https://nces.ed.gov/FastFacts/display.asp?id=98.
4. National Center for Education Statistics, table 322.20, "Bachelor's Degrees Conferred by Postsecondary Institutions, by Race, Ethnicity and Sex of Student, 1976–77 through 2019–20," *Digest of Education Statistics: 2021*, https://nces.ed.gov/programs/digest/d21/tables/dt21_322.20.asp?current=yes.
5. National Assessment of Educational Progress, The Nation's Report Card 2022, database, educational outcomes by race and gender, https://www.nationsreportcard.gov/ndecore/xplore/NDE.
6. National Center for Education Statistics, table 219.70, "Percentage of High School Dropouts among Persons 16 to 24 Years Old (Status Dropout Rate) by Sex and Race/Ethnicity: Selected Years, 1960 through 2021," *Digest of Education Statistics: 2022*, https://nces.ed.gov/programs/digest/d22/tables/dt22_219.70.asp.
7. National Center for Education Statistics, table 302.60, "Percentage of 18- to 24-Year-Olds Enrolled in College, by Level of Institution and Sex and Race/Ethnicity of Student: 1970 through 2021," *Digest of Education Statistics: 2022*, https://nces.ed.gov/programs/digest/d22/tables/dt22_302.60.asp; National Center for Education Statistics, table 104.20, "Percentage of Persons 25 to 29 Years Old with Selected Levels of Educational Attainment, by Race/Ethnicity and Sex: Selected Years, 1920 through 2022," *Digest of Education Statistics: 2022* https://nces.ed.gov/programs/digest/d22/tables/dt22_104.20.asp.
8. Angela Duckworth and Martin E. P. Seligman, "Self-Discipline Gives Girls

the Edge: Gender in Self-Discipline, Grades, and Achievement Test Scores," *Journal of Educational Psychology* 98, no. 1 (2006): 198–208, https://doi.org/10.1037/0022-0663.98.1.198.

9. David Deming and Susan Dynarski, "The Lengthening of Childhood," *Journal of Economic Perspectives* 22, no. 3 (2008): 71–92, https://doi.org/10.1257/jep.22.3.71.

10. Elizabeth U. Cascio and Diane Whitmore Schanzenbach, "First in the Class? Age and the Education Production Function," *Education Finance and Policy* 11, no. 3 (2016): 225–50, https://doi.org/10.1162/EDFP_a_00191; Sandra E. Black, Paul J. Devereux, and Kjell G. Salvanes, "Too Young to Leave the Nest? The Effects of School Starting Age," *Review of Economics and Statistics* 93, no. 2 (2011): 455–67; Deming and Dynarski, "Lengthening of Childhood."

11. Steven J. Spencer, Claude M. Steele, and Diane M. Quinn, "Stereotype Threat and Women's Math Performance," *Journal of Experimental Social Psychology* 35, no. 1 (1999): 4–28, https://doi.org/10.1006/jesp.1998.1373.

12. Eliana Avitzour et al., *On the Origins of Gender-Biased Behavior: The Role of Explicit and Implicit Stereotypes,* NBER Working Paper No. w27818, September 2020, https://ssrn.com/abstract=3692175.

13. Michael Baker and Kevin Milligan, "Boy-Girl Differences in Parental Time Investments: Evidence from Three Countries," *Journal of Human Capital* 10, no. 4 (2016): 399–441, https://doi.org/10.1086/688899.

14. Marianne Bertrand and Jessica Pan, "The Trouble with Boys: Social Influences and the Gender Gap in Disruptive Behavior," *American Economic Journal: Applied Economics* 5, no. 1 (2013): 32–64, http://www.jstor.org/stable/43189418.

15. Bonny L. Hartley and Robbie M. Sutton, "A Stereotype Threat Account of Boys' Academic Underachievement," *Child Development* 84 no. 5 (2013): 1716–33, https://doi.org/10.1111/cdev.12079.

16. Sylwia Bedyńska, Piotr Rycielski, and Magdalena Jabłońska, "Measuring Stereotype Threat at Math and Language Arts in Secondary School: Validation of a Questionnaire," *Frontiers in Psychology* 12 (2021): https://doi.org/10.3389/fpsyg.2021.553964.

17. Jill E. Yavorsky and Claudia Buchmann, "Gender Typicality and Academic Achievement among American High School Students," *Sociological Science* 6 (2019): 661–83, https://doi.org/10.15195/v6.a25.

18. Devin G. Pope and Justin R. Sydnor, "Geographic Variation in the Gender Differences in Test Scores," *Journal of Economic Perspectives* 24, no. 2 (2010): 95–108, https://doi.org/10.1257/jep.24.2.95.

19. Nicolás Sánchez-Álvarez, María P. Berrios Martos, and Natalio Extremera, "A Meta-analysis of the Relationship Between Emotional Intelligence and Academic Performance in Secondary Education: A Multi-stream Comparison," *Frontiers in Psychology* 11 (2020): 1517, https://doi.org/10.3389/fpsyg.2020.01517.

20. Carolyn MacCann et al., "Emotional Intelligence Predicts Academic Performance: A Meta-analysis," *Psychological Bulletin* 146, no. 2 (2020): 150–86, https://doi.org/10.1037/bul0000219.
21. National Center for Education Statistics, table 233.40, "Percentage of Students Suspended and Expelled from Public Elementary and Secondary Schools by Sex, Race/Ethnicity, and State: 2017–18," *Digest of Education Statistics: 2021,* https://nces.ed.gov/programs/digest/d21/tables/dt21_233.40.asp.
22. Florida Department of Education and University of South Florida, *Effects of Suspension on Student Outcomes,* updated April 12, 2022, http://floridarti.usf.edu/resources/factsheets/suspension.pdf.
23. Joseph A. Durlak et al., "The Impact of Enhancing Students' Social and Emotional Learning: A Meta-analysis of School-Based Universal Interventions," *Child Development* 82 no. 1 (2011): 405–32, https://doi.org/10.1111/j.1467-8624.2010.01564x.
24. Conduct Problems Prevention Research Group: Karen L. Bierman et al., "The Effects of a Multiyear Universal Social-Emotional Learning Program: The Role of Student and School Characteristics," *Journal of Consulting and Clinical Psychology* 78, no. 2 (2010): 156–68, https://doi.org/10.1037/a0018607.

CHAPTER 5: HYPERCONNECTION AND DISCONNECTION: BOYS ONLINE

1. Jean M. Twenge, "Have Smartphones Destroyed a Generation?," *The Atlantic,* September 2017. https://www.theatlantic.com/magazine/archive/2017/09/has-the-smartphone-destroyed-a-generation/534198/
2. Amy Orben and Andrew K. Przybylski, "The Association between Adolescent Well-Being and Digital Technology Use," *Nature Human Behaviour* 3 (2019): 173–82, https://doi.org/10.1038/s41562-018-0506-1.
3. Viviane Kovess-Masfety et al., "Is Time Spent Playing Video Games Associated with Mental Health, Cognitive and Social Skills in Young Children?," *Social Psychiatry and Psychiatric Epidemiology* 51, no. 3 (2016): 349–57, https://doi.org/10.1007/s00127-016-1179-6.
4. Jonathan Haidt, Zach Rausch, and Jean Twenge, "Social Media and Mental Health: A Collaborative Review," unpublished manuscript, New York University, accessed September 15, 2023, https://docs.google.com/document/d/1w-HOfseF2wF9YIpXwUUtP65-olnkPyWcgF5BiAtBEy0/edit.
5. Pew Research Center analysis of American Time Use Survey 2014–17 (IPUMS), summarized in Gretchen Livingston, "The Way U.S. Teens Spend Their Time Is Changing, but Differences Between Boys and Girls Persist," Pew Research Center, February 20, 2019, https://www.pewresearch.org/short-reads/2019/02/20/the-way-u-s-teens-spend-their-time-is-changing-but-differences-between-boys-and-girls-persist/.
6. Livingston, "Way U.S. Teens Spend Their Time."

7. A. Lenhart et al., "Teens, Technology and Friendships," Pew Research Center, August 6, 2015, http://www.pewinternet.org/2015/08/06/teens-technology-and-friendships/.

CHAPTER 6: ANGRY LONELY BOYS: CONVERSATIONS WITH INCELS

1. Amia Srinivasan, "Does Anyone Have the Right to Sex?," *London Review of Books* 40, no. 6 (2018): https://www.lrb.co.uk/the-paper/v40/n06/amia-srinivasan/does-anyone-have-the-right-to-sex.
2. Dennis E. Reidy et al., "Man Enough? Masculine Discrepancy Stress and Intimate Partner Violence," *Personality and Individual Differences* 68 (2014): 160–64, https://doi:10.1016/j.paid.2014.04.021; Dennis E. Reidy et al., and P. D. Kernsmith, "Masculine Discrepancy Stress, Teen Dating Violence, and Sexual Violence Perpetration Among Adolescent Boys," *Journal of Adolescent Health* 56, no. 6 (2015): 619–24, https://doi.org./10.1016/j.jadohealth.2015.02.009; Dennis E. Reidy et al., "Masculine Discrepancy Stress and Psychosocial Maladjustment: Implications for Behavioral and Mental Health of Adolescent Boys," *Psychology of Men and Masculinities* 19, no. 4 (2018): 560–69, https://doi.org/10.1037/men0000132; Ronald Levant, "Extending the Gender Role Strain Paradigm to Account for U.S. Males' Gun Violence," *Psychology of Men and Masculinities* 23, no. 2 (2022): 151–59, https://doi.org/10.1037/men0000385.
3. Dennis E. Reidy et al., "Masculine Discrepancy Stress, Substance Use, Assault and Injury in a Survey of US Men," *Injury Prevention* 22, no. 5 (2016): 370–74, https://doi.org/10.1136/injuryprev-2015-041599.

CHAPTER 7: "RAPE-CON"

1. "Yo-Ho/The Pirate Chant," Tau Kappa Epsilon fraternity song. The Reno, Nevada, chapter was suspended for one year after a songbook was found that contained songs—this and others—that promoted violence against women.
2. David Lisak et al., "False Allegations of Sexual Assault: An Analysis of Ten Years of Reported Cases," *Violence Against Women* 16, no. 12 (2010): 1318–34, https://doi.org/10.1177/1077801210387747.
3. Janet Halley, "Trading the Megaphone for the Gavel in Title IX Enforcement," *Harvard Law Review* F 128, no. 4, 103 (2015): http://nrs.harvard.edu/urn-3:HUL.InstRepos:16073958.
4. Title IX Lawsuits Database, https://titleixforall.com/title-ix-lawsuits-database/.

CHAPTER 8: SEX AND SEXISM

1. Plan International, *The State of Gender Equality for U.S. Adolescents*, 2018, https://planusa-org-staging.s3.amazonaws.com/public/uploads/2021/08/state-of-gender-equality-summary-2018.pdf.

2. Debby Herbenick et al., "Changes in Penile-Vaginal Intercourse Frequency and Sexual Repertoire from 2009 to 2018: Findings from the National Survey of Sexual Health and Behavior," *Archives in Sexual Behavior* 51, no. 3 (2022): 1419–33, https://doi.org/10.1007/s10508-021-02125-2.

3. Scott J. South and Lei Lei, "Why Are Fewer Young Adults Having Casual Sex?," *Socius* 7 (2021): https://doi.org/10.1177/2378023121996854.

4. Rita C. Seabrook, L. Monique Ward, and Soraya Giaccardi, "Less Than Human? Media Use, Objectification of Women, and Men's Acceptance of Sexual Aggression," *Psychology of Violence* 9, no. 5 (2019): 536–45, https://doi.org/10.1037/vio0000198.

5. Amber L. Ferris et al., "The Content of Reality Dating Shows and Viewer Perceptions of Dating," *Journal of Communication* 57, no. 3 (2007): 490–510, https://doi.org/10.1111/j.1460-2466.2007.00354.x.

6. Eric W. Owens et al., "The Impact of Internet Pornography on Adolescents: A Review of the Research," *Sexual Addiction and Compulsivity* 19, nos. 1–2 (2012): 99–122, https://doi.org/10.1080/10720162.2012.660431.

7. Joshua B. Grubbs et al., "Pornography Problems Due to Moral Incongruence: An Integrative Model with a Systematic Review and Meta-analysis," *Archives in Sexual Behavior* 48, no. 2 (2019): 397–415, https://doi.org/10.1007/s10508-018-1248-x.

8. Pornhub Insights, "The 2022 Year in Review," accessed September 15, 2023, https://www.pornhub.com/insights/2022-year-in-review#age-demographics.

9. Lux Alptraum, "5 Porn Stars Debunk the Myth of the Perfect 'Porn Pussy,'" Refinery29, October 18, 2018, https://www.refinery29.com/en-us/2016/06/113241/porn-pussy-perfect-vagina-myth.

10. Jochen Peter and Patti Valkenburg, "Does Exposure to Sexually Explicit Internet Material Increase Body Dissatisfaction? A Longitudinal Study," *Computers in Human Behavior* 36 (2014): 297–307, https://doi.org/10.1016/j.chb.2014.03.071.

11. Sean M. McNabney, Krisztina Hevesi, and David L. Rowland, "Effects of Pornography Use and Demographic Parameters on Sexual Response during Masturbation and Partnered Sex in Women," *International Journal of Environmental Research and Public Health* 17, no. 9 (2020): 3130, https://doi.org/10.3390/ijerph17093130.

12. Niki Fritz et al., "Porn Sex Versus Real Sex: Sexual Behaviors Reported by a U.S. Probability Survey Compared to Depictions of Sex in Mainstream Internet-Based Male-Female Pornography," *Archives of Sexual Behavior* 51, no. 2 (2022): 1187–1200, https://doi.org/10.1007/s10508-021-02175-6.

13. Debby Herbenick et al., "Diverse Sexual Behaviors in Undergraduate Students: Findings from a Campus Probability Survey," *Journal of Sexual Medicine* 18, no. 6 (2021): 1024–41, https://doi.org/10.1016/j.jsxm.2021.03.006.

14. Debby Herbenick et al., "'It Was Scary, But Then It Was Kind of Exciting,'": Young Women's Experiences with Choking During Sex," *Archives of Sexual Behavior* 51, no. 2 (2022) 1103–1123, doi:10.1007/s10508-021-02049-x.

15. Herbenick et al., "Diverse Sexual Behaviors."

16. Robin W. Simon and Anne E. Barrett, "Nonmarital Romantic Relationships and Mental Health in Early Adulthood: Does the Association Differ for Women and Men?," *Journal of Health and Social Behavior* 51, no. 2 (2010): 168–82, https://doi.org/10.1177/0022146510372343.

17. Andrew P. Smiler, " 'I Wanted to Get to Know Her Better': Adolescent Boys' Dating Motives, Masculinity Ideology, and Sexual Behavior," *Journal of Adolescence* 31, no. 1 (2008): 17–32, https://doi.org/10.1016/j.adolescence.2007.03.006.

INDEX

ABOUT THE AUTHOR

RUTH WHIPPMAN is a British journalist and cultural critic. A former BBC documentary director, she has written for *The New York Times, Time* magazine, *New York* magazine, *The Guardian, HuffPost,* and other publications. *Fortune* described her as one of the "25 sharpest minds" of the decade. Called a "whip-sharp British Bill Bryson" by *The Sunday Times,* she is the author of the book *America the Anxious,* which was a *New York Post* Best Book of the Year and a *New York Times* Editors' Choice and Paperback Row pick. She is also a regular contributor to radio and podcasts. Ruth Whippman lives in California with her husband and three sons.

ABOUT THE TYPE

This book was set in Sabon, a typeface designed by the well-known German typographer Jan Tschichold (1902–74). Sabon's design is based upon the original letter forms of sixteenth-century French type designer Claude Garamond and was created specifically to be used for three sources: foundry type for hand composition, Linotype, and Monotype. Tschichold named his typeface for the famous Frankfurt typefounder Jacques Sabon (c. 1520–80).